THE SCALP HUNTERS

Abenaki Ambush at Lovewell Pond—1725

Alfred E. Kayworth
Raymond G. Potvin

Raymond G Potvin

BRANDEN BOOKS, INC
Boston

Library of Congress Cataloging-in-Publication Data

Kayworth, Alfred E. 1920-
The scalp hunters : Abenaki ambush at Lovewell Pond, 1725 / Alfred E. Kayworth, Raymond G. Potvin.
p. cm.
Includes bibliographical references and index.
ISBN 0-8283-2075-6 (Paperback : alk. paper)
1. Pigwacket Fight, 1725.
2. Abenaki Indians—Wars.
3. Abenaki Indians—Queâbec (Province)—
Saint Francis River Valley—History.
4. Scalping—New England.
I. Potvin, Raymond G.
II. Title.
E83.72.K39 2002
976.7'9—dc21

2002005030

BRANDEN BOOKS
Division of Branden Publishing Company
P.O.Box 812094
Wellesley MA 02482

To

Eleanor and Montse

TABLE OF CONTENTS

ACKNOWLEDGMENTS
Raymond G. Potvin

The process of doing research can prove rewarding in many different ways. To talk daily with leaders in the field of archaeology and history in a region that is considered to be the birthplace of America is great fun. Although my research activities at the R.S. Peabody Museum of Archaeology have been most gratifying, there are other individuals and institutions that I would like to thank as well:

Robert S. Peabody Museum of Archaeology, Andover, MA—Melinda Bluestain, interim director and curator; Sandra Kornyu, collection manager; Leah Rosenmeier, Dr. James Bradley, Dr. Edward Sisson, the late Dr. Richard "Scotty" MacNeish, Eugene Winter, Teri DeYoung, Pat Perreault.

Massachusetts Archaeological Society Northeast Chapter—Bill Eldridge, Bob Burns, Bill Bourassa, Pat Smith, Jules Gordon.

N. H. Archaeological Society—Marc Greeley, Pat Hume

Massachusetts Historical Societies—**Andover**, Juliet Mofford; **North Andover**, Carol Majahad; **Dunstable/Tyngsboro**, Cindi Connel; **Groton**, Isabel Beal.

N. H. Historical Societies—**Conway**, Dave Emerson; **Allenstown**, Carol Martell; **Pembroke**, Mr. and Mrs. Charles Hamilton; **Salem**, Beverly Glenn; **Ossipee**, Frank Fisher; **Sandown**, Bertha Deveau; **Nashua**, Bill Ross, Beth McCarthy, Frank Mooney, Jodi Lowery-Tilbury, Margaret Garneau.

Maine Historical Societies—**Fryeburg**, Nancy Ray, Diane Jones, Ginney and Ted Nixon.

Ft. Ticonderoga, N.Y.—Chris Fox, Red Hawk; **Friends of Ft. Ticonderoga**, Carl Crego and Joe Lyon.

Odanak, Quebec, Canada—Rejean Obomsawin, Esther Nolett.

Massachusetts Libraries—Andover Memorial Hall; **No. Andover** Stevens Memorial, **Dunstable** Free Public, **Haverhill** Public, **Tyngsboro** Public, **Woburn** Public.

N.H. Libraries—Hollis Social, **Hudson** Hills Memorial, **Litchfield** Aaron Cutler Memorial, **Nashua** Public, **Portsmouth** Public, **Salem** Kelly.

Farwell House of Tyngsboro, MA—Kathy Glass, Sarah Farwell, Brice Farwell.

Remick Farm Museum, Tamworth, Rhonda Jacobson.

Historic Homes or Property—Paul Downey, Richard Eastman, Mrs. Gregg, Mr. and Mrs. Herb Hayes, Mr. and Mrs. Herb Morton, Mr. and Mrs. Tom Whittaker.

My special thanks go to those individuals who shared their knowledge of historic events and to others who joined me on visits to historic sites. Among these are, Sam Busheri, Phil Busby, Martha Clark, Bob and Sue Crowley, Pete Day, Dot Deroche, Barry Dube, Joe Duquette, Fred Flather, Mr. and Mrs. Gallant, Rick Holmes, Mrs. Shirley Howe, Miss Helen Kellner, Arletta Paul, Frank Potvin, Walter and Sandy Potvin, Phil Richards, Babs Ryan, Matthew Thomas, Greg Laing.

Bill Burnett is a great friend. We traveled all over New England and hiked up hills and trails to get the pictures needed for this book. I am grateful for his photographic expertise.

My wife, Eleanor, traveled with me to all the New England states, New York, and much of eastern Canada while I did research. We visited forts, museums, historic sites, battle sites, monuments, houses, libraries and bookstores. We even went out in a small boat to photograph the mouth of the St. Francis River at Odanak. She followed my agenda without complaint. I thank her for her companionship and understanding.

I am indebted to my daughter, Carol Potvin, for her help with artwork and computer graphics. I am particularly grateful to her for her cover design for our book. It has been a lot of fun working on *The Scalp Hunters* with my friend, Al Kayworth.

My apologies to anyone I may have inadvertently failed to recognize.

ACKNOWLEDGMENTS
Alfred E. Kayworth

Telling a story based on another person's research was a unique experience for me, but without the benefit of Ray Potvin's extensive files and his ongoing help, there would be no book. In the process Ray and I became great friends as well as collaborators—thanks for everything Ray! Ray brought another asset to the partnership: his daughter Carol Potvin designed our cover and provided other artwork and computer graphics. To Carol, *Kchi wli wni!* (Great thanks). To my companion Montse Goodrich: mil gracias for your proofreading and your support.

The Scalp Hunters might have ended up gathering dust on a shelf if it were not for Adolfo and Margaret Caso at Branden Books, Inc. Thank you for your interest, and for all your efforts towards delivering an attractive package one more time.

Thank you, Gene (Grey Wolf) Charon for telling me about the French-Canadian *voyageurs*. Cheryl Lynch of the Derry Public Library located the research I needed to write the chapter on the *voyageurs* and the fur-traders—thanks Cheryl! My special thanks go to Marilyn Jones of Norway, Maine for letting me use the 275-year-old oral tradition of her Penobscot ancestor in *The Scalp Hunters*. The Odanak historian, Rejean Obomsawin, helped me with terminology and the Abenaki language—*Kchi wli wni ne do ba Rejean*! My thanks go as well to Doug and Jeanne (Obomsawin) Brink of the Mississquoi Band for their special insight into Rogers' character and their help with terminology. The web site, *Ne Do Ba* (friends), by Nancy LeCompte, was an excellent source of information on Odanak and Rogers' raid—*Wli wni Ne Do Ba* Nancy!

For helping me to understand the *Indian Way of Life,* I offer singular thanks to my native friends, who share *The First People* heritage. Christine (Kukukuo) Dube, Abenaki Betsy

(Soft Talker) Jackson, Apache, Comanche, Navajo and Chippewa; Onkwe Tase (Mohawk); Althea (Has No Horse) Doodson, Lakota; Ed Bears, Penacook; Louis Annance, (Anasaguntacook); Sue Manic, Cherokee; Gene (Grey Wolf) , Cree; Laura Brooks, Passamaquoddy. *Kchi wli wni Nedobak; Wlibamkanni. Great thanks my friends; may your journey go well.*

ABOUT THE COVER

The Scalp Hunters cover is a reproduction of a color image of a Diorama of a Pawtucket village along the Merrimack River 500 years ago, based on the Shattuck Farm site in Andover, Massachusetts. The color image is used with the permission of the ©Robert S. Peabody Museum of Archaeology, Phillips Academy, Andover, Massachusetts.

The diorama portrays the *First People* engaging in routine village activities of the 16th Century. The rivers and lakes of New England were ideal locations for these villages. Such sites offered fertile soil for gardens, as well as providing a waterway for canoe travel to the interior as well as to coastal estuaries.

Carol Potvin of Andover provided the overall cover design.

FOREWORD

In the summer of 2001, I picked up Ray Potvin at my boat dock on the mainland, and we spent an afternoon on tiny Escumbuit Island at Big Island Pond in Derry pouring over his research material. I was impressed with the depth and variety of his research; it was very obvious that Ray had spent many months and had traveled many miles to accumulate such a research treasure. I knew Ray to be an amateur archaeologist who was a regular volunteer at the Peabody Indian Museum in Andover and I had also learned that he belonged to a dozen or more historical societies in communities as diverse as Andover and Nashua, and as far distant as Fryeburg, Maine.

Ray had previously mentioned that he was putting together a slide presentation on an historic event that I had briefly described in *Abenaki Warrior*. It was the famous story of Lovewell's fight with the Pigwacket Indians at Saco Pond in 1725. During our phone conversation Ray said, "*This is an exciting story; it would make a great book.*" After grousing about the huge amount of work it would require for a man my age (81-years), I relented and asked Ray to bring his research up to the pond.

One summer afternoon—in a simple cabin in the middle of the lake—we sat browsing through documents written in the 1700s and 1800s. In the midst of working our way through the material, I turned to Ray and said, "*My gosh Ray; I'm impressed with your research; you have enough stuff here for a full length book!* As it turned out that wasn't quite true. The broad outline of any historic portrayal requires many fine brush strokes in order to complete the picture. My most pressing concern was whether Ray saw the American Indian as I did; would he be comfortable with my portrayal of the *Original People*? I did not want to compromise long-term beliefs that had been shaped and refined by my Native American friends. I soon learned that this would not be an issue. Although we had traveled different paths to pursue our personal interests, at the end of the trail we found ourselves in the same philosophical camp.

By mid-summer I found myself completely engrossed in the story of Lovewell's scalp hunters. My interest in Ray's research provoked other questions: how had the Anglo-Indian friendship gone sour in only 50 years? Why did Jesuit priests incite the Indians against the colonists? What does Fight Brook look like today? Does Indian oral tradition mention these events? Why did Rogers decide to raid Odanak? To resolve these and other questions, Ray drove me to Lake Ossipee, Lovewell Pond in Fryeburg, Maine, Lovell Lake near Wakefield, NH, and the Abenaki Indian reservation at Odanak, Canada. The book that came out of our collaboration turned out to be an overview of the Colonial Wars from 1675 to 1763 with a special focus on two key events—the fight at Saco Pond in 1725, and Rogers' raid on Odanak in 1759. *The Scalp Hunters* is the brainchild of two people, a researcher and a writer, working together in harmony.

INTRODUCTION

Scarcely fifty years after helping the Pilgrims survive their first harsh New England winter; the *Original People* were disillusioned by the European's negative impact on the traditional Indian way of life. In 1675 the Wampanoag Chief Metacom initiated a series of atrocities and raids on colonial settlements that was called King Philip's War. The British response to the Indian depredations was brutal and overwhelming. After Metacom was killed in a Narragansett swamp in 1676, hundreds of his supporters were rounded up and sold in the West Indies slave markets; some died in detention camps on Deer Island, and others found refuge with sympathetic tribes to the north.

The French, who claimed all the land in Maine down to the Kennebec River, cynically used Jesuit priests living among the Indians to incite their converts to raid the English frontier settlements along the Merrimack River and up the coast of Maine as far as Newfoundland. By heeding the Jesuit counsel, the Abenaki Indians became pawns in a global contest between France and England for control of the North American continent. The British, not to be outdone by the French, quickly formed an alliance with the Iroquois Nation to harass New France from the Hudson Valley to the Great Lakes. The two European antagonists and their American Indian allies then engaged in a series of wars—King William's War 1689-1697; Queen Anne's War 1702-1713; Governor Dummer's War with the Eastern Abenaki Indians 1722-1725; King George's War 1744-1748; The French and Indian War (The Seven Years War) 1754-1763.

The Scalp Hunters offers an unbiased perspective of the wars between the early colonial settlers and the *First People* of New England. The narrative, which portrays the Abenakis in a sympathetic way, describes how the family based culture functioned within a democratic hierarchy of sachems, sagamores, chiefs, shaman and tribal council. They were a spirit-driven people who saw themselves as individual strands in a great web of life woven from all the elements of *Mother Earth*—animate and inanimate. Their belief in *Kchi Niwaskw* (The Great Spirit) was not unlike the Anglo belief in God. Their concept of man living in harmony with *Mother Earth* and in accordance with the natural laws of *Kchi Niwaskw* constituted *The Indian Way of Life*. At key points in the narrative, Indian oral tradition is included to provide native perspective.

The narrative narrows its focus to dramatize two epic events; two milestones in the long struggle for the domination of the North American continent. Illegal appropriation of Indian lands, elitist attitudes, and the bias of certain religious leaders all contributed to the climate in which the two historic events took place. The first was Lovewell's Fight with the Pigwacket Indians at Saco Pond in 1725, and the second was Rogers' Raid on a Jesuit Mission Village deep inside French territory in 1759.

By the end of 1724 the winds of war had begun to turn in favor of the English. Indian raids against frontier settlements had become sporadic and weak. More importantly, the English had uncovered a new effective weapon to use against the Indians; they began to offer bounties for Indians dead or alive! The bounty of 100 pounds for adult male scalps was a huge incentive for early frontiersmen. They were barely scratching out a living on their farms, and except for hunting forays into the woods, they were idle during the long New England winters. The business of hunting scalps during the winter took on the appearance of a new industry. Private scalp hunting expeditions were financed by the sale of shares to investors. Brothers, cousins and friends got together as if to go on a turkey shoot or a deer hunt; it was not only a way to get out of the house, it was patriotic, and besides—100 pounds was a lot of money!

A number of scalp-hunting expeditions spent weeks in the woods without discovering a single Indian. The Indians were in their favorite element, and when a large force of scalp hunters approached, they simply disappeared into the forest. Also, if they were severely pressed, they could find temporary refuge at Odanak on the Saint Francis River in Quebec. Odanak eventually became a staging center for raids against English settlements along the Merrimack River and the coastal towns of Maine and New Hampshire.

In the winter of 1724-25, a well-known bush fighter named Lovewell went north from Dunstable, Massachusetts with 80 volunteers on snowshoes to raid Pigwacket Valley, where the towns of Conway, NH and Fryeburg, Maine are presently located. Somewhere between Lake Winnipesaukee and his objective, he was diverted by the tracks of an Indian raiding party out of Saint Francis that was headed for the Maine coast. After tracking and destroying the small Indian raiding party, Lovewell paraded the scalps of his victims aloft on poles in the streets of Boston. Basking in his newfound celebrity, Captain Lovewell immediately began to enlist volunteers for a new scalp-hunting expedition to Pigwacket Valley. The Pigwackets had a long history of depredations against English settlements from Andover to Newfoundland, and their War Chief Paugus had earned a chilling reputation as *The Scourge of Dunstable.*

The Fight at Saco Pond that pitted Captain Lovewell's scalp hunters against Paugus and eighty Pigwacket warriors was immortalized in ballad and prose for the next one hundred and seventy five years. It had all the elements of an epic: it featured drama, courage, heroism, mystery, romance, sadness and tragedy. Although the marathon fight marked a significant turning point in the long resistance against the English, the Abenakis continued to be a factor in the continuing hostilities. The final chapter provides a stirring account of Rogers' Raid on the Abenaki Mission Village deep in French territory. The conclusion to the story reveals Major Robert Rogers' sordid post-war record.

CHAPTER 1

WHITE TIDE RISING

I made war upon them,
but they fought with fire and thunder;
my young men were swept down before me,
when no one was near them. I tried sorcery against them,
but they still increased and prevailed over me and mine.
I, that can make the dry leaf turn green and live again,
I, that can take the rattlesnake in my palm as I would a worm...
I, who have had communion with the Great Spirit dreaming and awake,
I,...I am powerless before the Pale Faces.

--From Passaconaway's
Farewell address to his Penacook people

In the spring of 1725 a pitched battle between colonial bounty hunters and Pigwacket warriors was fought on the shoreline of a pristine sheet of water called Saco Pond in Fryeburg, Maine. The pond that is now called Lovewell Pond to honor the leader of the white scalp hunters was home to the Pigwacket Indians. When news of the fight reached Boston, the image of men trading insults and exchanging lethal volleys at the sandy verge of a picturesque pond fired the imagination of a fascinated public. Debated by historians and immortalized by balladeers and poets, Lovewell's fight with the Pigwacket Indians inevitably became a part of the New England folklore. A modern generation may find it difficult to understand why red and white brothers fought each other to the death on the shore of Saco Pond. To properly address this and other concerns, it is important to understand how deep resentment over basic cultural differences had spread like a malignant tumor in the social fabric of Colonial New England. It is necessary as well to place the event in the context of the intense global competition between France and England over control of the seas and their colonial possessions. French territorial ambitions in Maine as well as the influence of their Jesuit missionaries on the Abenaki Indians further complicated the problem. To complete this appraisal, early chapters of the book reveal that the early colonial settlers failed to recognize and appreciate the highly developed nature of the indigenous culture. The white assessment of the *Original People* as a race of *savage atheists* devoid of white values led them to a series of catastrophic errors in their relations with the Indians. The unrestrained white development of the wilderness often resulted in consequences that made it impossible for the Indians to continue their traditional way of life.

During the 17th and 18th Centuries, worldwide competition between France and England over maritime dominance and colonial possessions caused them to wage four wars against each other between 1689 and 1763. Wherever in the world these two world powers crossed swords, lesser nations were forced to choose sides. The indigenous people of the North American continent, as a result of choosing sides, were inevitably and clearly exploited by these two super powers during this period of history. The English relied heavily on their Iroquois allies in Ohio and upper New York State to harass the French Colonists in Canada. The French countered by inciting their Abenaki allies in Maine, New Hampshire and Vermont to pillage and burn English settlements along the New England coastline and along the Merrimack River. All of these events were tied to hostilities taking place concurrently in Europe. *King Williams' War* began in 1689 when England formed an alliance with the Netherlands and the Holy Roman Catholic Church to declare war on France over a dispute having to do with succession to the English throne. At that time the British conducted a series of raids in North America against French possessions. They captured the French fort at Port Royal in Nova Scotia and mounted an unsuccessful attack on the French settlement in Quebec, Canada. The French and their Abenaki allies retaliated by burning the English settlements at Schenectady, NY, Salmon Falls, NH and Fort Loyal in Portland, Maine. At sea French privateers attacked British shipping along the New England coast. The 1697 *Peace of Ryswick* returned Port Royal to the French, but failed to resolve other differences over colonial possessions. The French continued to claim all the land down to the Kennebec River while the English insisted that the St. Croix River (the present U.S.-Canadian border) was the northernmost boundary of their territory.

Queen Anne's War (1702 to 1713) was fought over colonial issues that were unresolved by the *Peace of Ryswick*. In 1704 the French Captain Hertel de Roueville and his four brothers together with over 200 Abenaki and Caughnawaga Indians made a major winter raid on the town of Deerfield, MA where they killed 53 and took 111 men, women and children captives to Canada where they were held for ransom. In 1710 an English colonial military force, supported by British war ships, captured Acadia (Nova Scotia), but their large land and sea expedition against Montreal and Quebec failed. Called the *War of the Spanish Succession* in Europe, it was resolved in 1713 by the *Treaty of Utrecht* in which France ceded Acadia (Nova Scotia) and Newfoundland to Great Britain. The diplomacy leading to these treaties and the signing ceremonies took place in Europe where diplomats had to deal with incomplete or inaccurate maps. Native leaders usually had no role in the negotiations. Their totems affixed to treaties were a crude attempt to imply that the Indians understood and agreed to the substance of the treaties. Many modern historians agree that Indian leaders were induced to sign these documents without having a clear understanding of how the terms of the treaties affected the ownership of their ancestral lands. In the nine years of "peace" that followed the signing of the *Treaty of Utrecht,* there were no major initiatives undertaken by either side, but Indian retaliation for white incursions into Indian lands prompted Massachusetts Provincial Governor Dummer to declare a separate war against the Eastern Maine tribes.

Governor Dummer's War with the Eastern Abenaki Indians lasted from 1722 to 1725.

In 1724, after almost 50-years of intermittent warfare with the natives, the colonial settlers of New England were still denied free access to territories they had previously acquired through Royal grants and treaties made with the French and their Indian allies. It was as if their superior numbers and firepower stood for naught in the face of a wily, persistent foe that continued to resist intrusions into its ancestral lands with the fabled fury of a wolverine. Despite swelling English manpower and modern weapons, the Massachusetts Colony had been unable to further advance and consolidate its frontier with the Indians. The rough outline of the frontier followed the course of the Merrimack River from Nashua to the ocean and up the New England coast to Nova Scotia in the shape of a giant upright fishhook. The indigenous inhabitants inside this imaginary line were stubbornly resisting white intrusions into the interior despite English claims of legal ownership through Royal grants or by means of treaties signed with the French and their native allies.

Despite the vaunted psychic powers and the sorcery of their most powerful shaman, Indian leaders like the Wampanoag leader Massasoit could not foresee what the arrival of the Pilgrims meant to the future of his people. His humanitarian act of feeding the starving pilgrims with food from his own stores during their first winter may have hastened the doom of his own people. Once established there was no turning back, and as news of the bountiful New World filtered back to the continent, the way was opened to a flood of immigrants from England and Western Europe. As the demand for sea transport for immigrants as well as mercantile supply ships increased, it became inevitable that early colonial entrepreneurs would develop the port of Boston. Once the Royal Provincial Governor of the Massachusetts Colony was firmly seated in Boston together with his Council, other colonial settlements became mere satellites to the burgeoning city.

Inevitably, buoyed by tales of fortunes to be made in the colonies, thousands of immigrants from England and Western Europe clamored for passage to the land of opportunity. Desperate to claim their share of the riches, indigent commoners indentured themselves to wealthy employers who extracted years of free labor in exchange for passage money. After their contract period was completed, these indentured servants were free to pursue whatever dream they cherished. Despite the hardships, many chose the frontier risking the chances of being scalped or taken captive by the so-called *Red Menace*. They came from Western Europe as well as Great Britain, and their reasons for coming were as varied as their customs and their accents. Among them were convicts freed from prisons with the proviso that they leave England for good. It was a pragmatic way to relieve overcrowded prisons, and English authorities congratulated themselves on their good fortune as ships laden with ex-convicts departed for foreign shores. In the natural course of events, many of these social castaways ended up in the crude frontier settlements along the New Hampshire and Maine coastline that were under persistent pressure from Indian attacks that threatened their survival.

At the other extreme, there were religious refugees who braved the uncertainties of the New World for more lofty motives. In August of 1718, five ships arrived in Boston Harbor loaded with Scotch/Irish Presbyterians. In 1612 the Scots had fled from England to the Irish port city of Derry in order to escape persecution from the Anglican Church. In 1688 after successfully defending Derry from the invading armies of England's King Henry 2nd, they renamed their adopted city Londonderry. In 1718, in the face of new persecution by Irish Catholics, they set a course for a new promised land in five sailing vessels. Confined to cramped ships frozen in the winter ice of Boston Harbor, they were saved from starvation by the Massachusetts legislature that voted funds to provision them through the winter. In the spring of 1719, two of their ships sailed up the coast to Portland, Maine where the Scotch/Irish immigrants were assimilated into settlements along the Maine coast. A small number were able to find work in Boston, and the remainder sailed in three ships up the Merrimack River to the frontier settlement of Haverhill. From Haverhill they went north to establish a settlement of Scotch Presbyterians at a place they called Nutfield (Londonderry, NH). This obsession to immigrate to the New World appeared to have no limits. Lamentably, there were no think tanks, governmental agencies, or environmentalists to counsel caution about the possible negative effects of the headlong rush to settle what appeared to be virgin wilderness. In their eagerness to grab their individual share of the bounty, most settlers gave little thought to the welfare of the *Original People*. Most English settlers thought of them as nomadic savages with little culture, a people who displayed no discernible redeeming qualities.

The Aboriginal natives claimed that their ancestors had been here since the beginning of time, and when one examines the evidence, one can hardly deny their claim. 13.000 years ago during the *Wisconsin Ice Age,* much of New England was overlaid by a massive ice cap that was more that a mile thick, and whose reach to the south is roughly defined by Cape Cod, Martha's Vineyard and Long Island. As the oceans of the world diminished during the cataclysmic climatic changes of the *Ice Age*, a land bridge called *Beringia* seemingly rose from the ocean floor to create a link between Asia and Alaska. The ancient nomadic hunters who ventured across the land bridge in search of the mastodon, the giant sloth, and the woolly mammoth were the progenitors of the indigenous people of New England. In the warming period that followed the *Ice Age,* some of these nomadic hunters ranged down the West Coast and into the South American continent. Others came down the Eastern slope of the Rockies to inhabit all the land to the Atlantic Ocean, while still others followed the great herds across Canada to Labrador and the Maritimes. The plethora of books describing their evolution from spear-carrying nomads to 17th Century Woodland Indians would fill a library. While it is not within the scope of this book to minutely examine their long history, one can safely say that there is ample archaeological evidence to prove that the presence of Native Americans in New England dates back at least 10,000 years.

An examination of their culture reveals that they had well defined family units, and that they lived in a highly structured society that worked well for them. They were hunters and gatherers, and their large communal gardens were essential to their survival. They preferred elevated sites close to rivers, lakes or streams for their villages. The rich silt of interval areas that were created by the overflow of rivers during spring floods provided ideal sites for their agriculture. They used the rich interval soil to cultivate corn, beans and squash that they called *The Three Sisters.* The ancient tradition of these three plants held great spiritual significance for the natives. They planted their corn in mounds or hummocks, and the corn stalks served to support the green beans; the broad leaves of squash acting as mulch. The women tended the gardens, but because of its wide use in ceremonies, it was customary for the braves to grow and harvest their own tobacco. Tobacco was an important part of Indian spirituality. Every man had a buckskin tobacco pouch, and the ubiquitous clay pipe was part of every brave's accessories. Their wigwams were domed structures made by covering bent saplings with elm or birch bark, and they insulated them against winter cold with woven mats made from swamp rushes and grasses. During the winter they often moved into communal long houses that were constructed in much the same manner as the individual wigwams. The wigwam was the property of the woman, and if she and her husband separated, the male retained only his personal possessions. Wives worked in the gardens, prepared the food and were experts at working deer hide into buckskin. Female chiefs ruled certain tribes. Men prepared the garden site, grew tobacco, hunted, fished, trapped fur-bearing animals and went on the warpath when it was deemed necessary. In some of the larger villages, the wigwams were encircled by a tall enclosure made of vertical logs. These log palisades were designed to provide protection against hostile raiding parties.

A council made up of both sexes selected the leaders of a typical Abenaki tribe that could vary in size from 100 to as many as 2,000 tribal members. Having observed the candidates from birth, the Indian women were particularly well qualified to choose their tribal leaders. The typical tribe had five chiefs that were subordinate to a sachem or grand chief. The sachem was usually an elder who had experience in subordinate roles, and who was highly respected by all members of the tribe. The sagamore executed the sachem's instructions, and served as a captain to supervise the activities of the other chiefs. He coordinated the activities of the assistant chiefs who were chosen for their special abilities. The civil chief acted like the mayor of a small town coordinating the social affairs of the village. Another chief supervised all food gathering activities. The war chief was chosen for his proven reputation as a brave warrior. The spiritual chief was called the *madolinu;* he was the medicine man or shaman who was concerned with the spiritual welfare of the tribe. Although those honored were usually chosen by popular vote, it was a natural consequence of effective leadership for the offspring of revered leaders to be named chief. Every aspect of Indian life was connected in some way to the spirit world. In the daily life of the native, virtually no task was undertaken without consulting the *madolinu* who was the spiritual leader of the tribe.[1] Through the Millennia, male and female *madolinu* accumulated great knowledge about the medicinal benefits of plants, and modern medical researchers confirm that many of their potions and natural cures are beneficial. By studying the burial details and artifacts of ancient native gravesites, archaeologists have concluded that the Aboriginal People believed in the afterworld. Natives believed in the reincarnation of all living beings including man. The Indian warrior who stalked the frontier border settlements felt a deep affinity for Mother Earth that was little understood by the

---

[1]Authors' note: This description of the political structure of the typical Abenaki tribe comes from Rejean Obomsawin, Abenaki historian and curator of the Indian museum that is part of the Canadian Indian Reservation in Odanak, Quebec.

Engish. His profound respect for his natural surroundings was at the root of his very being. Indian leaders were famous for their oratory. Their impressive oratory skills were developed by the disciplined protocol of their council meetings where order was maintained through the use of a "talking stick." He who held the talking stick commanded the attention of all members of the council circle. The power of Native American oratory is beautifully illustrated in Chief Seattle's famous address. The imagery and the reverent resonance of his address are an excellent example of how natives view their role on this planet even today:

Chief Seattle's Address

This we know. The earth does not belong to man;
man belongs to the earth. This we know.
All things are connected like the blood that unites one family.
All things are connected. Whatever befalls the earth,
befalls the sons of the earth. Man did not weave the web of life;
he is merely a strand in it. Whatever he does to the web,
he does to himself.
Every part of the earth is sacred to my people...
every shining pine needle, every sandy shore,
every light mist in the dark forest, every clearing
and every winged creature is sacred to my people.
We are part of the earth and it is part of us,
The fragrant flowers are our sisters,
The deer and mighty eagle are our brothers;
the rocky peak, the fertile meadows,
all things are connected like the blood that unites a family.

The Original People were a spirit-guided people who believed in a *Creator of All Things* whom they called *The Great Spirit.* Their folklore abounds in stories and myths about good and evil spirits who either support or are against the nature of man—this is the native way. The remarkable thing about native spirituality is the universality of their beliefs. Across the American continent local legends and myths may prevail, but the basic native belief in a *Supreme Power* is universal. In colonial days as today, there was never any attempt by the natives to solicit others to their spiritual beliefs. In this context Native American spirituality should not be viewed as a religion so much as it is *a way of life*.

One can easily understand why the English were both fascinated and put off by the appearance and customs of a people who some described in their writings as *wretched savages*. Indeed, earlier explorers took native captives back to England as trophies intended to amaze monarchs and their royal advisors. Invariably these captives succumbed to one of a variety of diseases for which they had no natural immunity. The English had every right to be proud of their heritage and their advanced culture. Their many colonies around the globe originated the saying: *The sun never sets on the British Empire*. The administration of their colonies was efficient and firm. Local opposition was eliminated ruthlessly. They undoubtedly raised the living standards of millions of subjects who lived under their rule, and they were tolerant of their subjects—so long as they toed the line. In the early 18th Century, Britannia ruled the waves and was a world power. But success often breeds a feeling of confidence that can easily become arrogance. England's class system tended to foster a feeling of superiority that was harbored by many British subjects fortunate enough to be well born. Like most ethnic groups, the English routinely installed their own customs in their far-flung possessions. It is little wonder that the early architecture and layout of Boston could have been mistaken for a typical English town. Slowly but surely, the English began to remake the wilderness in the image of their cherished English countryside. The native's attitude towards land and its intrinsic value astonished the English. The natives appeared not to understand the concept of the exchange of land for goods or money. There is evidence to support the idea that many Indians thought they were merely granting the right for the use of their land. Later, when they found their land converted to pasture and enclosed by fences[2], some crestfallen natives demanded the return of their land to no avail. Slowly disillusionment grew and festered. Inevitably, there were envious natives who began to compare their primitive villages to the well-ordered English farms owned by the newcomers. Bitter seeds of jealousy turned their acceptance of the newcomers to distrust and hatred that eventually turned to violent retribution.

Some of the inequities revealed by ancient documents are stunning! Chief Passaconaway's sale of land north of Haverhill, MA in 1642 is a typical example of the naiveté of even the most wise and powerful sachems. The Indians Passaqueo and SagaHew represented Passaconaway at the signing ceremony. They drew their bow and arrow totems on a document that conveyed 196 square miles of territory to citizens of Haverhill, MA. The tract extended 7 miles east and 7 miles west with Haverhill at its center. The 14-mile northward reach of the tract included territory as far north as the present-day towns of Windham and Derry. The purchase price was 3 pounds, 10 shillings (about 7 American dollars). The Indians were also given food, beads and other trinkets to seal the bargain. Some settlers acquired other Indian land using unethical tactics. Many were persuaded to affix their totems to sale agreements while in a drunken stupor, while others agreed to sell land after their gardens were deliberately overrun by colonial cattle. In the absence of any authority charged with protecting native rights, abuses were extensive, and in certain cases, native leaders betrayed the trust of their people by accepting frivolous gifts—frock coats, rum, whisky and petty cash payments—in exchange for selling out their own people.

Among the newcomers there were responsible people that were interested in the welfare of the indigenous people they encountered in the New World. Their concern was driven by

---

[2]Authors' note: In 1663 the British Parliament passed a law requiring property owners of 100 acres of land to enclose it by a fence. During this period only 5% of the population of Great Britain owned 50 acres of land or more. In New England, during the same era, 85% owned at least 50 acres.

the same unshakeable faith that had caused them to abandon their English homeland in order to seek religious freedom in America. Their hearts went out to the indigenous people who they viewed as a people deprived, not only of material things, but certainly a people deprived of spiritual guidance. Their limited understanding of Indian spiritual beliefs confirmed what they suspected from the beginning; these wretched people were heathens who desperately needed to be saved from the fires of hell. Through the well-intentioned efforts of the Puritan clergy and their parishioners, thousands of natives were converted to Christianity by the time of King Philips War in 1675. Through the encouragement and assistance of well-meaning people, a number of "*praying villages*" were established in Southern New England. Visiting white preachers often preached sermons in native churches, and the conversion of the Indians to white beliefs seemed assured. The apparent harmony was superficial, however, and there was no real joining of the two races. There were no integrated communities, and there was virtually no intermarriage. In time, inter-racial marriage did take place between Indians of the Wampanoag and Narragansett tribes and black slaves of colonial slaveholders.[3]

In 1675 the tension between the two cultures erupted into open hostility in a two-year conflict known as King Philip's War. Overwhelming English retaliation to the early Indian raids eventually reversed initial native successes, and the brutal war ended when Metacom, also known as King Philip, was killed in a Narragansett swamp where he and his warriors had taken refuge from pursuing English forces. Ironically, an Indian scout acting for the English killed King Philip. As a warning to ambitious successors, the English cut off his head and mounted it on the palisade that protected one of their settlements. His body was quartered with an axe and thrown to the elements. Thus did his "civilized" victors dispose of the "savage". Even though the inhabitants of the praying villages tried

---

[3]Authors' note: There are many descendants of the Wampanaog Indians that have Indian/African roots who maintain their native culture and attend the various powwows in the New England area.

to remain neutral, cautious English authorities decided to confine them to Deer Island in Boston Harbor, where many died during the winter due to lack of food and proper shelter. Some of the inhabitants of the praying villages fled to a mission village located in Canada on the Saint Francis River near its junction with the Saint Lawrence River. It was established by French authorities to harbor native refugees from both New England and New York and it was run by Jesuit priests. The descendants of many native refugee tribes of New England and New York, still live in the city that is now called Odanak.

In the wave of indignation that followed the early Indian attacks on English settlements, the English rounded up all Indians who they suspected of having supported Metacom. Entire native families were herded onto ships and sold as slaves in Jamaica and Barbados. Some slavers sold their Native American cargoes as far away as Algiers in the Mediterranean. The fate of King Philip's wife and son has never been determined. Many historians believe that they were among the slaves who were sold abroad. In a strange twist of fate the colonists, after a 55-year experiment, expatriated a race of people whose ancestors had occupied the New England forests and coastline for more than 10,000 years!

By the end of King Philip's War, the native presence in Massachusetts was greatly diminished. Many braves had been killed during the hostilities, and some of the survivors avoided slavery in the Caribbean by fleeing to New Hampshire and Maine, where they found refuge with sympathetic Abenaki tribes. Some took refuge at the French mission village built by the French on the Saint Francis River, a tributary of the St. Lawrence River in Canada. By 1724, after almost 50 years of intermittent warfare with the English, the fighting power of the Abenaki was seriously diminished. The mission village, called Odanak today, continued to grow as more and more refugees from the south made it their permanent home. Odanak eventually became a staging area from where war parties, often led by French officers, made raids on colonial settlements. By 1724, however, with the balance of power shifting in favor of the

English, Indian attacks were reduced to small harassing raids on small outlying settlements like Dunstable and Groton. The main purpose of these raids was to abduct women and children to be turned over to French authorities in exchange for money. The French in turn ransomed them back to their families—sometimes for substantial sums.

In many ways, the Original People of the North American continent were victimized by the unintended consequences of actions initiated by Europeans during the 16th, 17th and 18th centuries. Beginning in the 1500s, smallpox and other diseases unique to Europeans decimated the native population as a result of their contact with early English and Spanish explorers. Historians have estimated the pre-contact native population of Maine, New Hampshire, Vermont and the Maritimes at 45,000. A severe outbreak of sickness (probably smallpox) in 1612-1613 wiped out up to 80% of the population of the coastal Indian tribes. Chief Passaconaway of the Penacook Nation that dominated the Merrimack River Valley in pre-contact times, declared the territory in and around Haverhill cursed and prevailed upon the Pentucket band to resettle in Concord, NH. He later sold that property for a pittance. By 1724 the native population was reduced to 12,000 as a result of European-transmitted diseases. Virtually all of the early English settlements were established close to the many river outlets to the Atlantic Ocean.

At the earliest opportunity, settlers began to move up the rivers where they could claim virgin farmland, and where they could dam the rivers and streams to provide waterpower for their sawmills and gristmills. One must be charitable in assessing their motives. In their eagerness to achieve their dreams of wealth and security for their families, they may not have considered how their dams would affect the lives of the native inhabitants in the interior. The rivers and streams of New England were essential to the very existence of the Indians. Natives navigated their 80-pound birch bark canoes using the network of rivers and streams to trade with their neighbors as well as for hunting and food gathering activities. In May of each year, the entire native population moved to their favorite fishing sites on the Merrimack to spear and net salmon, shad, and sturgeon during the spawning season. The surplus was dried and smoked and stored in underground birch bark containers for use during the winter. With spring planting completed, the Indians traveled by canoe to seasonal villages on the coast where they lived well on the bountiful food supply provided by the sea and its estuaries. One need only look at the condition of New England's rivers today to assess the consequences of 380 years of unbridled colonial expansion. The salmon count at the recently installed fish ladder at the Amoskeag Dam on the Merrimack River in Manchester, NH is increasing slowly, but the comparison to 1700 is discouraging—dozens of salmon versus millions.

England's War against the French and their native allies had not gone well in the New World. Discord between London and Boston mounted when the British proposed taxes on the colonists to help offset the cost of their war with France. The Massachusetts legislature calculated that they were spending the staggering sum of 1,000 pounds for every Indian killed. When seen in this context, is it not surprising that the legislature decided to offer a bounty of 40 pounds for each Indian scalp delivered to Boston. In frontier towns like Haverhill, Andover and Dunstable, where men were working for shillings a week, it was a fortune. With the frontier under constant attack from raiding parties out of Canada, Maine, NH, and Vermont, the colonists sorely needed a victory—any victory to lift their sagging spirits. It had been 28 years since Hannah Dustin inspired colonial settlers from Newfoundland to Virginia with her miraculous escape from Indian captivity carrying with her the scalps of 11 of her captors. On an island in the Merrimack River near the mouth of the Contoocook River, together with captives Mary Neff and Samuel Leonardson, she managed to surprise and kill two adult male Indians and nine native women and children and make her way back to Haverhill, MA. Traveling in a birch-bark canoe and carrying 11 scalps in a piece of linen stolen from her own home, their first friendly sighting was a farmhouse close by the river. The first white man to comfort them and feed them was the grandfather to a boy who would later grow up to become one of America's early folk heroes. After feeding them and listening to the details of their harrowing adventure, John Lovewell warned them of perilous rapids and falls downstream and wished them God speed.

In later years, the young lad John Lovewell sat at his grandfather knee countless times asking him to retell the story of his encounter with Hannah Dustin and her young companions. The same boy grew to manhood steeped in the military tradition of his family. He grew up to become a woodsman, a hunter, and a soldier who carried his reputation as a bush fighter with quiet assurance. As he prepared to embark on his first scalp hunting expedition in 1724, John Lovewell had no inkling that he was embarking on a series of adventures that would cause the name Lovewell to be celebrated in song and verse for the next one hundred years.

1-1 Historic Marker, Nashua, New Hampshire

1-2 Wampanoag Chief Massasoit

CHAPTER 2

FIRST NATIONS REBELLION

We burned their villages; we took a thousand scalps,
We carried off their women and their children.
Still they came to steal out land.
Our shaman used their most potent magic against them,
but their sorcery was greater.

From *Abenaki Warrior* by Alfred E. Kayworth

In 1675 a loaded musket was the constant companion of the Dunstable settler; it was at his side as he worked his farm, it stood by his bedside at night, and he went to worship on Sunday carrying a bible in one hand and his musket in the other. The early settlers were a hardy lot of people; it took courage to leave the safety of Boston and go into the wilderness to eke out a living surrounded by an alien people some called savages. As more and more ships from Europe landed their human cargoes in Boston, pressure steadily mounted to find room for them. Their expectations were high; for many the prospect of owning their own farm was the ultimate dream. As the original proprietors of Boston prospered and began to raise large families, they were faced with a dilemma; they needed to find a way for their children to prosper through their own devices. In the agrarian society of the 17th and 18th centuries, the best way to achieve success was to homestead a fine piece of land and forge a new life. Many of the later immigrants chose to seek their fortunes in the coastal settlements of New Hampshire and Maine, but for the canny early proprietors of Boston, there was valuable territory much closer at hand. They were among the early visitors to the lush valleys of the Nashaway

River and the Merrimack River,[4] and on their return to Boston, they rhapsodized over the rich soil where they had seen the bountiful Indian gardens. They watched in silent envy in early May as Indians of the Pawtucket and Wamesit tribes netted tons of spawning salmon, sturgeon and shad from their naamkeeks (fishing stations) on the Merrimack River. With this insight, it is no surprise that the recipients of land grants in the lush valleys of the Nashua and the Merrimack were given to prominent Bostonians.

In August 1652 the General Assembly of Massachusetts authorized a survey by Captains Simon Willard and Edward Johnson to determine the northernmost point of the Massachusetts Colony. They carved an inscription on a large stone in the Winnipesaukee River at a point *three miles north of the head of the Merrimack River* to designate this point. The Massachusetts Colony then claimed all land laying three miles north and east of the Merrimack from its mouth to the stone marker on the Winnipesaukee River and thence due west to New York.[5] Inasmuch as the stone marker was located three miles north of where the Pemigewassit and the Winnipesaukee Rivers join just above Franklin, NH, the New Hampshire province vigorously contested the Massachusetts interpretation of the original charter. Over a period of many years, the two provinces made numerous legal challenges to each other's grants of territory along the Merrimack River north of Dracut. An English court finally resolved the long legal wrangle in 1741. The details of the English court ruling and its subsequent effect on the early Massachusetts grants, are covered in a later chapter.

---

[4]History of the Old Township of Dunstable by Charles J. Fox, 1846, p9; "The valley of the Merrimack was not an object of desire to the English alone. From the earliest days it seems to be have looked upon by the Indian as almost a Paradise. So far indeed had its fame spread that in 1604, years before the landing at Plymouth, a French Jesuit, writing from Canada to France could say; "*The Indians tell us of a beautiful river lying far to the south, which they call Merrimac*" Authors' note: The English translation of Merrimack is "*Profound River.*"

[5]History of the Old Township of Dunstable by Charles J. Fox, 1846, p8 footnote.

Between 1653 and 1673, having obtained a survey of land they perceived to be part of their grant from the King of England, the Massachusetts Council awarded 14,000 acres of land in grants that extended from the Souhegan River southward to Chelmsford. In the east the grants included parts of the modern towns of Dracut, Windham and Derry, and in the west, they reached as far as Amherst and Milford. During this 20-year period, the local Indians continued to plant their traditional *Three Sisters* (corn, squash and beans) each year. During the 2nd and 3rd weeks of May, they continued to man their naamkeeks (fishing stations) on the Merrimack as their ancestors had done for thousands of years. In the beginning, the natives accepted the few venturesome settlers who settled on what the English called "*plantations.*"[6] In the context of the period, there seemed to be plenty of land for all; the Indian way of life was not yet affected, and the natives who were fascinated by the strange ways of the white man, seemed to accept their presence with tolerance and curiosity. The Indians continued to practice their pastoral traditions unaware of the storm clouds that were building beyond their horizon. Chief Passaconaway, who had counseled peace in his farewell address to his people in 1660, was a strong advocate of friendship with the English[7]. The Indian leaders did not judge the strength of the English by the weakness of their unprotected settlements in Dunstable. They were sufficiently impressed by the large English settlement in Boston. They were well aware of the killing power of their muskets and cannon, and they were mindful that the English could only accommodate their insatiable appetite for more land by moving north—towards them. In addition to the increasing power of the English, the Pawtucket, the Wamesit, and the Na-

---

[6]Authors' note: *Plantation* was the accepted terminology used to describe individual land grants.

[7]Authors' note: Chief Passaconaway, the great Penacook Sachem and the most powerful and noted sorcerer of all the country, retired to tiny Wickasuck Island (now the site of the Vesper Country Club) where he lived until his death in about 1670. Estimates of his longevity vary from 100 to 120 years.

ticook Indians felt equally threatened from another quarter. Although they were nervous about having the English as neighbors, they were more fearful of their ancient enemy to the west—the Mohawks. This fierce tribe from the Hudson River Valley was *Guardian of the Eastern Portal* of the five-member *Iroquois Nation.* They were part of *The Great Umbrella of Peace*[8] that extended from the Adirondacks to the Great Lakes and from the Canadian border to Mississippi. For centuries they had made war against the tribes who refused to join their confederation, and their reputation as fierce warriors was legendary. Passaconaway's strategy to use the English as a shield against the Mohawk failed, and the warriors of the Merrimack Valley eventually were forced to support the Wabanaki Federation's efforts to drive the English back to Boston. However, Wannalancet heeded his father's counsel, and he also avoided conflict with the English. During the King Philip's war he and his Wamesit warriors avoided confrontation with the English by moving to Canada. He remained a steadfast friend of the English, and he lived peaceably with members of his tribe at Wamesit Falls until his death.

In September 1673, the owners of 26 individual plantations petitioned The Commonwealth of Massachusetts to combine all of their grants into a single large plantation that would include the area previously described, and to be officially known as the Township of Dunstable.[9] The 200 square miles of the new township embraced the towns of Nashua, Nashville, Hudson, Hollis, Dunstable and Tyngsboro. It also included parts of the towns of Amherst, Milford, Merrimac, Litchfield, Pelham, Londonderry, Brookline, Pepperell and Townsend. The consolidation of all the grants into a single township "*secured for*

---

[8]Authors' note: The Iroquois "Great Umbrella of Peace" was a misnomer. It eliminated the incessant wars between members of The Confederation, but continued to wage war on those tribes who refused the protection of their "Umbrella of Peace."

[9]History of the Old Township of Dunstable, by Charles J. Fox, 1846; p 16: "It received its name in compliment to Mrs. Mary Tyng, wife of Hon. Edward Tyng, one of the Magistrates of the Commonwealth of Massachusetts who came from Dunstable, England."

all the inhabitants the privileges and immunities of an incorporated township."[10] The new charter imposed certain conditions on the grantees. They were required to have a minister within three years and to provide at least 20 competent settlers, each of whom was required to erect a dwelling that was at least 18-feet square that was sufficiently sturdy to be defended against Indian attacks. In addition they had to set aside a farm for the use of the Commonwealth, and they were required to construct a meetinghouse.

An examination of the records of early colonial settlement reveals a recurring pattern. In his *History of Old Dunstable*, Charles Fox lists the names of the 26 individuals who petitioned the Commonwealth to grant township status to 14,000 acres of land they owned jointly. Of these 26 original proprietors, only 4 names show up in a subsequent list of 32 early Dunstable settlers. It appears that most of the original grantees induced others to settle small portions of their grant, knowing that once the settlement was secure from Indian attack, the value of their remaining property would skyrocket in value—a typical land speculator's tactic. The rigors and dangers inherent in frontier life produced very close-knit families; parents and children often lived within a short wagon ride of each other for life. When a couple settled a grant of land, it was not uncommon for them to have large families. Farms require a lot of hand labor, and the children were expected to help with the farm chores until they married. When they married, the parents encouraged them to press further into the frontier and develop their own farms. By encouraging others to tame the wilderness, the parents gradually reduced their own chances of being attacked by Indians, and the value of their own property inevitably increased in value. Typically, the oldest son stayed with his parents for life with he and his wife caring for his parents in their old age. When the parents passed on, the oldest son and his wife inherited the original homestead and the process was repeated in the following generation.

---

[10]History of the Old Township of Dunstable, by Charles J. Fox, 1846, p 12

The earliest settlements in Dunstable were located in the neck of land located between the Merrimack River and the Salmon River that ran almost parallel to the Merrimack from Massapaug Pond to its outlet in the Merrimack. There was such an abundance of interval[11] land along the Merrimack and the Nashua that the natives chose only the most fertile ground. English farmers gave a high priority to settling those unused interval areas, and when the Indians abandoned interval land for whatever reason, they quickly moved in. It was only after they acquired these prime lands that the English began to think of the Indians. They eventually rewarded Wannalancet for his steadfast loyalty to the English by allotting land to the Wamesit near Wickasuck Island, where he spent his final years. Under the guise of peaceful coexistence with their native neighbors, the English conquest of the Original People continued to make inroads like an insidious plague.

In 1675, the idyllic vision of Colonist and Indian peaceably harvesting the bounty of *Mother Earth* side by side was abruptly shattered when Metacom and his Wampanoag warriors launched an attack against English settlements throughout Massachusetts. The repercussions from King Philip's War eventually affected all of the First Nation tribes of New England. During the next 50 years, Abenaki Indians and their French-Canadian allies subjected Dunstable and other frontier settlements to innumerable raids. Towards the end of that era, growing English power began to force the Indians to the defensive. The marginal relevancy of these episodes to our central theme, as well as the constraints of space, make it necessary to limit the number of events described in this story. It will be sufficient to briefly describe the principal raids on Dunstable and neighboring towns in the larger context of the world competition between France and England for control of maritime trade and colonial possessions. In the process of portraying the worldwide competition between the two super powers, the

---

[11]Authors' note: Interval areas were alluvial deposits formed by the overflow of rivers through the Millennia. Very often they were void of trees and the soil was extremely fertile and suitable for farming.

storyline gradually narrows to a single bloody battle on the sandy verge of a picturesque pond in Maine.

In the summer of 1675, Groton, Chelmsford, and Lancaster were among the first settlements that were burned and pillaged by rampaging Indians led by the Wampanoag Sachem Metacom, better known as King Philip. The three towns were leveled by fire, and hundreds of their citizens were either killed or carried into captivity by Caughnawaga Indians. Shaken by the news, the Dunstable settlers petitioned the governor and his council for relief, and in August, eighteen militiamen were sent to reinforce the Dunstable garrison. The same order provided twelve militiamen to both Groton and Chelmsford.

At this stage of the conflict, Indian raids against these towns were coming from the Wampanoag and other southern tribes, and the reinforcements prevented further attacks. In September of the same year, the Governor and his council ordered Captain Thomas Brattle and Lt. Thomas Henchman to take the following additional measures:

1. To draft 50 additional men and establish new garrisons at Dunstable, Groton and Lancaster
2. To appoint a guardian over the friendly Indians of the so-called "*Praying Towns*" who were presumed to be neutral
3. To locate Wannalancet and invite him to come out of hiding to reside at Wamesit, where he would be under the protection of the English
4. To inform the Penacook Indians at Naticook and Penacook (Concord) that if they remained neutral, they would not be harmed by the English.

At this point in time, the "*Praying Indians*" were caught in a dilemma. The Massachusetts Colony had six "*Praying Villages*", one being located in Dunstable. When war broke out, most of the fighting braves went into the wilderness with Wannalancet who sought to remain neutral. The General Court placed ten Indian warriors and fifty native women and children under the care of Jonathan Tyng who kept them near their traditional home on Wickasuck Island. Fifteen additional males and fifty women were "*bound out to service*" with various English families during the war. Their protected status enabled them to earn their room and board in the service of their English patrons. At this point in time, many settlers regarded the natives with disdain. Increase Mather, a leading Boston clergyman and preacher, illustrated the efficacy of prayer by saying,

> "Nor should they cease praying to the Lord against Philip until they had prayed the bullet into his heart." He added, "We have heard of twenty two Indian captives slain together, all of them, and brought down to hell in one day."

Another appalling sentiment expressed frequently during this period by certain members of the clergy further illustrates the spirit of the times:

> It has often been remarked that, in the settlement of New England we may discover the hand of an overruling Providence. The Plague that swept off the Indian tribes in and around Plymouth and Piscataqua in 1612 and 1613 prepared the way for the coming of the forefathers, and similar providential events occurred as population moved westward.[12]

Caught between the conflicting interests of the two greatest world powers of the period, the legendary Sagamore Passaconaway and his son Wannalancet did the best they could for their people. Although the Penacook in Concord eventually joined in the French/Abenaki crusade against the English, the great Passaconaway was so highly regarded by the English that they arranged for him to spend his last days on a small island

[12] History of the Old Township of Dunstable, by Charles J. Fox, 1846; p 23

in the Merrimack together with some of his people. His son Wannalancet, by heeding his father's advice, managed to save himself and other Wamesit from annihilation. In time, as the mist in a forest glade fades with the rising sun, so too faded the Indian way of life before the mounting power of the white man. Whittier's *Bridal of Penacook,* that was written on the occasion of the wedding of Passaconaway's daughter Wetamoo to Winnepurkit, paints a idyllic portrait of a *Paradise Lost:*

The Bashaba's Feast

With pipes of peace and bows unstrung,
Flowing with paint, came old and young,
In wampum, and furs and feathers arrayed,
To the dance and the feast Bashaba made.

Bird of the air and beast of the field,
All which the woods and water yield,
On dishes of birch and hemlock piled,
Garnished and graced that banquet wild.

Steaks of the brown bear fat and large,
From the rocky slopes of the Kearsarge;
Delicate trout from Babboosuck brook,
And salmon spear'd in the Contoocook;

Squirrels which fed where nuts fell thick,
In the gravelly bed of the Otternie,
And small wild hens in reed-snares caught
From the banks of the Sondagardee brought.

Pikes and perch from the Sunacook taken,
Nuts from the trees of the Black Hills shaken;
Cranberries picked in the Squamscot bog,
And grapes from the vines of Piscataquog.

And drawn from that great stone vase which stands
In the river scooped by a spirit's hands,
In white parched pile, or thick suppawn,
Stood the birchen dishes of smoking corn.

Thus bird of the air and beast of the field,
All which the woods and water yield,
Furnished in that olden day,
The bridal feast of the Bashaba.

And merrily when that feast was done,
On the fire-lit green, the dance begun;
With the squaw's shrill stave, and deeper hum
Of old men beating the Indian drum.

Painted and plumed, with scalp locks flowing,
And red arms tossing, the black eyes glowing;
Now in the light and now in the shade,
Around the fires the dancers played.

The step was quicker, the song more shrill,
And the beat of the small drums louder still,
Whenever within the circle drew
The Saugus Sachem and Weetamoo.
--John Greenleaf Whittier

During the winter of 1675-76, the people of Dunstable lived in fear of Indian raids. Only the intrepid Jonathan Tyng remained in Dunstable to defend his home at Wickasuck Falls near Tyngsboro Village. His petition for assistance was quickly granted, and several men were dispatched to help him defend his property. His plantation was never deserted during the war, and by his rather foolhardy bravery, he earned the distinction of being the first permanent settler within the limits of Dunstable. At the end of 1676, with the Narragansett and the Wampanoag Indians subdued and Philip's severed head on public display to remind the natives of English might, the town of Dunstable and surrounding communities quickly returned to normal. The people of Dunstable switched their priority to building a meetinghouse and a church, but they continued to maintain five garrison houses in the town.

King William's War began in 1688 after the fall of the House of Stuart. The far-reaching effects of that war began to be felt in New England, and Dunstable was now faced with attacks from a new quarter. At the bidding of Canadian authorities, resident Jesuit priests of the major Abenaki Tribes of Maine and Vermont began to incite their Indian disciples to attack English settlements on the Merrimack River and up the coast as far as Newfoundland. During the month of September 1694, Abenaki war parties murdered a total of seven Dunstable residents in two separate raids. A brief period of peace followed the signing of the Treaty of Ryswick in 1698, but unresolved issues between the two powers ignited a new war that lasted for 10 years; it was known as Queen Anne's War. During the month of August in 1703, Canadians together with their Abenaki allies launched a series of destructive raids on the coastal settlements carrying into captivity more than 200 settlers. As a consequence of these raids, the Massachusetts Council offered a 40-pound bounty for Indian scalps, and in the winter of 1703-1704, Captain John Tyng and a small group of men traveled to the Pigwacket stronghold in Maine and took 5 Pigwacket scalps. On the 3rd of November 1704, the General Court approved an appropriation for four additional blockhouses to be built on the Merrimack, two for Chelmsford, and one each for Billerica and Dunstable. On July 3, 1706, two hundred and seventy Abenaki Indians surprised a garrison house in Rowley and overwhelmed Nathaniel Blanchard's garrison in Dunstable killing nine people. By 1711 there were seven fortified garrison houses in Dunstable. During this trying period, every citizen of the town routinely slept in a garrison house.

When the Treaty of Utrecht once again restored peace in April 1713, Dunstable grew its population quickly. In the following eleven years, despite having signed their totems to a peace treaty, the Abenaki Indians continued to commit smaller depredations against the settlements on the colonial frontier. At the same time, the English took advantage of the relative quiet afforded by the treaty, and they continued to build stone forts on the rivers. Young Indian braves that were indoctrinated from birth with the warrior tradition and the importance of demonstrating their bravery in battle, could not understand the acquiescence of their elders. Their strong objection to the ongoing construction of fortified outposts in their territory was the principal reason for Indian complaints.

The English finally responded to the Indian violence by sending a combined force of English and Mohawk Indians[13] to the Norridgewalk village on the Kennebec River. They destroyed the village and killed Jesuit Father Rale, a man who had incited his native followers against the English for many years. As a result of the raid, Norridgewalk Indians abandoned their village and moved to the French mission village on the St. Francis River in Canada. A similar raiding party sent to punish the formidable Penobscot Indians found only empty wigwams; like the Norridgewalk, they appeared to have vanished. Yet, despite these major pullouts, smaller raiding parties continued to make life miserable for settlers along the frontier. No farmer was safe working his fields during the day, and any relaxation of vigilance was an invitation to murder, pillage and abduction. The raiding parties came well prepared; the extra moccasins they packed were intended for the captives they planned to ransom in Montreal and Quebec. They routinely killed and scalped most of the adult males they encountered. They preferred adult women and children of either sex who were generally submissive captives. Although they were not known to sexually molest captive women, they had no scruples about dispatching them with a tomahawk if they were unable to maintain the pace on the return trip to Canada; it was a business! The French paid them for the captives they brought in,

---

[13]Authors' note: They came from the Hudson Valley in Northern New York State. The Mohawks were members of the Iroquois Nation and traditional enemies of the New England tribes. They were natural allies for the English in their war against the French/Abenaki alliance.

and the captives were generally well treated by the French. Children were placed in convent schools where concerted efforts were made to convert them to Catholicism. Although many captives were eventually redeemed by ransom, there were some women who married Frenchmen and refused to return to their homes when their families offered to ransom them.

In 1722, because of the continuing depredations by the Abenaki Indians, Governor Dummer declared war on the eastern tribes. It was called *Governor Dummer's War with the Eastern Abenaki Indians*. The Massachusetts Colony poorly coordinated the war, and by 1724 a stalemate existed. The Abenaki Indians continued to raid settlements along the Merrimack and up the New England coast. When the English retaliated with punitive probes into the interior, the Indians faded into the forest. For the colonial militia, it was like trying to net a butterfly blindfolded. The English complained bitterly about the treacherous savages and their skulking tactics and their refusal to engage in a fair fight—a ludicrous complaint! Stealth and surprise had been the Indian's best weapon for thousands of years. Now, with 70% of their population victim to the white man's plagues and attacks, for them to engage in frontal attacks against the English would have been suicidal. Like two pit bulls locked in a fight to the death, neither side would concede defeat, and both sides sorely needed a victory to boost their morale.

Captain John Lovewell had lived amidst danger since his birth on October 14, 1691. He had spent much of his youth sleeping in garrison houses with his parents and neighbors wondering when the Indians would attack. He was old enough to remember how the Indians had killed his grandparents and three other relatives. As a young lad he could load and prime a musket that was taller than him, and at age twelve, he had stood transfixed with awe when Captain William Tyng and his snowshoe militia returned from Winnipesaukee proudly exhibiting their scalp trophies. He was a farmer first as well as a woodsman, a hunter, a soldier, and an Indian fighter. Lovewell and his wife Hannah lived with their two children on a 200-

acre plantation on the south side of the Nashua River in Dunstable.

The John Lovewell saga began rather routinely. In the evening of September 4, 1724, Lovewell went to his sawmill to check on two men who were sleeping there with his permission. Nathan Cross and Thomas Blanchard made their living by "boxing" pine trees to collect resin that was used in the production of turpentine. The pine forest in which they had been working ran along the north side of the Nashua River where there were no settlers. Sensing Indian trouble, Lovewell sounded an alarm, and Lieutenant French took nine men to locate the missing men. Signs at the work site indicated that Indians abducted Blanchard and Cross. Bands on the wooden resin buckets were broken, and the thick resin was still oozing into the pine needles. Noting the flow of the resin, Josiah Farwell suggested that the kidnappers could not be far away, and Lieutenant French perhaps feeling the importance of his command, impetuously gave the order to pursue. Farwell, brother-in-law to Lovewell and an experienced Indian fighter, suggested that they take a circuitous route to reduce the chances of being ambushed. Annoyed by what he perceived to be a challenge to his authority, French threw down the gauntlet saying, "*I'm taking the direct route. If any of you are not afraid—follow me*"[14] Farwell, unimpressed by French's bravado, trailed the headlong pursuit cautiously. They did not realize that they were chasing a large Canadian raiding party of Caughnawaga Indians led by French officers.[15] At Thornton's Ferry just south of where the Sou-

---

[14]Authors' note: The chronicles of the Indian wars recount many instances of the ambush that was so natural to a race of people bred to the forest environment. The wily Indians, understanding the impetuous nature of their foe, routinely ambushed rescue parties sent out to retrieve kidnapped relatives and friends.

[15]Authors' note: The Caughnawaga Indians were also known as Maguas. They were a band of Mohawk Indians who had been converted to Catholicism by the Jesuits. From their new base at the Saint Louis Mission in Montreal, they launched many raids against English settlements. Their dev-

hegan joins the Merrimack River, the Indians ambushed them. Suddenly confronted by the live reality of his worse fears, Farwell watched his companions fall in a maelstrom of musket fire, war whoops, black powder smoke, and death cries. A few managed to flee, but they were pursued and cut down. After surveying the bloody scene from behind the protection of a tree, Farwell fired his musket and then ran for his life. Two Maguas intent on killing him followed him with great purpose for a considerable distance without gaining an advantage. At length he burst through a thicket, and the Indians, fearing he might have reloaded, finally gave up the chase.[16]

When the sole survivor of the ambush reached home, the townspeople were stunned by Farwell's account of the massacre. Sick at heart, they sent an armed contingent of men to retrieve the victims of the massacre. Seven of the victims were laid to rest in a common grave marked by a unique headstone. The quaint, rather untutored inscription of the headstone is still legible:

> Momento Mori: Here lies the body of Mr. Thomas Lund who departed this life September 5, 1724 in the 42nd year of his age. This Man with Seven more that lies in this Grave was Slew in A day by the Indiens.

The interred men were: Lieutenant Ebenezer French, Thomas Lund and Ebenezer Cummings of Dunstable, Daniel Baldwin and John Burbank of Woburn, Mr. Johnson of Plainfield and Benjamin Carter. Three nearby stones bearing the same date are placed for Benjamin Carter, aged 23, Ebenezer Cummings, aged 29, and Oliver Farwell, aged 33.

---

astating raid on Deerfield, Massachusetts in 1704 resulted in 53 English killed and 111 taken to Canada as captives.

[16]Authors' note: During his flight from his Indian pursuers, Josiah Farewell lost his gun, his coat and 3 pounds in cash he was carrying with him. Upon his petition to the court he received an allowance of 5 pounds. Unfazed by his narrow escape from death, or perhaps to revenge the death of his brother Oliver in the same incident, he went on to serve as a lieutenant with Lovewell in his three raids into Indian country.

The kidnap victims, Thomas Blanchard and Jonathan Cross, ultimately provided an ironic epilogue to the sad affair. After suffering greatly as captives of the Caughnawaga Indians, the pair managed to negotiate their release in exchange for building a sawmill in Canada for the French. The French released them at the same time they released William Lund, who had been taken in early 1724. The three returned safely to Dunstable after a long difficult trek from Montreal, Canada.

In the aftermath of the massacre at Thornton's Ferry, the public mood gradually changed from shock and sorrow to bitterness and anger. The public outcry for revenge against this and other depredations was rampant in the colony, and the General Court looked for ways to retaliate for the depredations. During the winter, John Lovewell and his brother-in-law Josiah Farwell often talked about the desperate situation with Jonathan Robbins. Having shared the bitter brew of humiliating defeat, their talk centered on ways to retaliate for the deaths of their relatives and close friends. When they heard that the General Court was raising the bounty on Indian scalps to 100 pounds, they were galvanized to action. Their farms were idle until spring; the hay and the cattle were safely in the barn; what better season and reason to seek revenge? After pooling their thoughts, the three men went to Boston to petition the court. They offered to raise a group of volunteers to hunt the enemy in his own lair provided the court would approve a per diem payment of 2 shillings 6 pence for each man in addition to the 100 pound bounty for scalps. On November 17, 1724, the General Court approved their petition and commissioned John Lovewell Captain of the expedition, and assigned Josiah Farewell and Jonathan Robbins as his lieutenants.[17]

Lovewell and his two lieutenants lost no time in raising a volunteer force of thirty men for his first expedition into the wilderness. Most of the men who volunteered harbored a grievance against the Indians that they were anxious to redress.

---

[17]History of Dunstable, Nason p43: Lovewell or Jonathan Tyng was probably the originator of the volunteer system of this state, men having hitherto been raised only by draft or impressment as it was sometimes dominated.

There was little to do on their farms and they each hoped to claim some of the bounty money. When Lovewell called the muster of the heavily armed volunteers, they looked like trouble for the Indians. Swinging their muskets and dressed in homespun frontier clothes, they headed north on the Merrimack Trail with Lovewell, Farwell and Robbins in the vane. By the middle of December, they found themselves north of Lake Winnipesaukee. About forty-four miles north of the lake they came across a single wigwam, and in the brief encounter that followed, they killed one adult native and captured a fifteen-year-old Indian youth. After two weeks in the wilderness, they were short of provisions and Lovewell decided to return to his base. Like a proud retriever carrying a mallard to his master in a duck blind, Lovewell and his lieutenants appeared before the council with their boy captive and a single scalp. A Boston News Letter of January 7, 1725 reported that *"the Lieutenant-Governor and his Council were pleased to award the scalp hunters 50 pounds above the 150 pounds allowed by law."* After a series of humiliating defeats and reverses along their frontier, it was a small but significant success. Warmed by the praise of the council and with 200 pounds ($275) in hand, John Lovewell, Josiah Farewell, and Jonathan Robbins headed home. Out in open country after crossing the Charles River, they urged their horses into a canter buoyed by the praise of the council and feeling supremely confident about the new venture they were already planning.

Bad news languishes while good news has wings, and the yeomen of the Merrimack Valley responded to Lovewell's 2nd call for volunteers enthusiastically. By the end of January, he managed to enlist a volunteer company of eighty-seven men. Some of the Dunstable men who responded to the call were his brother Zacheus Lovewell, Thomas Colburn, Peter Powers, Josiah Cummings, William Ayers, Samuel Fletcher and Henry Farwell. Groton volunteers were Jacob Ames, Ephraim Farnsworth, Reuben Farnsworth, Benjamin Parker, Samuel Shattuck, Samuel Tarbell, and Henry Willard. They were farmers, woodsmen, and bush hunters, and they were all equipped with snowshoes. They were men who had quickly adapted the best ideas of the native to their own use. They had seen the Indian glide the surface of deep winter snow on webbed feet pulling his toboggan. They had watched him return pulling the same toboggans laden with moose and deer meat taken in their deep winter retreats. They had learned the lessons of the wilderness; like the wolverine, they too could travel and live in the snow bound stillness of the forest. In the eyes of these frontier-bred men, John Lovewell didn't need a captain's commission to command respect. He was a man who led by example, and his methodical approach to his task imbued his men with the confidence that he knew what he was doing. The surviving journal of his 2nd raid to Pigwacket country reveals much about John Lovewell; he was methodical, he was brave, and he cared for his men.

His journal reveals that the volunteers from surrounding towns arrived at the Dunstable staging area in groups. The Groton and Lancaster men arrived on January 27th followed by the men from Haverhill and Billerica on the 28th. On the 29th they crossed the Merrimack River by ferry where Lovewell mustered the company. On the 30th the column of men headed north on snowshoes into the frozen wilderness. On the 2nd they arrived in Penacook (Concord) and camped there for the night. On the following day they covered twelve miles camping at Contoocook (Boscowen). On the 4th Lovewell sent out a small scouting party while he held his main force back. It was a sound way to move his large company towards its target without falling blindly into an ambush. His journal reveals he used this tactic frequently. On the 7th one of the volunteers was badly cut with an axe while cutting firewood. Lovewell sent him home with a six-man guard. He couldn't take the risk of having the enemy slip in behind his main force and kill or capture one or two isolated men. It snowed on the 8th and the company lay about all day passing the hours in makeshift shelters or in crude tents. Difficult as it must have been to carry a heavy pack and walk up to 16 miles a day on snow shoes, spending 24 hours in a makeshift two-man canvas shelter in a snow storm seems infinitely worse. According to Lovewell's journal, they were at that point camped "*on the northwest corner of Lake Winnipesaukee.*" By the 10th some of the men betrayed their nervousness when they thought they saw signs of smoke and imagined they heard gunfire. On the 12th the main force stayed in place, and Lovewell sent out scouts who found nothing. In planning their provisions, Lovewell had counted on supplementing their diet with wild game, but at that point in the march, their hunting efforts had failed to produce enough meat to feed eighty-seven hungry men. By the 13th because of the dwindling food supply, thirty names were drawn by lot and sent home. The following roster lists the names of the sixty-two men who were chosen by lot to continue the march. Although the list does not identify the towns they came from, they were all residents of communities along the Merrimack River. The commissioned officers were not part of the draw:

Jno. White
Sam Tarbol
Jer. Hunt
Eben. Wright
Joseph Read
Samuel Moore
Phin Foster
Fra. Dogett
S. Hilton
Jno. Pollard
Ben. Walker
Jos. Wright
Jno. Varnum
Robt. Ford
Ben. Parker
Sam. Shattock
Jacob Ames
Jno. Stephens
Jos. Wheelock
Sam. Sawyer

Jno. Houghton
Henry Willard
Jacob Gates
Jos. Whitcomb
Sam. Learned
Rob. Phelps
Moses Graves
Moses Hazzen
Jno. Levingston
Jere. Pearly
Wm. Hutchins
Jacob Cory
Oliver Pollard
Sam. Trail
Ben. Parker
Wm. Shalden
Sam. Fletcher
Jno. Duncan
Jethro Ames
John Sawyer

Moses Chandler
Jos. Wilson
Joshua Webster
Jona. Parks
Stephen Merrill
Jacob Pearly
John Hazzen
Ebn. Brown
Jona. Ferren
Sam. Stickney
Joshua Hutchens
Ephm. Farnsworth
ReubenFarnsworth
Thomas Farmer
Richard Hall
Neh. Robinson
Jona. Parks
Caleb Dustin
Lenony Boynton
Sam. Johnson

Lovewell's target appears to have been the Pigwacket Village located inside of the great north to south loop of the Saco River in the area that is now Fryeburg, Maine. Several previous expeditions to the stronghold of the Pigwacket Indians had met with little success. The Indians were like phantoms that simply vanished into the forest when they met a larger force. The woodsman Lovewell knew a great deal about his wily foe. He was planning to catch the entire tribe in their wigwams and longhouses where they normally stayed from January to February. In wigwams insulated with mats woven from rushes and swamp grasses, and protected by wolf and bearskins, they passed the winter comfortably warmed by the heat of their cooking fires. *N'datlogit* (The Storyteller) entertained them with the fascinated myths and legends of their folklore; in this way the Indians passed the winter in comfort together with their elders, their women, their children, and their smoking pipes.

For Lovewell's men it was a far different story. Hiking six to ten hours a day on snowshoes is an exhausting business. For the uninitiated, the discomfort and pain produced by walking for hours in awkward ash frames laced with rawhide can be excruciating. The French called it, *mal a la raquette.* The mere fact that a company of English volunteers could survive weeks in the wilderness where temperatures sometimes dropped to 30 degrees below zero was an extraordinary feat. They were reduced to melting snow over campfires for water, and they swept up handfuls of snow as they marched to quench their thirst. At night they erected small canvas flies or canvas tents, and one can only imagine the discomfort they endured in having to respond to nature's call in sub zero temperatures. The vaunted English grit and the willingness to endure the most trying conditions must have been a source of wonder for Indians and their French allies as well.

On the 14th, after more than two weeks in the wilderness, their luck took a turn for the better. That day one of the men killed a moose, and the men went to their tents with full stomachs that evening.[18] That night they camped on "a branch of the Saco River". The Company rested over the 15th, but the 16th brought electrifying news. The terse description in Lovewell's journal gives a laconic account of their actions:

> *We traveled 6 miles and came upon the tracks of Indians, and we left 16 men with our packs and the rest pursued the tracks till dark that night and staid there all night, and on the 17th we followed their tracks till about 8 o'clock." We then found where the Indians had lain twenty-four hours before, and we having no vituals, returned again to the 16 men we had left our packs with and refreshed ourselves. We all pursued the remaining part of that day and the night.*

Like baying hounds in a foxhunt, they were in full chase with all thoughts of Lovewell's original plan forgotten. Now, instead of moving steadily toward Pigwacket in a northeasterly direction, they were following a fresh trail south. On the 18th they traveled 20 miles and camped at a pond, and they followed that with an incredible 22-mile sprint on the 19th. On the 20,th after a fast five miles, they came upon a camp that appeared to have been freshly abandoned. In full pursuit they sighted a thin plume of smoke only two miles beyond the abandoned camp. Lovewell journal gives no clue as to why the Indians chose to stop again so close to their previous camp, but it is possible that the picturesque site located on high ground beside a lake attracted them. Once Lovewell's scouts determined that the enemy had stopped for the night, he called a halt and waited for darkness. They shunned the comfort of fires that might betray their presence, and they waited through the long day for darkness to become their ally.

---

[18]Authors' note: After bagging the moose, their food situation improved greatly. Later accounts report that they were "well entertained with moose, deer, and salmon-trout measuring 3 feet in length and weighing up to 7 pounds!"

At this point Lovewell demonstrated his skill as a bush fighter; he was methodical, stealthy, and cold-blooded. In his quiet dispassionate way, he issued instructions to his men. By 2 a.m. he and his men had moved within point blank range of the enemy encampment. Guided by his carefully worded instructions, they split into three groups and surrounded the campsite. The golden glow from a campfire bathed the silent arena with its dim light.[19] The ten Indians lay close to the warmth of a central campfire wrapped in blankets and furs and oblivious to the looming danger. The attack was executed efficiently according to Lovewell's plan. A ball from Lovewell's musket triggered the assault and mortally wounded two sleeping warriors. A volley from the first reserve that killed five was followed by another volley from a second contingent that killed two more. The surviving brave started up from his sleep, but he too was dispatched when an attack dog jumped into the fray and prevented his escape. One can only imagine the scene that followed when the rangers moved in to finish off the wounded and take the scalps; the incident can only be described as an execution or a massacre!

The possessions of the dead Indians indicated that they were planning to pillage, burn and take captives for ransom. The new muskets, spare blankets, moccasins and snowshoes of the raiding party showed that they were well prepared to return to Canada with prisoners. Their pursuit of the Indians had diverted Lovewell and his rangers far from their original target. The massacre had taken place on the shore of Lake Lovell[20] in

---

[19] Authors' note: The Lovewell journal states simply that they "*tarried until 2 o'clock in the morning and then came upon their wigwams and killed 10 Indian men, which were all that were there, and not one escaped alive.*" On his return to Boston, Lovewell was undoubtedly asked to describe the event in more detail to the Governor's council and other interested parties. This version is a composite of the more detailed accounts of at least ten historians beginning with Penhallow's account written in 1727.

[20] *History of Wakefield New Hampshire* by Elizabeth Banks MacRury, P. 17; "The well related story of Captain John Lovell or Lovewell, as it has also been spelled." Authors' note: The early pronunciation of Lovewell was Lovell.

the present town of Sanbornville just south of Wakefield, New Hampshire. The Indian raiding party had been traveling south via the old Indian Cocheco Trail that would have ultimately brought them into the vicinity of Dover and Portsmouth. Another day or two would have exposed these and surrounding communities to their attacks. Regardless of one's personal sympathies, it was a gruesome bloody business however it might have ended. After fifty years of intermittent warfare, all sense of decency was gone. The colonists had learned to kill as dispassionately as the Indians.

It is interesting to note that Lovewell and his men did not hang about the scene of their early morning massacre of the ten sleeping braves. His journal reveals that after daylight illuminated the bloody scene, he and his rangers resumed their trek on snowshoes toward Cocheco (Dover) that same day. One might expect that they would make all possible speed to announce their success, but instead, after marching only six miles, they camped for the night. Lovewell's next move reveals a great deal about his conservative nature and the pressure he must have felt. With success in hand and with prospects for a triumphal return to civilization only thirty miles away, he did the prudent thing. He sent a scouting party on his back trail to make sure he was not being followed, and he rested his men for a whole day! Who would not want to follow this man? Though he appeared to enjoy personal fame, he was concerned for the safety of his men, and he still managed to get the job done! On the following day after a sound night sleep, the rangers followed the Cocheco Trail thirty miles into Dover. The Scalp Hunter's entrance to the town resembled a Roman triumph. They marched along dirt roads flanked by rude log cabins with the stretched scalps of their victims held aloft on poles to the universal delight of the town's inhabitants. The townspeople's delight was palpable. The collective frustration caused by fifty years of incessant Indian raids was released in a flood of joy as they celebrated the gruesome spectacle. The townsfolk feted Lovewell's men, and the legend of John Lovewell the Indian fighter was born. The next day apparently tired by the welcoming celebration in Dover, they traveled only six miles to Oyster Harbor where they stopped to camp. The following entries in Lovewell's journal describe the condition of his men after their epic journey on snowshoes and tells how they got home:

> 25th, "Lay still as our men were lame in their feet." 26th we marched down to Captain Knights at Newington, and 27th went on board a sloop to come to Boston where we arrived the 9th current. Mar. 10th, 1725.

In Boston, they were reviewed by enthusiastic crowds who gathered to watch them walk from the harbor to the Governor's Council meeting chamber. The spectacle of booted bush fighters in homespun clothing striding through the urban streets of Boston caused a sensation. The intrepid rangers fascinated the Boston populace; the ubiquitous scalping knife in every belt, and the worn muskets together with their rustic attire made them appear like killer angels. The cheers, the commentary, and the news articles all echoed the same theme—Thank Almighty God for John Lovewell and his volunteers—they are the sword our country needs to wreak justice on the miserable wretches whose depredations we have suffered so long!

After a series of stirring speeches glorifying the heroic exploits of Lovewell and his company, the General Council approved a payment of 1,000 pounds plus a per diem payment of 2 shillings 6 pence for each day the volunteers had been in the field. In addition, Lovewell found willing buyers for the excellent French muskets they had captured in the massacre. He received an additional 70 pounds for the ten pieces. In a farewell talk to the men of his company, John Lovewell spoke of bigger and better raids yet to come thanking the men for their participation and wishing them well. As he strode towards home with his men, John Lovewell's mind was full of plans for yet another expedition to the remote valley of the Pigwacket Indians.

In Canada, unease over the overdue return of their raiding party grew, and native women wearied of answering the questions of children asking when a father or older brother might return. Like their English counterparts, the native mothers, wives, and sweethearts of New France silently noted how the lure of bounty and glory drew their men like moths to an open flame. They too wondered if the danger was worth the risk. After a time, the French sponsors closed their file on the lost raiding party, and they turned their attention elsewhere. One can imagine a French official's exasperated expletive—damn those English! Will they never give up? And far to the south on a pine-covered knoll beside a frozen lake, the still forms of ten young warriors lay unnoticed by man. For them there would be no funeral chant by shaman, family and elders. For them there would be no solemn burial together with fire making equipment, favorite amulet, and sacred calumet. Their physical forms would remain until the spring thaw when *Mother Earth* would reclaim all that was hers—plant, animal and man. The sentinel pines and the nearby lake provided immutable silent monuments. And one day, from a special place prepared for them by *The Creator,* the unique essence of each slain warrior would return to *Mother Earth* as living beings; it would be their destiny to return in the form of a deer, a soaring eagle, or even as a legendary warrior.

2-1 James Frye House, Andover, Massachusetts

2-2 Hannah Duston stone, Nashua, New Hampshire

CHAPTER 3

THE FRENCH CANADIANS

God has confided this flock to me.
I will follow its lot,
too happy to lay down my life for it.
--Jesuit missionary, Sebastian Rale,
1657-1724

At the beginning of 1725, the people who lived in the settlements on the Merrimack River and up the coast into Maine must have wondered whether there would ever be a lasting peace with the Indians. Despite the death of King Philip in 1676, and even after the Treaties of Ryswick and Utrecht, most settlers had never felt completely secure in their homes at the edge of the wilderness. After almost 50 years of Indian depredations against their settlements, one can understand how the English raid on Norridgewalk in August 23, 1724 would have raised their spirits. News of Lovewell's bold display of scalps in Dover must have traveled like a wind driven wildfire along the banks of the Merrimack. But after fifty years of having the changing tides of war color their expectations, they needed more than one or two isolated victories to make them feel truly safe. When would the news about isolated abductions and murders along the frontier stop? Even if the average settler knew the details of the game being played by the two most powerful nations in the world, he would have been little more enlightened. He was, in fact, a tiny cog in a gigantic game of chess that involved four nations with different agendas. The four players were France, the Abenaki Confederation, England, and the Iroquois Five Nations. There was no single solution that would accommodate the national interests of each of these players; someone had to lose.

The settlers who were the targets of French sponsored Indian hostility would probably have been very surprised to learn that their Canadian counterparts were also plagued by many problems. While it would be tedious to detail every aspect of the history of New France, it is important to have a general understanding of the strategic problems its settlers faced. They had hostile Iroquois Indians on their border, they had major problems trying to develop a diversified economy, and the strategic objectives of the colonial administrators and the French King were often at odds. The pressures generated by these problems inevitably drove the French to use their Abenaki allies in a way that countered English territorial aspirations. On the surface the French support of their Abenaki allies appeared to be a gallant humanitarian gesture, but the cynic would argue that the Indians were merely pawns in France's colonial strategy. Because of the complexity of the four-nation power struggle, it is important to have a general understanding of the powerful forces in play.

In 1534, Jacques Cartier, master-navigator and former corsair, planted a giant wooden cross on a Gaspe Peninsula headland to claim all the territory in the St. Lawrence Gulf for France. Like other English, Dutch, and Spanish explorers to the new world, it probably never occurred to Cartier that the Aboriginal inhabitants he encountered on his arrival had prior claim to the land their ancestors had occupied since a time beyond memory. During his voyages he visited native settlements along the St. Lawrence River that stood where the cities of Quebec and Montreal are now located. Since he had failed to discover a Northwest Passage to the Orient, and also had failed to uncover any valuable mineral deposits, official interest in his discovery languished until 1603 when Samuel de Champlain began his explorations. In 1608 Champlain and his men built the first permanent Canadian settlement in Quebec. Because of his exceptional ability to document his travels in well-written chronicles, the King of France appointed him an official geographer. During his extensive explorations, he visited Georgian Bay on Lake Huron, and Lake Ontario. In one instance he and his men accompanied Huron Indians and Algonquian Indians on a raid into Iroquois territory. The huge inland body of water they traversed in canoes was later named Lake Champlain in his honor. In the vicinity of Ticonderoga they chanced upon a war party of Iroquois who attacked them. The Iroquois, who had never experienced gunfire, were confounded by the noise and smoke. Terrified by the din and lethal reach of the muskets, they fled in disorder. Many historians credit the animosity between the French and Iroquois to that initial contact, but their distrust of each other was actually caused by factors much more complex. Subsequent passages will reveal how the long enmity was caused by irreconcilable differences over the fur trade.

Prior to the arrival of the Europeans, the *Iroquois Five Nations* was the largest democracy in the world. At the apex of Iroquois influence, their so-called *Umbrella of Peace* extended from the Hudson River in the east to Lake Ontario in the west, and from the Canadian border south to Mississippi. They spoke a different language than the Algonquian tribes of the northeast. For centuries bitter rivalries and warfare between the member-tribes weakened their confederacy. To curb the constant squabbles between member tribes, the federation elders devised a democratic council system in which each tribe was allowed a single representative. The members of the general council negotiated all disputes between member-nations, and when the general council reached a resolution to the problem, the decision was enforced by all member nations. The Iroquois had a reputation for being fearsome fighters and the torture of their prisoners could be ingenious and cruel. Although they had built their great confederation largely by intimidation, they were never able to convince the Abenaki Indians to seek the protection of their Umbrella of Peace. The agrarian society of the Iroquois did not appeal to the more free ranging Abenakis.

As quickly as Champlain and LaSalle discovered the lake and river routes that led into the *Pays d'en Haut* (high country), the coureurs-de-bois[21](wood runners) and the voyageurs (canoe paddlers) went deep into the territory to trade with the Indians. This created a great dilemma for the Iroquois. How could they continue to act as middleman between the western tribes and the English with the French in the picture? Clearly, the coureurs-de-bois trade with the western tribes threatened the Iroquois/English monopoly. Beginning in the east, the five members of the Iroquois Nation were the Mohawk, Oneida, Onondaga, Cayuga and Seneca tribes. The *Guardians of the Eastern Portal* were the Mohawks in the Hudson Valley, and the *Guardians of the Western Portal* were the Seneca who bordered on Lake Ontario. The English had traditionally bought furs from the Iroquois at their trading post on the Hudson River in Albany. By the time the French entered the trade in Canada, all the beaver in Iroquois territory had been trapped out! The English didn't dare pass through Iroquois territory to gain access to the abundant supply of furs in the lakes region, so they were forced to compromise by allowing the Iroquois to act as middlemen with the western tribes. Having conducted hostile raids against the western tribes for generations, the Iroquois were doing all they could to mend their relations with those tribes. There were other complications as well. The French King and his ministers envisioned their new colony to be a cluster of settlements confined to the St. Lawrence River. They issued specific instructions to discourage settlements in the interior of the New Land. After the King appointed Count Frontenac colonial governor of New France, the "The Iron Governor" ignored this Royal edict. Frontenac immediately recognized the importance of keeping the water route open to the west. He saw the need to establish a fort at Cataraqui where

---

[21]Authors' note: Before liberalization of the fur trading laws by the French government, trading was restricted to government-approved monopolies. The "legal" *marchand-voyageur* (traveling merchant) was in charge of the trading expeditions into the Pays d'en Haut. The voyageurs were the canoe paddlers and laborers. The activities of the *coureurs-de-bois* were considered illegal by the authorities, but the "wood runner" literal translation of the term became the most common term to describe the fur trader.

the waters of Lake Ontario discharge to form the St. Lawrence River. In a 1673 meeting with the Iroquois chiefs, Frontenac overcame the Iroquois natural suspicion and hostility with his diplomacy and with his liberal distribution of presents. In the face of his charm offensive, the Iroquois relented and allowed the French to build their fort at Cataraqui. In spite of this concession, the Iroquois continued their aggression against the French with isolated attacks that reached the outskirts of Montreal.

Frustrated by the Iroquois raiding parties, the French sent an expedition of 1,000 men on snowshoes into Mohawk territory to teach them a lesson. Forewarned of the raid, the Mohawks disappeared into the forest, but the Frenchmen and their Algonquian Indian allies burned their villages and dug up and destroyed all their winter supply of food. The French punitive raid made the Iroquois wary of an enemy that could raise a war party of that size and invade their territory in mid-winter. Trapped between the French to their north and the English in Albany, the Iroquois chiefs decided to throw their lot in with the English while maintaining a fragile truce with their northern neighbors. This suited the French who were not anxious to fight a war on two fronts. Instructions to New France administrators by King Louis 14th stressed the need to keep the peace along their border with the Iroquois while continuing to incite their Abenaki allies against the English in New England. The Massachusetts Colony and their Abenaki adversaries were seriously affected by these policies. The success of the French strategy hinged on their ability to keep their Abenaki allies stirred up against the New England colonies. By 1725, however, the strategic position of the Abenaki Indians had become critical; the English were growing stronger by the day, and they were beginning to carry the fight to the Abenaki Indians.

In spite of persistent official attempts to diversify the economy of New France, the fur trade remained the major commercial activity that sustained the colony during its first 150 years. Almost every official correspondence during that era complained about the trader's use of brandy in their dealing with the Indians. Every issue of *Les Relaciones des Jesuites* contained articles deploring the immorality of the coureurs-de-bois and the negative influence of their immoral behavior on the native converts. It was an issue that was never completely resolved despite laws and other attempts to control the trade through the use of trading licenses known as *official leaves*. The *voyageur* and the *marchand-voyageur* were key members of a rather large enterprise that began with a merchant in France and ended with the native trapper. To appreciate the scope of the Canadian fur trade and its romantic appeal to the youth of New France, it is helpful to understand the terms and jargon that were in common use at the time.

The French government was trying to run the fur trade as a cartel. The official chain of authority began with the Parisian merchant who made his living importing a variety of commodities such as sugar and tobacco as well as furs. His contact in New France was the *marchand-equipeur* or outfitter. He was the manager of the North American end of the business. He was responsible for putting together a crew and providing them with a cargo canoe complete with supplies and trade goods. He imported items that were suitable for trading with the Indians, and he also signed up local investors to share the cost of the enterprise. The man who actually managed the trading expedition was called *marchand-voyageur*. He was the key man in the enterprise. He was authorized by the authorities to negotiate with the natives for their furs. Over a period of time however, the term *coureur-de-bois* (wood runner) seems to have replaced the term *marchand-voyageur* in general usage. During the English regime the coureurs-de-bois were called *freemen*. At the bottom of the chain of command were *engages* who paddled the canoes and performed most of the manual labor. When the British took over, the name *engage* was replaced by *voyageur*. The voyageurs were generally young men in the twenties and many came from the ranks of the French/Indian population of the colony called *Metis*. The term *voyageur* appears to have been used to describe anyone who traveled in the wilderness. The terminology was not limited to the laboring class. The famous explorers in New France history that opened up the interior of the North American continent were called *voyageurs.* It was a term loosely applied to woodsmen, travelers and explorers such as Jacques Cartier and Samuel de Champlain.

Official attempts to control the conduct of the fur trade in New France are reminiscent of Federal attempts to control the sale of alcohol in the United States in the 1920s. In both cases the general public ignored the law and continued to conduct illegal traffic in forbidden substances. *The Prohibition Act* of 1920 created the bootlegger phenomena in the United States, and the 1656 French decree against illegal fur trading produced the coureur-de-bois. It took the appeal of the prohibition act to put the bootleggers out of business, and despite fines and imprisonment, the coureurs-de-bois continued to operate until there was no longer a demand for furs.

In the early days of the fur trade, the French decided against stocking their outposts with large quantities of trade goods. The Iroquois might have found them irresistible targets for attack. Each outpost had a garrison of soldiers to deal with attacks, but the main purpose of the outpost was to provide headquarters for the coureurs-de-bois. Another function of the outposts was to provide a rendezvous for the annual trading expedition to Montreal. Before the coureurs-de-bois began to trade for furs at the source, one of the most spectacular and colorful events of human history took place each year in the Pays d'en Haut. Deep in the forest hundreds of natives shouldered their winter catch of furs and headed overland to their rendezvous with the coureurs-de-bois. Many other natives brought their furs to the rendezvous in their *canot du Nord* (birch bark canoes). The buckskin-clad Indians were greeted warmly by the *marchand-voyageur* in reunions of men whose shared risks made them friends. Together they weighed and packed the furs in 50-pound bundles and carefully loaded and balanced the 34-foot *canot de maitre* (Montreal canoe). Each canoe was capable of carrying three tons of goods together with crew as far as 60 miles a day.[22] The fragile canoes had to be light enough to be portaged around rapids and falls.[23] The margin between safe passage and disaster for the crew and cargo in perilous rapids was the skill of the voyageur. When the last of the individual caches of furs had been loaded into the cargo canoes, they all proceeded to the grand rendezvous at Michilimackinac or at Green Bay. When the last straggler had arrived, the great spectacle began. Hundreds of canoes loaded with furs, voyageurs, marchand-voyageurs, and Indians began the grand procession to Montreal traversing the southern lake route or traveling via the Ottawa River. The coureurs-de-bois acted as pilots to show the way. Tall pines along the route from which the lower branches had been removed were solitary navigation markers, and the coureurs-de-bois had to be alert and prepared to provide leadership if the Iroquois attacked. News of the flotilla's progress raced ahead of it like a ripple on a lake, and the arrival of the great flotilla above the *Lachine Rapids* set off a boisterous welcome by the people of Montreal who came out of the city to greet the spectacle.[24] In makeshift booths on the shore, *cabaretiers* sold brandy to the voyageurs and Indians as officials turned a blind eye to the illicit trade. While the supply lasted chaos reigned as natives and voyageurs celebrated the completion of their 1,000-mile voyage from deep in the wilderness.

The official reception for the flotilla came in Montreal where the governor of the colony made an appearance at a great council resplendent in scarlet cloak and a plumed hat. In solemn ceremonies vows of friendship were renewed, and the

---

[22]Authors' note: The specifications of the *canot de maitre* are taken from the Canadian Museum of Civilization web site. The site includes a photograph of a "Montreal Canoe" built in 1957 by Chief Matt Bernard and his kin on the Algonkian Indian Reserve at Golden Lake, Ontario.

[23]Authors note: Some portages in the Pays d'en Haut were as long as 12 miles. After unloading and transporting the cargo, all hands were needed to transport the *canot-de-maitre* across the 12-mile carryover.

[24]Crusaders of New France by William Bennett Munro; 1921, p. 167. The flotilla of 1693 consisted of more than 400 canoes, with about 200 coureurs-de-bois and 1200 Indians.

peace pipe was passed from native to voyageur in a warm atmosphere fueled perhaps as much by brandy as genuine friendship. In a holiday atmosphere on the banks of the St. Lawrence River, the bargaining for the furs began in earnest. In anticipation of the annual fair, ships from France had landed trade goods that appealed to the whimsical as well as the practical needs of the Indians. Along with the muskets, gunpowder, hatchets, kettles, needles, and blankets, the merchants offered cheap trinkets that appealed to the Indians. Like children on their first visit to a department store, the profusion of gaudy necklaces, bracelets, bells, and small mirrors fascinated the Indians. The liberal use of brandy by the merchants created chaos among the Indians placing them at a disadvantage in the trading process. At the conclusion of the 14-day fair in Montreal, the coureurs-de-bois, the voyageurs, and the Indians continued their holiday in Montreal until their funds were exhausted. After final toasts and tearful farewells by female camp followers, the hung over voyageurs manned their canoes for the long voyage back into the wilderness.

Although there was a limited amount of trading conducted at the frontier outposts, the authorities preferred to entice the Indians and their furs to markets closer to home. Concurrent with the Montreal fair, the French sponsored other fairs in Trois Rivieres for the Indians of the St. Maurice region; fairs were also held at Sorel for the Richelieu and at Quebec and Tadoussac for the natives of the lower St. Lawrence River. As the coureurs-de-bois and the fur buyers prospered so prospered New France; the health of the economy hinged on two things: whether the water routes to the west were open, and the strength of the demand for furs in European markets.

The liberalization of the trading rules in 1652 changed the way furs were traded and encouraged scores of young Frenchmen to go wood running. Fur trading was no longer restricted to the annual trade fairs in Quebec, Montreal, and Trois Rivieres. Instead, a limited number of licensed traders were authorized to carry goods into the *Pays d'en Haut* (the high country) to trade directly with the trappers. In 1654 Governor Jean de Lauson allowed two intrepid young Frenchmen to go into the Pays d'en Haut with some Ottawa tribesmen on a fur-trading run. One of them was Medard Schouart Des Groseilliers, and the other was named Nicolas Forget alias Despatis (Forget). Groseilliers later gained fame from the adventures that spurred him to found the renowned Hudson Bay Company. When Groseilliers and Forget returned to Quebec in August 1654 with fifty canoes filled with furs, the arrival of the flotilla set off a great celebration in Quebec. They were saluted by a great salvo of cannon fire, and the general populace hailed them as heroes. Their success touched off an enormous increase in illegal wood running that resulted in a great deal of hand wringing by Canadian officials. A secretary to the Intendant[25] Jean-Batiste Patoulet, asked Minister Jean-Bastiste Colbert for permission to intervene in the crisis complaining that 10% of the men capable of defending the country were out wood running. He noted that these men seemed to have no inclination to take wives nor seemed to have any desire to cultivate the land; their disorderly conduct as well set a bad example for the natives and the Metis.

The story of French coureurs-de-bois during the 17th and 18th centuries has all the adventure, romance and color associated with the early American cowboy. The literal translation of the term *coureur-de bois* is *wood runner*. The common elements shared by the cowboy and the wood runner were self-reliance, romance, freedom, and a willingness to brave danger. The danger came from the physical demands of their calling as well as the hostility they might encounter from native inhabitants. Like their American cowboy counterparts, the reputations of the coureurs-de-bois ran the entire gamut from heroic to corrupt. There was nothing in the early history of New-

[25]Authors' note: Like their British counterparts, the King and his ministers appointed the early governors of New France. The French king, however, also appointed a personal representative called an *Intendant* who reported directly to the King. He acted like a personal spy for the monarch. There was often a great deal of friction between the colonial governor and the *Intendant.*

France that was more controversial than the bohemian lifestyle of the coureur-de-bois and his negative influence on the indigenous inhabitants of the country. In spite of official contempt for his excesses, the coureur-de-bois was widely admired for his joie de vivre and his independent lifestyle. In the eyes of young French colonials, the coureur-de-bois represented unrestrained freedom from authority. The Frenchman La Houtan once remarked that a more apt name for the men who lived with such reckless abandon might have been *coureurs-de-risques*. After seeing the early coureurs-de-bois reap huge profits from fur trading, the youth of the country turned away from farming and garrison duty—they all wanted to go off wood running! For a governing hierarchy that was desperately trying to develop an agrarian economy, the wood running craze presented a huge problem. The frustration of early authorities over the problem was a favorite theme of their correspondence. One governor of New France commenting on the romantic appeal of the coureur-de-bois wrote:

> I cannot tell you how attractive this life is to all our youth. It consists of doing nothing, caring nothing, following every inclination and getting out of the way of all restraint.

A typical example of the more notorious coureur-de-bois was a colorful individual named Michel Accault. After migrating from France to Quebec in 1665, he borrowed money from friends and went into the Pays d'en Haut to try his luck as a coureur-de-bois. He never returned to the civilized world. He went down the Mississippi River with La Salle and became an excellent canoe handler. After the Sioux Indians captured him, he was rescued by the famous Daniel Greysolon Dulhut whose name is associated with the City of Duluth. Accault worked as a guide and partner to Dulhut, and when American authorities put a price on his head, he managed to escape justice. He had a reputation as a miscreant and a troublemaker. He fathered children in several different Indian tribes, and in 1693 he married the daughter of the chief of an Illinois tribe. He later changed his ways and became an exemplary father and helped support Indian missionaries. Several of his former mates married Illinois women, and some named him godfather to their children.

It took a rugged breed of men to survive the harsh Canadian winters, and in contrast to the English in the south, men outnumbered women inhabitants by a wide margin. Hoping to encourage men to settle down and farm the land, King Louis 14th sent more than 900 single women to New France to ease the shortage. Most of the women who arrived between 1663 and 1673 were married within six months of their arrival, and the importance of *Les Filles du Roi* (The King's Women) is evident in the fact that all of the founding families of Canada include them in their family trees. But in spite of *Les Filles du Roi,* there were still not enough women to satisfy the demands of a lusty male population. The desperate shortage inevitably led to the acceptance of a more relaxed set of standards. Many of the young female English captives raised in convents accepted proposals of marriage from eligible Frenchmen. In the crude environment of the New World, the liberal French attitude towards mixed marriages was far more practical than the rigid English standards. There was little stigma to being identified as *Metis* (mixed breed), and the assimilation of the indigenous population into the national culture was significant. Virtually all of the early voyageurs came from the Metis.

No chronicle about this special breed of men can be complete without briefly examining the career of the most famous voyageur—Robert Cavalier de LaSalle. Among other noted pathfinders of the era like Tonty, Du Lhut, La Mothe-Cadillac and others, La Salle had no peer. He began his career as the commander of the fort at Cataraqui, and in 1678, Governor Frontenac commissioned him to build a fort at Niagara Falls. He and his men then built a small ship in which they sailed to Michilimackinac at the juncture of Lake Michigan and Lake Huron. He later made his way down the Wisconsin shore of Lake Michigan, where after many hardships, he discovered the headwaters of the Mississippi River. He eventually reached the

Gulf of Mexico where he planted the banner of French imperialism. He failed to find the Northwest Passage to China, but more than any other man, he opened up the middle of the North American continent. In the winter of 1687, while attempting to retrace his route from the Gulf of Mexico to New France, he and his men suffered many hardships. Beset by constant danger from Indian attacks, some of his men challenged his leadership, and on March 19, 1687, the intrepid LaSalle was slain by a mutineer. Far from home at a place later to be named Texas, the greatest voyageur died at the age of 41 far from his Rouen, France birthplace. The early 21st century historian Francis Parkman wrote of him:

> America owes him an enduring memory; for in this masculine figure she sees the pioneer who guided her to the possession of their richest heritage.

Through the explorations of men like Cartier, Champlain, and LaSalle, France had not only claimed a vast *New Land*, but she also had colonized it and had learned that her new possession was a source for what seemed to be an inexhaustible supply of furs! Champlain and LaSalle had blazed new paths deep into the rich fur country of the Great Lake region that the enterprising fur traders quickly exploited. The all-water route to rich fur country followed the St. Lawrence River to Cataraqui where the voyageurs had to portage their canoes around Niagara Falls to gain access to Lake Erie. At the western limit of Lake Erie, they traveled north on Lake Huron to Michilimackinac. From there they were able to voyage to Green Bay, Wisconsin via Lake Michigan. When the Iroquois blocked this southern water route, the voyageurs used a northern route that went overland from Montreal to the Ottawa River and thence via Lake Nipissing to Georgian Bay. It was a long passage either way, but in their fearless way, the coureurs-de-bois and the voyageurs refused to let the Iroquois block their access to the Pays d'en Haut.

Although the English appeared to be at a disadvantage having to buy furs through their Iroquois partners, they had an edge on the French in other ways. They were able to offer the Indians two and three times more value for their furs than the French. There were many reasons for their competitive edge. For one thing, shipping costs were higher from France to its colonial possession. Also, navigating the St. Lawrence River was time consuming because of the many hidden rocks and sandbars. English privateers were constantly preying on French merchant ships, and English trade goods were much cheaper than those produced in France. The most important price advantage the English had over the French was the cheap rum imported from the West Indies versus French brandy imported from Europe. To magnify the problem, French authorities established prices that gave the French merchant an unreasonable profit. The following table[26] shows the number of furs the Indians had to give the English in comparison to the French in exchange for an equal amount of trade goods:

The Indian pays for	To the English	To the French
1 musket	2 beavers	5 beavers
8 lbs. gun powder	1 beaver	4 "
40 lbs. lead	1 "	3 "
1 blanket	1 "	2 "
4 shirts	1 "	2 "
6 pairs stockings	1 "	2 "

The only way that the French could overcome the huge price advantage was to do everything in their power to minimize contact between the English and the Indians. The biggest French ally in discouraging contact between the Indians and the English were the Jesuits who had missions at all of the major Indian villages. The coureurs-de-bois also did all they could to discourage contact between the Indians and the English, but

[26]Authors' note: The table comes from *Documents Relating to the Colonial History of New York*, p 408-9

the Jesuits and the coureurs-de-bois were constantly at odds over the sale of brandy to the Indians. Minimizing contact between the Pays d'en Haut Indians and the English was a difficult task, but with the help of the Jesuits, the French managed to keep the English out of their trading sphere for almost 100 years.

Trading activity between the Abenaki Indians and British sea traders was outside the French sphere of influence, but in comparison to the Canada, the fur trade in New England was quite small. Because of their desperate need for English trade goods, the Abenaki were willing to set aside their differences with their English adversaries. Cheap British goods were one of the chief reasons that the Abenaki Indians signed treaties of pacification with the English. There was language in most treaties addressing the problem of providing trading posts in neutral territory that would allow the Indians to buy English goods such as blankets, muskets, black powder and metal utensils at fair prices.

For one hundred and fifty years everything in New France revolved around its fur trade with the Indians. Early in the 17th Century the trading was centered in the St. Lawrence River area, but as the beaver and other fur bearing animals were trapped out, the trade began to move west to the Great Lakes. By 1725 the fur trade had moved to the headwaters of the Mississippi, and New France fur revenues were declining. Like the relentless ebb and flow of the ocean's tides, France's prestige in the New World crested and declined with the flow of her fur trade revenues.

By the nature of his temperament, the young 17th Century Frenchman was ideally suited to the life of the coureur-de-bois. His open personality and his sheer joy in the freedom of his lifestyle gave him a flexible approach to every problem he encountered. He quickly learned the secrets of the forest from the Metis voyageurs that were his companions in the wilderness, and he embraced the hardships and dangers of his trade with casual abandon. His joie de vivre and his ability to adapt quickly made him more Indian than the Indian when he was in their company. He quickly adopted the time tested native techniques of forest survival. By the early 1600s, the native snowshoe was a standard part of the French voyageur's equipment. In contrast, until the early 1700s, the English farmer/woodsman was snowbound in his settlement during the winter. The voyageur's familiarity with Indian woodcraft together with his personal bravery and intelligence made him a lethal opponent, especially in the forest environment.

No less effective in supporting the official dream of monopolizing the fur trade was the Jesuit missionary who lived among the Indians. In his mission to spread the gospel, the Black Robe never forgot his obligation to France. His zeal for his Christian mission was only matched by the fervor of his patriotism. One of his most pressing goals was to discourage contact between his native disciples and the English. In his mind he knew what was best for his flock—his children. From a practical point of view, he believed that French policies best served the Indians, and in discouraging contact with the English, he was leading his flock to salvation while blazing the path of a commercial empire for his country. So happily for the French administrators during much of its early history, New France had two powerful forces supporting its national mission.

From a geographical perspective the French had all the advantages. They controlled most of the major river routes into the heart of the continent. Early in the game their Abenaki allies controlled all the major rivers on the Atlantic coastline from the Merrimack River to the St. Lawrence River. Champlain and LaSalle then opened the water routes to Green Bay, Wisconsin via the St. Lawrence River and the Great Lakes. After LaSalle claimed the Territory of Louisiana for the French Crown, they controlled all the water routes into the interior except the Hudson River.

Far up the Hudson River at their trading post in Albany, the English felt they could almost reach out and touch the prize, but they dared not offend their Iroquois ally. Although the French had a relatively safe northerly route to Michilimackinac and Green Bay, it required an overland carry to reach the Ottawa River and they realized that they had to defend their southern water route with a series of military outposts. In the period 1674 to 1686, they built fortified posts in Cataraqui, Detroit, Niagara, Sault Ste.Marie, and Michilimackinac. Then a succession of fortified outposts were built at Baye des Puants (Green Bay), Fort St. Antoine, Fort St. Nicholas, Ft. St. Croix, Fort Perrot, Fort St. Louis and others. The French may not have realized it at the time, but they were staking everything on a single venture, and like a phantom dream that beckons just out of reach, the supply of beaver was fading deeper and deeper into the forest.

At the height of the fur craze in 1680, more than 800 men out of a total population of 10,000 were engaged in the fur trade. These were not the misfits of society; they came from all stations in life. Many were men of good birth who were well educated. They were officers at military posts who were tired of garrison duty and had succumbed to the lure of high adventure and the promise of quick wealth. Men abandoned their families, and seigneurs sold their grants and became coureurs-de-bois.

In some respects, the "live for today" attitude of the voyageurs resembled the rebellion of American youth in the 1960s. In their headlong pursuit of immediate self-gratification, many American youths rejected adult values choosing instead to indulge themselves in drugs and free love. Perhaps it was the same driving need for freedom from restraint that caused youths from all levels of New France society to embrace the life of the coureur-de-bois. In most cases it was far more demanding than the life they scorned. For the young voyageur, the red knit cap and his colorful ceinture (sash) and his pipe were his proud identity. In the summer a homespun shirt, breechcloth and moccasins completed his outfit. His sparse personal belongings were stored in a small sack under his canoe seat. Day after day, week after week, he and his companions paddled the great canoe on the rivers and lakes deep in the wilderness. They seemed to relish the danger that always lurked ahead—perilous rapids and Indian attacks. To relieve the tedium of paddling ten hours a day, the helmsman frequently led the crew in singing boisterous French folk songs. In response, the sweating backs of the voyageurs straightened; their heads rose, and from their upturned faces issued the lyrics of *Claire fontaine,* or perhaps *Ma boule roulant.* In such moments, each man experienced the adrenaline rush that bound him to the life of the voyageur. The vast sweep of the lake, the fragile canoe and its eight paddlers, the surrounding dark forest and the soaring voices under the blue bowl of *The Creator's* sky was like a narcotic to the voyageur. Once hooked by the danger, the romance, the camaraderie, and the free spirited life, the wilderness became the voyageur's mistress for life. One of the noted coureurs-de-bois, Nicholas Perrot, took 143 voyageurs with him when he went out to Green Bay, Wisconsin in 1688. There were twenty to thirty coureurs-de-bois at most of the posts along the trading routes in the fur country. Once infected by the virus of the carefree life, few were able to shake their attachment to it. Most ended up broke and perhaps disillusioned, but addicted to the end.[27]

During the entire 150 years of New France's preoccupation with the fur trade, the sale of *firewater* to the natives invited criticism by the Jesuits and the authorities in France. Everyone agreed that the sale of brandy to the Indians was their ruination, but the authorities were never able to enforce a prohibition against it. The reason why the trade was allowed to continue was purely economic in nature. The coureurs-de-bois and the merchants argued that if they (New France) refused to sell brandy to the Indians it would force them to trade with the British who would be happy to supply them with rum. Their justification to the Jesuits was the same with a different twist.

---

[27]Authors' note: Most of the voyageurs were single and relatively young, and many of them were *Metis* (part Indian). Most of them lived in Trois Rivieres and surrounding villages like Batiscan, Champlain and Cap-de-la-Madeleine. Some of the famous voyageur family names were; Aubuchon, , Chorel, Crevier, Folsy, Gateineau, Lafond, Pepin and Trottier. Many came from the ranks of those without trades.

They argued that by prohibiting the sale of brandy, the indigenous people would be exposed to the heresy of Protestantism as well as English rum. Although everyone from the coureurs-de-bois to the colonial governor knew that brandy destroyed all that was noble in the Indian, they continued to let economic reality and their pocketbook control their ethics.

The entire economy of New France was dependent on the fur trade for almost 150 years, and the amount of trade goods the Indian received for his furs was controlled by the prevailing fashions and demand for furs in Europe. When the fashion for men's beaver hats changed to a low crowned style, the value of beaver skins was halved, and the economy of New France declined dramatically. Like the enthusiasm for stocks that obsessed the American public at the end of the 20th Century, the people of New France could see no end to the fur trade bonanza, but the statistics belied their vision. At a typical annual Montreal trade gala, 500,000 livres worth of furs were exchanged for trade goods. To generate this amount of trade on an annual basis would have required the Indians to remove 100,000 beavers from their natural habitat each year—an unsustainable figure! The people of New France were living a transitory dream that could not last! There was also a limited market for mink, marten and otter furs, but the demand in Europe for beaver pelts was so strong that the prices for the less popular furs were lower. Moose and bear hides were also in demand, but they took up so much space that the Indians were unwilling to transport them 1,000 miles to market.

In time many coureurs-de-bois tried to get a jump on their competition by taking trade goods and brandy into the Pays d'en Haut to trade directly with the Indians. After failing to eliminate this practice by imposing fines and other penalties, the government decided to issue twenty-five licenses each year to legalize this practice. These licenses were given to the church and to dependent widows of former military officers. The original licensees soon found that they could sell these special permits to forest traders for 1,000 livres or more. As time went on, even this limited privilege was abused as government officials in Quebec got into the act and began to issue licenses to their friends. It was one thing for the Indians to get drunk during the 14-day Montreal fair, but when traders began to provide brandy to western tribes in their own territory, the Jesuits finally balked. Brandy became the great issue between the church, the government authorities, and the coureurs-de-bois. During fifty years every issue of the church-sponsored *Relationes de les Jesuits* referred to the problem, as did other official memos and dispatches of the government. The defenders of the trade always fell back on the same tired arguments:

> The problem is really not as widespread as it has been reported and besides, if we don't supply the western tribes with brandy, they will buy rum from the English.

In modern society there are those who would tell the church to stick to their theology, but in New France in the early 1700s, authority and the Jesuits went hand in hand; they had the power to exert great influence on both the civil authorities and the rank and file. Notwithstanding the power of the Jesuits, they were never able to completely convince the colonial authorities nor the King and his ministers. King Louis the 14,Th pressed by his confessor on one hand and by his ministers on the other, was never able to take a firm stand. Perplexed by the contradictory advice of his religious and political advisors, he referred the debate to the theologians of the Sorbonne who promptly opined that to sell alcohol to the heathens was a heinous sin. The results of a limited plebiscite in which Count Frontenac requested the leading citizens of New France to express an opinion revealed that most citizens thought the problem was greatly exaggerated. Frontenac forwarded the results of the plebiscite to Louis 14th who promptly issued a royal decree that forbade the coureurs-de-bois to take brandy with them on their voyages into Indian country. The decree had no apparent effect on the illegal activities of the coureurs-de-bois, and the debate raged on. Authorities estimated that the consumption of brandy by the native population was only one pint per capita for adult Indians, less than what the typical Frenchman drank in a single day at the Breton fair. The problem lay in the fact that those Indians who drank the brandy were a minority who drank to get drunk; those that would literally sell the furs off their back to satisfy their craving for the white man's fire-water. For thousands of years the Original People lived on this continent untouched by European maladies. With the coming of the Europeans, native populations were decimated by small-pox, diphtheria, influenza and other white-transmitted disease. These unintended consequences of their contact with the native population can be excused as ill-starred, but the deliberate exploitation of the Indian's genetic intolerance for alcohol by both the English and the French left a dark stain on their national history.

Aside from the coureurs-de-bois, no group of individuals had a greater impact on the development of New France than the Jesuits. The founding of the new colony coincided with great religious troubles that were taking place at home. In addition to the Huguenot's break with the old religion, the Catholic Church in France was split into two opposing factions. One group was fighting to preserve the Gallican liberties including the special rights of the King and the French bishops to control the ecclesiastical affairs of France. The opposition stood for the Pope's supremacy over the King and his ministers in everything having to do with earthly spirituality. Since the King and his ministers were solidly aligned with the Gallicans, it was natural that French royalty would select a Gallican Order to be the first missionaries to New France. From 1615 to 1625, the Recollet Order strove to plant the seeds of their doctrine in the uncultivated wilderness of what they believed to be a pagan culture, but because of their lack of manpower and resources, their missionary efforts yielded sparse results. The grand scope of the problem needed stronger measures, and in 1625, Richelieu used his political influence to send the first contingent of Jesuits to the New France. The Jesuits were not men who sought personal glory and salvation by endless prayer and self-deprivation in monastic isolation. Their founder Loyola had given the world a vision of a crusading Order that was willing to face unknown danger in any continent of the world in order to spread its message. The soldiers of the Order were physical men, quick to action, willing to go alone into situations that might invite torture and martyrdom. Historians of all creeds have acknowledged their moral heroism, their self-sacrifice and dedication to their mission.

The force behind this driven group of men was Francois Xavier de Laval, Abbe de Montigny, and a scion of the house of Montmorency. Although he was not a Jesuit, since no Jesuit could be a bishop, he shared their views on every important religious and civil matter. A rugged physique reinforced his haughty manner; his intellect and his instinct to lead gave him a special authority. It was through his example that the Jesuits became the most formidable institution in New France.

One can judge the effectiveness of the Jesuits among the New England tribes by the scathing way English historians reported their influence on the Indians. Modern historians like Francis Parkman who wrote about the French and Indian wars during the early 1900s, took a more objective view. A writer seeking objectivity can come close to the truth by analyzing the opinions of both English and French historians. In doing so it becomes apparent that political spin was just as prevalent in the 1700s as it is in the new millennia. To illustrate this point and to return the focus of our story to the 1722-1725 era, the story of Father Rale's twenty-nine years with the Norridgewalk Indians provides us an excellent example of Jesuit martyrdom. Most of the details of his missionary work with the Abenaki Indians are from the works of Reverend P. F. X. de Charlevoix S. J. who was the official historian of King Louis 14th.

Father Sebastian Rale was born in Franche Comte, France in 1657, and he entered the Society of Jesus in the provinces of Lyons in 1674. After teaching in the College at Nismes, he came to New France in 1689 and was assigned to the French

Mission Village on the St. Francis River.[28] In 1695 he became the resident Jesuit missionary of the Norridgewalk tribe of Abenaki Indians on the Kennebec River. During his twenty-nine years of missionary work with this tribe, he learned to speak the Abenaki language. He is also credited with developing an Abenaki to English dictionary. Throughout his missionary work with the Indians he shared their Spartan life, their living quarters, their food, and their trials. Among the Abenaki tribes of Maine that harassed the English settlements between 1703 and 1724, none was fiercer or more daring than the Norridgewalk Indians were. The location of their village between two sets of rapids at a bend in the Kennebec River placed them in a precarious position between the two world powers. The land along the lower Kennebec was highly desirable property that English farmers, sawyers, and others coveted. The Norridgewalk were torn by conflicting thoughts about the English. They loved the price and the quality of their trade goods, but they didn't trust the English. The French, who were unable to compete effectively with the English in trade with the Indians, relied heavily on the Jesuit influence with the Indians. There were no such conflicting values or motives among the Jesuits. Besides being apostles of their faith, they were ambassadors of their country, and by following the dictates of their religious beliefs, they were serving their country as patriots. It was this focus of purpose that drove the English to distraction.

Periodically the English sent raiding parties to the Norridgewalk Village hoping to engage them in direct battle, or even better than that, they hoped to capture or kill the incendiary Black Robe Sebastian Rale. In the winter of 1704, Colonel Hilton and two hundred and seventy men on snowshoes mounted an expedition to Norridgewalk in four feet of snow only to find the village deserted. They encountered empty wigwams and a large chapel that they burned. Forewarned of the raid, Father Rale and the Indians had fled to the woods, and

---

[28]Authors' note: This mission village, now called Odanak, is an official reservation for the Abenaki Indians. Its history and role during the 17th and 18th Centuries will be covered in more detail later in this chronicle.

the large raiding party was forced to return with little to show for their efforts.

The frontier settlements from Dunstable to Newfoundland had been subjected to their greatest trial from 1703 to 1713. The Abenaki Indians and their French allies had kept the English on the defensive during those ten years. The French Governor, Vaudreuil, had not only insured that they had a continuous supply of powder and lead to carry the attack to the English, but he had been largely responsible for the overall strategy. Mission Indians from Canada with French officers often joined the Maine Indians in their raids. The French officers were often the high-born-nobility of France, the coureurs-de-bois and voyageurs whose forest skills made them especially lethal in the guerilla-type war they were conducting against the English. As if this combination was not sufficiently deadly, the Indians went about their business with the conviction of fanatics who truly believed that *The Creator* was on their side. The religious influence was the handiwork of the Jesuits who did inspired work as propagandists for the French cause. Among other things, the English accused Father Rale of inciting the Norridgewalk braves to kill the English heretics by promising them certain salvation for their sacrifice. Rale was so effective in his work that he gained the reputation with the English of being the leading instigator of Indian depredations against their people and property.

Samuel Penhallow was a New Hampshire militiaman during this dark period. Passages in his 1727 *History of the Indian Wars* reflect the bias and festering anger of a man who was personally involved in the conflict. The following passage that was selected specifically to illustrate Penhallow's bias is balanced by a later quote from the French historian Charlevoix that depicts English atrocities from the French perspective. Penhallow's anger illustrates the bias of a New Hampshire militiaman:

> That when she was going to Canada on the back of the Mont Real River she was violently insulted by Sampson

> her bloody master who without any provocation was resolved to hang her; and for want of a rope made use of his girdle (belt) which when he had fastened about her neck attempted to hoist her up on the limb of a tree that hung in the nature of a gibbet, but in hoisting her the weight of her body broke it asunder; which so exasperated the cruel tyrant, that he made a second attempt, resolving that if he failed that to knock her on the head. But before he had power to affect it (kill her), Bomazeen[29] came along who seeing the tragedy on foot prevented the fatal stroke.

A later passage by Charlevoix, who was the official historian for King Louis 14th, contains even stronger language and underscores the bias of both sides. Prolonged wars inevitably reduce man's instinct to its darkest nature, bringing forth a contemptible quality that human progress and so-called civilization seems incapable of eliminating.

Not long after the *Submission and Pacification of the Eastern Indians Treaty* was signed on July 13, 1713, English settlers began using every means available to push their settlements up the Kennebec River. The Norridgewalk Indians approved the initial request to build a trading post that offered English goods at fair prices, but shortly thereafter without further consultation with the Indians, new settlements were built in Brunswick, Topsham, Augusta, and Georgetown. Emboldened by the Indian's acquiescence, sawmills and fisheries were quickly built, and finally, the owner of a major fishery on the Kennebec built a stone garrison in Augusta. Penhallow wrote:

> The French missionaries perceiving the growth of these plantations soon animated the Indians to distrust them by insinuating that the land was theirs, and that the English invaded their properties which was a vile and

---

[29]Authors' note: Bomazeen was a Norridgewalk Chief.

wrong suggestion for that their conveyances were from the ancient sagamores at least seventy years before."

Charlevoix in his chronicle of the period contended that although the French had ceded Acadia to the English in the Treaty of Utrecht, that the treaty defined the territory of Acadia as being limited to Nova Scotia. According to him, the English were encroaching on Indian lands with their settlements on the Kennebec River. Notwithstanding the *Treaty of Pacification by the Eastern Indians,* the level of Indian hostility rose steadily, and the smoldering fires of their resentment were fueled by the insinuations of their French sponsors and by the Black Robes. Despite the protestations of innocence by the English, the careful researcher begins to perceive hypocrisy in their denials of wrongdoing. Even the New Hampshire militiaman Samuel Penhallow acknowledged the English failure to follow the terms of treaties as well as the English use of alcohol to aid in the commission of fraud on the Indians. The following quote by him illustrates his views:

> The country at this time was in a surprising ferment and generally disposed to war, but the Governor and Council could not readily come into it considering the vast expense and effusion of blood that would unavoidably follow. Besides some were not satisfied with the lawfulness of it at this time. For although they believed the Indians to be very criminal in many respects yet were of the opinion that the English had not so punctually observed the promises made to them of trading houses for the benefit of commerce and traffic *and for the preventing of frauds and extortions too common in the private dealings of the English with them. But the grand abuse to them is the selling of strong drink to them which has occasioned much quarreling and sin and loss of many*

> *lives to the great scandal of religion and reproach of the country.*[30]

Penhallow went on to explain that Governor Shute was unwilling to enforce the terms of the treaty that were included to benefit Indians because of the level of opposition he knew he would face from his council. This hypocrisy is typical of English dealings with the Indians. Unfortunately the native custom of recording their history through telling beads and story telling did not serve them well in their dealing with the white man. The writer's attempt to reconstruct native history is like a blind man trying to describe an elephant using only his touch and his hearing. Over time the Indians abandoned their oral history tradition as they were assimilated into the white culture. That is the reason that the native perception of their history was never properly recorded. The charges and counter charges issued by Penhallow and Charlevoix reflect the hopeless muddle the two sides found themselves in. On July 25, 1722, the Massachusetts and New Hampshire colonies issued a proclamation declaring war; it was called *Governor Dummer's War against the Eastern Abenaki Indians*. In 1723 hostile acts by the Indians resumed at a furious level, and the General Assembly in Boston raised the bounty on Indian scalps to 100 pounds. The increased bounty attracted many volunteers other than those who went up to Pigwacket country with Lovewell in February of 1725. During that same winter Captain Moulton took a company of men up the Kennebec River to the Norridgewalk Indian village where he hoped to find the incendiary Jesuit. The firebrand Sebastian Rale and his Indians were warned of the approach of the English raiding party and they left an empty village to Moulton and his men. In his haste to avoid capture, the Jesuit had not cleaned out his files, and the raiders recovered a letter that Governor Vaudreuil had sent to the missionary. Penhallow characterized the letter as follows:

---

[30]Authors' note: Italicized by authors for emphasis

> A vile and pernicious letter from the governor of Quebec directed unto the Fryer, exhorting him to push on the Indians with all imaginable zeal against the English whose advice he as industriously pursued.

In late summer of 1724, the English decided to change their tactics. All of their previous raids on Norridgewalk had been designed to catch Rale and the Indians in their winter quarters. In early August 1724, a two hundred-man force made up of English volunteers and Iroquois braves went up the Kennebec in seventeen whaleboats. The four captains who led the party were Harmon, Moulton, Brown and Bene—all experienced bush fighters. They disembarked from the whaleboats near Brunswick and went forward on foot. During their march they had an encounter with a well-known Norridgewalk war chief called Bomazeen who had killed an Englishman a few days earlier. The English killed him as he was trying to make his escape across a river. In this same encounter they killed Bomazeen's daughter and captured his wife. Penhallow wrote that Bomazeen's wife cooperated with the English, and she briefed the English on conditions at the Norridgewalk village. With Iroquois warriors in the English party, it is little wonder that the Indian woman decided to talk. Encouraged by the information they got from her about the state of preparedness in her village, the raiders proceeded quickly to the target. On August 12th they approached within two miles of the village without being detected. With Chief Bomazeen gone from the village, security measures were lax. Captain Harmon with a contingent of forty men went to investigate the smoke they saw coming from a cornfield. At the same time Captain Moulton crept closer to the village with one hundred men. When they reached the perimeter of the village, Moulton divided his men into three squadrons of thirty men each, and he ordered the remaining ten men to guard the baggage. He positioned the two squadrons on his left and right flanks placing them in a position to ambush the escape lanes. He and his thirty men got within pistol shot before they were discovered by the Indians, who Penhallow described as being in "amazing terror." Snatching up their guns the Indians fired wildly and ineffectively, and in their headlong flight, they ran into the muzzles of the two squadrons that lay in ambush. Many were slain on the spot, some escaped in their canoes, and others who attempted to swim the river were drowned in the rapids and falls downstream.

The untimely death of prominent people usually invites contrary opinions, and the death of Sebastian Rale was no exception. Revered by the Norridgewalk Indians his superiors and the French authorities, Rale was the object of intense English hatred. He had steadfastly refused to accept an easier posting that would have allowed him to live out his life in comfort and safety. Regardless of belief, the unbiased observer must concede that the pattern of Rale's life was that of a martyr. The writings of Penhallow and Charlevoix effectively illustrate the divergence of opinion over Rale's influence upon the Norridgewalk Indians. Penhallow's comments reflect his long standing hatred for the Jesuit:

> The number of dead we scalped were twenty six besides Monsieur Rale, the Jesuit, who was a bloody incendiary and instrumental to most of the mischiefs that were done to us, by preaching up the doctrine of meriting salvation by the destruction of heretics. Some say that quarter was offered him which he refused and would neither give nor take any. After this they burnt and destroyed the Chapel, canoes and all the cottages that lay round, they also took four Indians alive and recovered three captives. The numbers that were killed and drowned were supposed to be eighty, but some say more. The greatest victory we have obtained in the three or four last wars, and it may be as noble an exploit (all things considered) as ever happened in the time of King Philip.

The Jesuit Charlevoix lived in New France as a student, and he later served as a missionary. As historian for King Louis 14,th one should not be surprised at the level of his indignation over the death of his clerical colleague:

> Warned by the danger in which his neophytes were by the cries and tumult, Father Rale went fearlessly to meet the assailants, in the hope of drawing all their attention on himself alone, and thus saving his flock at the peril of his life. His hope was not vain. Scarcely had he appeared when the English uttered a loud cry which was followed by a shower of musket-balls, under which he fell dead, near a cross that he had planted in the midst of the village. Seven Indians who accompanied and wished to shield him with their bodies were slain beside him. Thus died this charitable pastor giving his life for his flock after a painful apostleship of 37 years. His death spread consternation among the Indians who at once took flight and crossed the river by swimming or fording, but constantly being pursued by the enemy till they reached the depths of the woods where they rallied to the number of 150. Although more than two thousand shots were fired at them, only 30 were killed and 14 wounded.
>
> The English, seeing no further resistance, proceeded to plunder and burn the cabins. They did not spare the church, but did not set fire to it till after they had unworthily profaned the sacred vessels and the adorable Body of Christ. They then retired with a precipitation resembling flight, and as though they had been smitten with a panic terror. The Indians immediately returned to their village, and their first care, while the women were seeking herbs and plants proper to cure the wounded, was to weep over the body of their holy missionary.
>
> They found him pierced with a thousand blows, his scalp torn off, his skull crushed by hatchets, his mouth

> and eyes full of mud, his leg-bones broken, and all his members mutilated in a hundred different ways. Thus a priest was treated in his mission, at the foot of a cross, by those very men, who on all occasions exaggerate so greatly the pretended inhumanities of our Indians, who have never been seen to use such violence to the dead bodies of their enemies.[31] After his neophytes had raised up and repeatedly kissed the precious remains of a Father tenderly and so justly beloved, they buried him on the very spot where the day before he had celebrated the holy mysteries; this is to say, on the spot where the altar stood before the church was burned.

As summer faded to fall, Mother Earth began to erase the morose tableau of man's folly. Multi-hued leaves gradually softened the shattered outlines of the abandoned village. The Kennebec flowed as always, but now its surface was unbroken by the surging bows of birch bark canoes. Reminders of a once thriving village lay here and there provoking memories of another time—an idyllic time. There were reminders of the ancient culture that had lived for centuries hard by this bend in the river. Indian papoose were born here, were strapped to their cradleboards while their mothers tended the *Three Sisters* in the rich interval soil. Here successive generations had danced in festive regalia to the songs and beat of a thousand drums in countless celebrations. In infinite councils the oratory of elders had enthralled men and women. Now their oratory was replaced by the rustling sounds of nature's creatures busy on the forest floor and in the canopy overhead. Meanwhile.... in a misty glade the essence of earthly forms met in ghostly council...the spirits of an ancient people were conducting an ethereal inquest:

---

[31]Authors' note: Other chronicles of the raid claim that the mutilation of Rale's body was the work of Iroquois warriors who were part of the English expedition. During the retreat the Iroquois detached themselves from the main English party and returned to the village to carry out the mutilations described by Charlevoix.

Why has the sorcery of our shaman failed us; how is the white man's magic so powerful; how have our people displeased *Kchi Niwaskw* (The Great Spirit)? Surely He, in his infinite wisdom, will reveal the answers to these and other questions that fill our troubled minds. With the tribes to the south broken, their braves sent far across the great water in chains, with the mighty Penacook and Passamaquoddy scattered and the village of the Penobscot abandoned.... who is left to raise the hatchet against the English? Our shaman must brew their strongest potions and use their most powerful sorcery against the scalp hunters. Only the Pigwacket in their distant valley have strength to defy the English. The Pigwacket warriors and their chiefs Paugus, Adeawando and Wahwa are our last hope.... the people of *All Nations* must pray for powerful magic to strike down the English who grow stronger every day. *We, The People of the Dawn Land pray to Kchi Niwaskw to reveal an auger.... an omen that portends the destruction of the English.*

3-1 Fort Ticonderoga Militiamen
The French Canadians

3-2 Colonial French, Indians and Jesuit

3-3 Colonial French, Indians and Jesuit

CHAPTER 4

THE FIRST PEOPLE

'Twas Paugus led the Pequa'tt tribe—
As runs the Fox, would Paugus run;
As howls the wild wolf, would Paugus howl,
A large bearskin had Paugus on.

The valley of the Saco River had nurtured *The First People* for thousands of years before the coming of the white man. *Kchi Niwaskw* (The Great Spirit) had crafted a paradise on *Mother Earth* for his people. Secure in their mountain-girded valley, their subsistence was either at close hand, or accessible via their river highway. From the high valley of the Passaconaway River that discharged its brawling waters into the Saco, came the furs and deer hides they needed to clothe them in all seasons. The fertile interval soil of the river nourished an abundant crop of corn, squash, and beans that supplemented their meat and fish diet. The profusion of lakes and ponds in their valley attracted migratory waterfowl and a variety of fresh water fish that were part of their diet. Their domed wigwams, and the vertical log stockade that enclosed them, were built from materials provided by *Mother Earth*. A classic example of their artisan skill was the birch bark canoe. The rawhide lashed gunwales and thwarts were crafted of white ash; the ribs were formed from cedar, and the birch bark skin was laced to the frame with *wattup* (split spruce roots). The eighty-pound masterwork was made watertight with spruce gum. This efficient transport carried the Indian to the far reaches of his valley, and to the estuaries of the coastline for his seasonal food gathering activities. The native's reverence for his physical environment, as well as his respect for the living creatures that shared his life on the *Great Turtle Island*, lent a mystic quality to his image.... that of the noble savage. However, as we examine the social structure and spirituality of the 17th Century Indian, it is clear that words like *Stone Age* and *savage* are not appropriate terminology to describe the Native American and his culture.

The Pigwacket Indians were the descendants of the Sokoki Indians who once made their home on the lower Saco River. The river provided a natural highway that gave them easy access to the upper Saco Valley for their winter hunting and trapping activities. In the summer, their canoes carried them to their food gathering activities in the marshes and estuaries of the seacoast. The appearance of European fishermen and explorers along the New England coastline in the 1500s may have been the catalyst that caused them to move into the interior. On the other hand, it was not uncommon for native tribes to change the location of their village when the fertility of the land declined, or when supplies of local game ran out. Having hunted and trapped in the upper Saco Valley for as long as anyone could remember, the Pigwackets believed that their ancestors had occupied the valley since the beginning of time. George Hill Evan, who wrote Pigwacket in 1939, found sixty-eight variations in the spelling of Pigwacket. By the late 1800s, most historians were using the Pigwacket spelling. Beginning about 1903, people began to spell the name Pequawket, and today, that is the accepted form. The names of Indian tribes, nations, and federations can be confusing to the uninformed. Although many tribes joined together under the banner of the Wabanaki and Abenaki Confederations, the individual tribes still retained their special identity. Abenaki was used in the same context as we use the term *American*. In modern society a "Floridian" or a "Georgian" can also be an American, just as a Penobscot or Pigwacket tribal member was also Abenaki. The names of individual tribes were usually a reference to their geographical location, or it might refer to some feature of the tribe that was unique to them.

Many historians have declared that the name Pigwacket was derived from certain Indian root words that referred to the convoluted course of the Saco River; they claimed that the literal meaning of the word was, "*the place at the bend in the river.*" Fanny Hardy Eckstorm, who spent sixteen years researching the Pigwacket culture, insisted that the Indian translation for Pigwacket was, "*at the punched up through ground.*" She referenced the name to the up thrust outcropping of rock known locally as Jockey Cap. According to Eckstorm, Pigwacket Hill was a landmark used by the natives to locate the canoe carry over point into Saco Pond from the Saco River. It is doubtful that disagreement over the correct spelling and translation of the name will ever be completely resolved.

The main Pigwacket village of Lovewell's era had approximately two hundred and fifty wigwams inside a log stockade enclosure that was built to protect them from the Mohawk Indians. The village was built in approximately the same location as the current Fryeburg fair grounds. There was a smaller village to the south that was situated between the main village and Stark Mountain. Various native artifacts discovered in the Conway, New Hampshire area indicate that the Pigwackets had another village there. Estimates of the population of the Pigwacket tribe in its hey day range as high as 2,500. The reckless expenditure of their manpower in forty years of warfare against the English seriously diminished their fighting strength. In their defense, one could argue that the unrelenting English appetite for land left them with no other option. There is no evidence to suggest that they were driven by anything other than a desire to preserve their ancestral lands from foreign invaders. Their French allies artfully played on their fears by constantly reminding them of previous English acts of aggression against other tribes. After receiving the news of the destruction of the Norridgewalk Tribe in 1724, the Pigwackets must have felt that continued resistance was their only option.

Lovewell's journal of his second raid described their destination as being "towards the eastern part of the White Mountains." The remote mountain-bound valley had two portals of access, one from the west and the other in the south where the placid Saco River meandered out of the valley to the southeast.

The upper valley was guarded on the west by the stately mountain peaks of Chocorua, Paugus, Passaconaway, and Whiteface. The drainage of the high mountain watershed of Albany and Waterville was the source for the Swift River[32] that flowed through a deep gap in this mountain chain to discharge into the Saco River. Amidst a profusion of low wooded peaks near the town of Madison, the placid Pigwacket Stream wandered into the valley from the southwest. In the north, the valley rose towards the mountain defiles of Jackson, Bartlett and Chatham. The imposing dark ramparts of these northern sentinels and their western rivals veiled the surpassing beauty of *The Hidden One*. Cold and aloof, its peak shrouded by clouds, *Agiochook* (Mount Washington) dominated the lesser peaks. The daily spectacle of the rising sun held an important clue to the identity of the Abenakis. They believed that their home was at the edge of a great Turtle Island floating in the universe. Since a time beyond memory, the sun had cast it first rays on the Pigwacket people as it rose above the rim of *The Great Turtle Island*. The appearance of the fiery ball from behind the dark highlands of the eastern horizon was an immutable sign of their unique identity.... *The People of the Dawn land*. The modern Abenaki is offended by the notion that he or she is a member of a vanishing race. "We are still here," they will say with a smile, and for emphasis, they may quietly add.... *remember that when the last Abenaki is gone, the sun will rise no more.*

The convoluted course of the Saco River; and the traditional short cut through Saco Pond to their village, was a crucial factor in the way the two forces ultimately joined in mortal combat. After entering the valley from the west, the Saco wandered aimlessly towards the north. After prescribing a 32-mile loop, it doubled back to the south passing within six miles of its starting point. It is very likely that the Indians decided to

---

[32]Pigwacket, 1919 by George Hill Evans: p2; The stream anciently known as the Swift Saco discharges into the true Saco, the watershed drainage of the high mountain valley in Albany and Waterville. The basin of the Swift River, now named Passaconaway after one of the highest peaks of its horizon, was formerly called Swift River Interval, or locally, The Great Interval.

build their village in the neckline of this loop because of the duel accessibility to the Saco River. One could launch a canoe at the west boundary of the village, and after traversing the thirty-two-mile loop, it was possible to return to the village through Saco Pond to within a mile of the southeast edge of village. Northbound travelers on the Saco could eliminate the thirty-two-mile loop in the river by going through Saco Pond and making a two mile portage to the west side of the village.

The rivers of New England were vitally important to the native way of life. The clean unpolluted waters not only served as highways for native canoes, but the plentiful fish and game were a dependable source of food for the First People. For thousands of years the Saco cradled and nurtured countless generations of indigenous people in her timeless way. From its brawling beginnings in the mountains, the spirited flow of the Saco was tamed by its meandering passage through the idyllic valley of the Pigwacket. At long length, having concluded its lingering visit to the peaceful valley, the river flowed though a low corridor between minor eastern peaks and continued its placid journey to the coast.

The earth seemed to love her,
And heaven smiled above her,
As she lingered towards the deep.
--George Hill Evans in *Pigwacket*

The routine of a Pigwacket family was controlled by the food-gathering activities of the tribe. The male Indians were adept at making wigwams from nature's materials. The frame was fashioned from bent saplings that were covered with either elm or birch bark. The interior was insulated against winter cold with mats woven from swamp rushes and grass. The crown of the wigwam had an opening to vent the smoke of cooking fires. The interior was furnished with low sleeping pallets made out of wood lashed with wattup or rawhide and padded with straw mats. The wigwam had a center pole that was used to store the meager personal belongings. Hanging from this center pole might be the scalp trophies of the warrior, or the ash and rawhide snowshoes he used in the winter. The outfit of the male Indian was made from natural materials. His moccasins were made of moose hide that were sometimes used with buckskin liners for added protection from the cold. In the summer his outfit was a breechcloth held in place by a rawhide girdle or belt at the waist. In colder weather he wore buckskin leggings suspended by thongs from his belt. To protect his upper body he wore a soft buckskin shirt, and in severe weather, a variety of furs kept him warm. For festive occasions, he wore regalia that could be decorated with colorful designs made from dyed porcupine quills or beads. For celebrations and other rituals, he applied war paint made with a mixture of animal fat and natural pigments such as red ochre or charcoal. To insure that a warrior would be properly outfitted to enter the afterworld in case of death on the battlefield, they wore their most colorful outfits into battle.

Indian women wore wrap-around buckskin skirts, and when their season required, they used squirrel skins lined with moss. Before the arrival of the Jesuit missionaries, Indian women went topless during the summer, and in the winter, they wore buckskin shirts, furs and blankets. After the arrival of the Jesuits, the women wore outfits that covered their breasts. In the years before puberty, male and female children ran naked about the village. When they reached puberty, there were rituals designed to initiate maidens to womanhood and males to manhood. The young Indian maiden was required to spend time in the long house with the elder females of the tribe, where she learned her womanly duties and the secrets of her special magic.... the natural cycles of her body and, her ability to create life.

When he reached the age of puberty, the young brave embarked on a solitary *vision quest*. He subsisted on water alone, communing with nature until he experienced a visitation, or he recognized a sign that identified his spiritual guardian.... his *manatou*. Throughout the long cycle of his life, he relied on signs and messages from his unique manatou to guide his decisions in times of crisis. In addition a special *totem* was passed down through many generations of an Indian family that identified them as members of a particular clan. Many modern native descendants consider their family clan name a part of their identity.... for example *the turtle clan.*

The native thought of himself as a strand in a great *Web of Life* that was composed of the totality of his physical surroundings and other living beings. Nuances in his language defined mountains and rivers as inanimate beings, and birds, animals, and fish as animate beings. He believed that man should live in harmony with these animate and inanimate beings in order to maintain the web of life undisturbed.... this was the measure of man's worth during his time on *Mother Earth*. The circle had great symbolism for all Indians. From the protective circle of the mother's womb, the young brave or maiden emerged to travel the great circle of life. From cradle board to grave, living beings were controlled by nature's cycles: the cycle of the seasons, the movement of celestial bodies, the maiden's reproductive rhythm, and the seasonal return of spawning fish. The native man or woman approached the end of his or her journey on *Mother Earth* with calm acceptance.... for the Indian knew no hell. When the night owl came to call their name, they knew it was their time. When that moment arrived, they calmly followed their guide to the other side, confident of their immortality.... knowing that one-day, the essence of their being would return to *Mother Earth* in another physical form.

All tribal members felt responsibility for initiating the Pigwacket youth to Spartan virtues. The entire community taught him to withstand pain, hunger, fear and sorrow stoically. He learned to exalt valor and to scorn weakness, to suffer hunger, exhaustion, and cold without complaint. Before the young brave could call himself a man and a warrior, he was expected to demonstrate his mastery of the Spartan virtues by performing well in a war party, or by facing danger bravely. The eagerness of young braves to prove their manhood, often worked against the designs of the elders. During sensitive peace negotiations with the English, elders were often unable to restrain their young warriors from murderous acts that were sure to disrupt negotiations.

Historical records reveal that the Pigwacket Indians were an implacable foe of the English for more than fifty years. There are many documented accounts of Pigwacket involvement in raids that ranged from the Merrimack River to Newfoundland. An analysis of their raids against the English reveals that it would be incorrect to portray them as innocent victims of Lovewell's scalp hunters. The scope of their history of resistance against the English is impressive. There are extensive published reports that they were involved in raids along the Merrimack River from Dunstable (Nashua) to Andover and Haverhill. Their warriors ranged up and down the New England coast from Portsmouth to Pemaquid, and the two expeditions of Pigwacket warriors to Newfoundland with the legendary Chief Escumbuit are well documented by Samuel Penhallow and the Jesuit historian Charlevoix. Although Chief Escumbuit was not involved in the final showdown between Paugus and Lovewell, his legend is part of the historic mystique of the Pigwacket Indians. The selected Pigwacket actions against the English were chosen to validate their reputation as an aggressive warlike tribe with a long history of bloody warfare.

One of the English forts that frustrated the French during King William's War was located at Pemaquid Point at the tip of a peninsula that jutted into Casco Bay south of Damariscotta, Maine. The French and Indians had built the wooden stockade to replace an outpost that was destroyed in 1676. The new Fort St. Charles drew the attention of the French after a series of frontier events made it vulnerable. Tensions that were once again rising along the frontier after a ten-year interlude of peace reached a flash point as a result of three events. In the first instance, the trading post of a Frenchman named Saint Castin was looted and burned in a surprise raid by the English. Castin had solidified his relations with the Indians by marrying the daughter of the Abenaki Chief Madockawando. Saint Castin avoided capture by fleeing into the forest from where he helplessly watched the English destroy his outpost. Infuriated by the destruction of his property, Castin offered gunpowder, lead and tobacco to any Indian that would take up the hatchet against the English. Castin's father-in-law, Madockawando, had little difficulty turning native anger to his son-in-law's advantage, and his warriors were eager to raise the tomahawk against the English.

At about that same time, an atrocity committed by English sailors against an Indian woman and her papoose occurred near the mouth of the Saco River. Intoxicated by rum, the sailors were out in a whaleboat on a lark where they sighted an Indian woman in a canoe with her papoose. On an impulse they decided to test the theory that Indian babies have the natural swimming ability of a baby otter. In a classic example of their low regard for Indians, they proceeded to capsize the canoe amidst great hilarity. The mother managed to get to shore with her papoose, but the child did not survive the ordeal. Inasmuch as the papoose happened to be the grandchild of the famous Chief Moxus, the entire Abenaki Indian Federation was outraged by the brutal act of the English sailors.

These two acts by the English were played out against political uncertainty in England and the Massachusetts Colony. Prior to the two incidents, authorities had recalled five hundred military personnel from frontier garrisons after receiving news from England of an attempt to unseat the despotic King James the 2nd. Only thirty of the former contingent of one hundred fifty six soldiers at Fort St. Charles remained after the force reduction.

Father Thury, Jesuit missionary to the Penobscot Indians, wanted to destroy the Pemaquid fort, and he asked for help from the Pigwacket and the Norridgewalk Indians. Fired by the recent English acts on the frontier, the Pigwacket and Norridgewalk councils agreed to join the Penobscot. Two hundred Indians executed the surprise attack. Many of the soldiers had wives and children living in houses located outside the walls of the fort. The Indians quickly overwhelmed the civilians in those houses and mounted a siege on the fort. The situation soon grew desperate for Captain Weems and his thirty men. The Indian crossfire from second floor windows of the captured houses and from behind a large outcropping of rock on the seaward side of the fort was devastating. They managed to pick off sixteen of Weems' small force with their fire. The next day Weems accepted the Indian offer of quarter, and he and fourteen men walked out of the fort in the company of a large group of women and children who had sought protection inside the fort. Despite the promise of quarter, the Indians attacked and killed many until Chief Madockawando restrained them. Captain Weems and five of his men were taken to Canada from where they were later repatriated. The French historian Charlevoix wrote that the total English dead, including men, women and children, was eighty. The American historian, Francis Parkman, appeared to take a rather conciliatory view of this raid when he wrote the following:

> Except for the slain, the behavior of the victors is said to be credible. They tortured no one and their chiefs broke the casks of wine in the fort in order to keep their warriors under control. Father Thury, who was present, writes that he exhorted the Indians to refrain from drunkenness and cruelty. He adds that, as a consequence, they did not take a single scalp.

If the Charlevoix tally of eighty men, women and children dead is correct, Parkman's comments seem curiously out of place. He marginalizes the dead by writing, "Except for the slain, the behavior of the victors is said to be credible." He then appears to praise the Indians because they didn't get drunk or take any scalps. The implication is that, without the presence of Father Thury on the scene, the carnage would have been much greater. This 1688 attack was typical of some of the early Indian raids on English settlements. Later, when the French discovered that the families of captives were willing to pay ransom money for their release, they paid bounties to the Indians for the captives they delivered to Canada. The Penobscot missionary, Father Thury, was typical of the more militant Jesuits. He not only instigated raids, but he actually played an active role in the execution of the raid. One can understand why the English judgment of the Jesuits was so harsh and unyielding. One suspects that our modern society would call them terrorists.

In January of 1689, the Governor of New France decided to send three war parties south to try to buoy up the sagging spirits of his people. Since his own colony was under almost constant attack from the Iroquois, one wonders why he did not use these forces to protect his people in New France? Referred to as the "Iron Governor," he was famous for his obstinacy and temper, and knowing that the Iroquois were English allies, he perhaps thought to give the English a taste of their own medicine. One of the war parties headed for Schenectady, NY, and the remaining two companies headed for the Maine coast traveling independently. Approximately seventy five Frenchmen and one hundred mission Indians made an incredible three months march through winter storms to arrive within striking distance of settlements on the lower Maine coast. Pigwacket, Norridgewalk and Penobscot warriors joined the Canadian strike force as it neared its target. Presently one of the war parties lay undetected on the outskirts of Salmon Falls, NH. After reconnoitering the town, the commander, Francois Hertel, split his force into three groups that attacked the unprepared town simultaneously. There was no night watch posted anywhere in the town, and the fortified garrison houses as well as local farms were easily overwhelmed. The thirty dead victims of their attack included elders, men, women and children who died brutally under a hail of blows from war clubs, tomahawks and gun butts. Fifty-four women and children and a few men were taken captive, all the buildings of the settlement were burned, and all the cattle were killed. This deliberate scorched-earth policy was part of the French strategy to force the English to give up their settlements and return to Boston.

As they made their way north with their prisoners, a force of one hundred and fifty English militia attacked them near the

Wooster River. Hertel's son was badly wounded in a firefight that caused heavy casualties on both sides. Hertel managed to escape under cover of darkness and he continued north with his captives. When he heard that the other French war party was planning to attack Fort Loyal in Portland, he posted a guard on his prisoners, and he hastened to link up with the other group. A French officer named Portneuf and Lieutenant Courtemanche were in command of the 2nd war party. The combined force of Frenchmen, mission Indians, Pigwackets, Norridgewalk and Penobscot Indians was later estimated to total four hundred and fifty men.

Fort Loyal was located near the present day India Street in Portland, Maine. The fort was the centerpiece of a small village that included four garrison houses. It was a typical fort of the period that consisted of wooden barracks surrounded by a wooden stockade of vertical logs. The fort had eight cannon mounted in the walls of the stockade. To minimize the possibilities of a surprise attack, the defenders had cleared the surrounding area of all trees and vegetation. About eighty men under the command of Sylvanus Davis were charged with protecting the fort, the blockhouses and the village. The townspeople were alerted to the raiders by the sound of Indian scalping cries, and everyone in the village immediately fled to the safety of the fort. The yelps were from Indian scouts who had killed and scalped a straggler in the fields. Although the enemy had not yet appeared, a young lieutenant named Thaddeus Clark called for volunteers to locate the Indians. Against the advice of Sylvanus Davis, he set out across the half-mile cleared area around the fort with thirty eager volunteers. The woods at the perimeter of the cleared area held four hundred fifty experienced French and Indian bush fighters lying concealed with primed and loaded muskets. Alerted by the curious behavior of cows grazing near a section of woods, Clark and his men impetuously charged the area hoping to flush out a handful of Indians. From the murderous ambush that took place in a cacophony of musket fire, black powder smoke, and war whoops, four wounded men fled to the safety of the fort.

Once again, the impetuous action of brave young Englishmen had cost them dearly.

As darkness fell on the overcrowded fort, the occupants pondered their fate. They were safe for the moment, but in the milling legions of buckskin-clad attackers outside, they could only envision an outcome of capture, torture or death.... It was a long night for the besieged occupants.

The next day on Portneuf's orders, the Indians sacked and burned all of the houses in the vicinity of the forts. Using shovels taken from the village, they dug trenches within yards of the fort. The defenders were unable to depress the muzzles of the cannon low enough to direct fire on them, and musket fire was ineffective. Portneuf rejected an English request for a six-day cease-fire, and the methodical assault continued. During the next four days, the occupants prayed for help as the trenches crept ever closer to the wooden palisade of the fort. When the Indians had managed to place firewood and tar against the palisade wall, Captain Davis knew he had to act. He was not only running low on food and water, but his men were low on powder and musket balls.... he requested a parley!

For the first time, he realized that he was dealing with Frenchmen; Portneuf and the other Frenchmen were dressed in Indian outfits, but their accented English gave away their identity. Davis offered to surrender the fort if the French would agree to give quarter to all the occupants of the fort. He stipulated that they be allowed to go to the closest English settlement accompanied by a French escort to protect them from the Indians. Portneuf not only accepted the English terms, but in response to Sylvanus Davis' plea for assurance, he raised his right hand and swore to God that he would faithfully carry out the agreed upon terms. One can only imagine the paralyzing fear that gripped the occupants of the fort as they filed out to face the milling hundreds of buckskin-clad warriors in war paint. Once the safety of the fort was behind them, their worse fears were realized when the Frenchmen turned their backs and allowed the Indians to have their way with the prisoners. The Pigwackets, Norridgewalk and Penobscot warriors immediately assaulted the prisoners with war clubs and tomahawk killing many on the spot. Remarkably, Sylvanus Davis and three adult men were spared and they were taken to Canada as prisoners. Davis eventually had a meeting with Count Frontenac, the French governor. When informed of Portneuf's betrayal, Frontenac expressed great anger, but he later wrote that he was quite pleased by the way the success of his raiding parties had buoyed the spirits of the French people:

> You cannot believe the joy that these slight successes has caused and how much it contributes to raise the people (Canadians) from their dejection and terror.

It is a strange quirk of man's nature that he can find comfort in the destruction of other human beings, and that terror inflicted on others can produce a joyous reaction in fellow beings. For thousand of years the aboriginal warrior had gratified his primitive need to dominate through raids on his traditional enemies using spears and clubs as weapons. Now that he was caught in a power struggle between rival European nations, the native was expected to observe "civilized" rules of war. But there is plenty of evidence to prove that the English and the French were often treacherous in their dealings with one another. As the succeeding episode will demonstrate, the English were not above dishonesty and treachery in their own conduct of the war.

The raids on Pemaquid, Salmon Falls and Fort Charles were a launching platform for the rising star of a legendary Pigwacket warrior. He had distinguished himself by his bravery in these actions, and he was subsequently made a war chief by the Pigwacket Chief's Council. He was given the name *Assacumbuit* by the Council, but was later called *Escumbuit*[33] by

---

[33]*Histoire des Abenaquis* by Abbe N.F. Maurault; p. 330; Maurault was in charge of the St. Francis Mission in Odanak. In his book he spelled Escumbuit as Naskanbiwit, and he interpreted it to mean: **"He who is so important and raised so high by his merit, that thought cannot reach his greatness."**

the English, and the French knew him as *Nescambiouit*. He and his Pigwacket warriors are associated with a series of attacks on English outposts from Andover, MA to Newfoundland. The French historian Charlevoix wrote that Nescambiouit and his warriors were favorites of the Sieur de Montigny and the famous French sea captain Pierre Le Moyne d'Iberville. Any chronicle of Pigwacket military action between 1688 and 1708 would not be complete without prominent references to the Sieur de Montigny and his favorite Indian…Chief Nescambiouit.

In 1696 the English rebuilt the fort at Pemaquid Point, and they renamed it Fort William Henry. The Massachusetts Colony used one third of the yearly budget to rebuild the fort with stone and mortar. There were eighteen cannon mounted in the gun ports of six-foot thick walls that rose ten to twenty feet above the ground. The fort was rebuilt under the direction of Captain March who was a ship builder on the Merrimack River in Andover, MA before joining the militia. When the fort was completed, March turned command of the fort over to another Andover man named Chubb. March was later quoted as saying that no man was more ill equipped to command such an important fort than Pasco Chubb. Shortly after Chubb assumed command of the fort, Governor Stoughton of Massachusetts wrote a letter in which he proposed a parley with the Indians at Pemaquid to discuss a prisoner exchange. After an exchange of letters between the governor and the Jesuit priests Bigot and Thury, a date was arranged for the parley. Among the twelve Indians who came to the negotiation were the three Norridgewalk chiefs Bomazeen (Abomazine), Abenquid and Taxous. Chief Egeremet of the Machias Indians came as well as the Pigwacket Chief Escumbuit. Other chiefs and captains brought the total count of the Indian negotiating party to twelve. Pasco Chubb and eleven of his subordinates made up the English negotiating party. At the request of the Indians, the meeting took place outside the fort under a white flag of truce. According to a pre-arranged plan, Chubb extended a cordial greeting to the Indians through his interpreter, and he then had rum served to all the negotiators. After Chubb and his lieutenants offered a few toasts, the Indians felt compelled to respond in kind, and the rum continued to flow. When Chubb judged the moment to be right, he signaled a pre-planned attack on the Indians. The English pulled out concealed daggers and clubs, and they attacked the defenseless Indians. Several Indians including Egeremet and Abenquid were killed, and a few Indians including Bomazeen[34] were captured. Escumbuit and Taxous managed to escape.

The shocking news of Chubb's betrayal swept through the native and white communities like a tornado, and even the English were dismayed by Chubb's treachery. The French celebrated the news of Chubb's blunder saying that his action accomplished more to stir up the Indians than the best efforts of the Jesuit missionaries to incite them. In spite of the general condemnation of his conduct, Pasco Chubb was allowed to continue as the commander of Fort William Henry. His treacherous act while under the sacred protection of a white flag of truce went contrary to every concept of Abenaki honor. In every tribal debate in councils of the Abenaki Confederation the vote was unanimous.... Only Chubb's death could appease the Abenaki thirst for revenge.

Fort William Henry presented a direct challenge to the territorial claims of the French in Maine. If they had mounted an attack against the fort during its construction, they could have

---

[34] *Whose Who in Indian History* by Carl Waldman, p. 33; Bomazeen, Bomazine, Abomazine "Keeper of the ceremonial fire." Like Assacumbuit, Madockawando and Moxus, Bomazeen was a prominent sachem of the Abenaki Confederacy. His village of the Norridgewalk Tribe was located along the Kennebec River. In 1693 he signed a treaty with Maine's Colonial Governor, William Phips. The garrison at Pemaquid, Maine seized him while negotiating under a flag of truce and imprisoned him in Boston. Upon his release he led his warriors in attacks on Chelmsford and Sudbury in Massachusetts in 1706, and Saco in Maine in 1710. In 1713 Bomazeen signed a peace treaty with the British at Portsmouth, NH, but before long took up arms again in support of the French. He died in an engagement near Taconnet, Maine. Colonial troops then attacked and destroyed Bomazeen's village. His daughter was killed and his wife taken captive in the same raid.

easily shattered the British presence there. As the fort was nearing completion, Pierre Le Moyne d'Iberville had sailed into the harbor with three French war ships, but after reconnoitering the site, the ships returned to Newfoundland. Based on his reconnaissance, D'Iberville knew he would require land-based cannon to take the fort. For d'Iberville, Chubb's continued presence in the fort only made it a more attractive conquest to contemplate. The war councils of the Abenaki Nation greeted the news of the impending attack on Fort William Henry with great excitement. At last, Abenaki warriors would have a chance to avenge Chubb's insult to their sacred honor.... Now they would have the trickster's scalp!

In early August of 1696, three French sloops under the command of d'Iberville sailed out of Placentia harbor on the southern coast of Newfoundland. Off the port of St. John's, Newfoundland they engaged two British frigates and an auxiliary tender. They captured one frigate after blowing away its mast, but the remaining frigate and tender got away in the fog. Buoyed by their sea victory over the British, d'Iberville directed his small fleet south for a rendezvous with the Abenaki Indians in Castin, Maine. Most of the tribes of the Abenaki Confederation had sent contingents of warriors to the rebuilt trading post of the French trader Saint Castin. Chief Escumbuit, who had survived Chubb's nefarious attack, was there with more than one hundred Pigwacket warriors. When d'Iberville arrived with one hundred Canadian soldiers, the French hosted a huge powwow for the Indians. The reunion between Escumbuit and the Sieur de Montigny was warm because of their mutual respect for each other's bravery and fighting ability. The French historian Charlevoix knew Escumbuit and Montigny personally, and he often wrote glowingly about the gallant Montigny and his faithful Nescambiouit.

The attack on Fort William Henry unfolded like a cinematic spectacle. The sequence of events began with five hundred Abenaki warriors paddling canoes from Castin, Maine across the bay towards New Harbor at Pemaquid Point. The sight of hundreds of warriors in fragile birch bark canoes in the open ocean was unforgettable. When they landed at New Harbor, hundreds of warriors immediately surrounded the fort. As d'Iberville had planned, their presence accomplished two things. First it pinned the English inside the fort, and secondly, it secured the small port at New Harbor where d'Iberville planned to unload his cannons. D'Iberville's plan worked extremely well. The Indians had already secured the port by the time the three French sloops arrived, and the combined force immediately began to unload their heavy siege guns. The two Jesuit priests, Thury and Simon, labored alongside the Indians to unload the guns and drag them to the fort that was located only one half mile from the harbor. Before the cannons and mortars were moved into position, the Indians called on the English to surrender. With flair for the dramatic, Chubb is reported to have responded: "*We will continue to fight though the ocean may be covered with French ships and the land by Indians.*" By mid-afternoon of the following day, there were two cannon and two mortars in position. Saint Castin sent a message to Chubb offering him quarter, advising him that all inhabitants including women and children dependents would be turned over to the Indians if he did not yield at once. When Chubb failed to respond to Saint Castin's offer, the French began to lob exploding mortar rounds into the interior of the fort. The interior wooden barracks provided little protection from exploding shell fragments, and incredibly, the garrison's only water supply was a well located outside the fort! After several mortar shells exploded inside the compound, Chubb raised a white flag and asked to parley. Despite his previous mistakes, Chubb was no fool. Given the enemy numbers and their firepower, he knew that his situation was hopeless. He offered to surrender the fort in exchange for a d'Iberville guarantee that the English garrison would be given a safe escort to Boston where they could be exchanged for French and Indians prisoners held there. When he learned that d'Iberville had accepted his terms, Chubb breathed a huge sign of relief knowing his certain fate if the French turned him over to the Indians. D'Iberville then executed his end of the agreement faithfully.

To safeguard the English, he herded them into small boats and canoes, and he sent them out to a small island in the bay where one of his sloops was assigned to guard them until they could be transferred to Boston. A serious crisis arose when Escumbuit and his men found a chained Indian prisoner in a stone dungeon. Scurvy and festering sores on his arms and legs from manacles and leg irons devastated the prisoner's body. When Escumbuit and his warriors saw the man's condition they flew into a rage, and they remonstrated with the French to take their revenge on Chubb and the other prisoners. Under the tense circumstances, the French decided it would not be wise to tell the Indians about an official letter they had found among Chubb's effects. The letter contained official instructions directing Chubb to hang the Indian prisoner.

The bloodless surrender was a letdown for the Indians who had taken part in the raid. Many had traveled a great distance to the rendezvous in Castin, Maine. The festive powwow hosted by the French and the proud oratory of their leaders had girded them for a fierce fight with the English. For them it was a proud moment in Abenaki history. Every warrior had thoughts about his personal involvement in the historic event. For a thousand years *N'datlogit* would tell the story of how five hundred Abenaki warriors in battle regalia had crossed Penobscot Bay to revenge the treachery of the English. Every warrior had expected the victory to come amidst chaotic noise, fire, smoke, blood and scalping cries. It was the bloodless surrender that was disconcerting to the Indians. The sudden reversion to European protocol puzzled them. Was there any honor in protecting an enemy that surrendered without firing a shot? Were the Indians not entitled to vent their anger, and should they not be given an opportunity to test Chubb's manhood through torture? Instead, the white man's inexplicable behavior had robbed them of the celebration they expected to come with victory!

The fate of the English prisoners had been in doubt for some time after the surrender. Ultimately, in spite of the Indian protests, d'Iberville followed through with his promise to protect the English prisoners. With the prisoners beyond their reach, the Indians could only vent their frustration by helping the French destroy the fort and by loading the captured English guns onto the French ships. For the Indians there were no bounties, no scalps, and there was very little loot. Escumbuit was completely bewildered by the French decision to shield Chubb.... his revenge would have to wait.

After destroying the fort at Pemaquid, d'Iberville sent some of the prisoners to Boston with a message that the remainder would be turned over to the English when certain Indian and French prisoners were released in Boston. After waiting for some time in Penobscot Bay, he ran low on provisions, so he put Captain Villieu in charge of the remaining prisoners and departed for Placentia, Newfoundland. Chubb and the rest of the prisoners were eventually transported to Boston. On his arrival in Boston, Chubb was tried and imprisoned for dereliction of duty because of his role in giving up Fort William Henry without a fight. It was an uninspired end to a colorless career, but at least for the time being, he was safe from Escumbuit's revenge.

D'Iberville was anxious to take full advantage of the large number of fighting men he presently had under his command. His easy victory at Pemaquid had convinced him that he could virtually wipe the slate clean by driving the British out of St. John's, Newfoundland. After conferring with the Sieur de Montigny, he decided to bring Escumbuit and his Pigwacket warriors together with as many Indians they could make room for on the crowded sloops. Already far distant from their mountain-girded valley, the Pigwacket warriors were headed for Newfoundland. For Escumbuit, it was only one campaign out of an incredible fighting career that would eventually result in him being knighted by King Louis 14th at the Palace of Versailles in France. As the French sloops sailed north in a freshening breeze, the chief remained aloof from his companions. He stood apart, smoking his pipe, his face impassive, his eyes revealing a burning malice that smoldered within. Montigny was fascinated by Nescambiouit's intensity, sensing that the chief would never rest until Pasco Chubb's scalp hung from his belt.

The galling presence of St. John's on the northeast coast of Newfoundland was an irritant to the French. From this far north settlement and port, the British were able to harass French shipping, and their position there allowed them to control access to the vast cod fishing areas off the coast. In a curious juxtaposition of power, the French also had a port and settlement they called Placentia on the south coast of the island. Neither the French nor the English had been successful in establishing contact with the indigenous people of the island.[35] The natives had retreated to the mountainous interior of the island. The fortifications of the British garrison at St. John's were designed to withstand a naval bombardment from the sea, but d'Iberville had an entirely different campaign in mind. His point of attack would be from the south against the soft underbelly of the settlement. First he had to deal with the egotistic, power-hungry Governor De Brouillan who schemed to be the overall commander of an expedition that included his own Placentia force. Brouillan finally had to abandon his personal ambition when the Canadians and Indians under Montigny and d'Iberville declared that they would fight only under their own commanders

After a nine-day march through severe winter conditions, they reached the small settlement of Florillon. All chance of a surprise attack on St. John's was lost when one of their prisoners escaped and alerted the settlement. The cumbersome weight of the small cannon they were dragging over the rough terrain slowed their advance. At the Bay de Toulle, d'Iberville left the cannon behind with a small guard in order to speed his advance on St. John's. On November 26th they engaged in a firefight with a company of thirty Englishmen who retreated to

---

[35]Authors' note: Although the indigenous people of Newfoundland avoided contact with both the French and the English, the presence of the Europeans proved disastrous to their culture. Deprived of their traditional fishing sites along the coast, their attempts to survive in the interior of the island eventually failed. The last Newfoundland indigenous survivor died in about 1909.

St. John's after losing six of their men. That night Escumbuit and his Indians scouted the area in a heavy snowfall returning with several English prisoners. The snowstorm kept them in place for a full day, but on the second day, they resumed their advance with Montigny and thirty Canadians as advance scouts. About mid-morning Montigny and his men came under fire from the muskets of ninety Englishmen hidden behind rocks. When De Brouillan and his men joined the action, they made a frontal assault on the English position while Escumbuit and the Pigwacket Indians attacked the English flank. Perceiving their danger from the Indians, the English retreated to St. John's with the French and Indians in full pursuit. The survivors of the last ditch defense effort ran for the protection of the fort—about fifty made it. By the time the French surrounded the fort, it held most of the remaining civilian and military inhabitants of the settlement. As the French watched, a large sailing vessel loaded with civilians put on sail leaving the occupants of the fort to their fate as it sailed out of the harbor. When the commander of the fort refused to parley, d'Iberville dispatched men to recover the cannon from Bay de Toulle in order to place a siege on the fort..

On the nights of the 29th and 30th of November, the Canadians and Indians burned all the wooden houses of the settlement. The English commander decided to surrender the fort after reviewing his available options. He had lost almost one half of his force in futile skirmishes outside the fort; he was running low on provisions, and he was hoping to buy some time. The hopes of the defenders were raised after spying two large English ships maneuvering to enter the harbor. The commander requested a parley outside the fort because he did not want the French to see the miserable state of his defense. After De Brouillan delivered his terms, the English commander requested a twenty-four hour cease-fire to give him time to study the terms. Having been informed of the approaching English ships, De Brouillan deflated the commander's faint hopes, warning that the attack would begin immediately if he did not surrender. When the English ships drew close enough to appraise the situation, they changed course and sailed out of the harbor.

After the surrender, d'Iberville's overruled De Brouillan's proposal to establish a permanent outpost at St. John's; he argued that he needed every available man for other campaigns he had in mind. He decided instead, to burn the fort and the remaining houses in the settlement. Escumbuit and the warriors under Montigny's command were given the job of neutralizing the smaller English settlements in the area. They rounded up more than seven hundred civilians, and they marched them across the island to Placentia where they became prisoners of war. At that juncture, a French sloop brought the startling news that the Treaty of Ryswick had ended the war between France and England, and that the two nations were officially at peace!

Upon hearing the electrifying news, d'Iberville was obliged to alter his plans for additional campaigns. He loaded the Abenaki Indians aboard a sloop and sent them to Maine where they were free to return to their villages. For Montigny, the parting with Escumbuit was difficult. He had developed a deep admiration for the warrior he called Nescambiouit. In parting, Montigny spoke warmly to the chief using the few Abenaki phrases he had learned during their many hours together: "*Kchi wli wni nidoba*" (*great thanks my friend*) "*Wlibamkanni*" (*may your journey go well*).

The return of the Pigwacket warriors to their tranquil valley coincided with Mother Earth's awakening from her deep winter sleep. Compared to the hardships they had experienced in Newfoundland, the beauty of their valley and the warmth of their reception seemed like paradise to the tired warriors. The village rejoiced at their minimal casualties, and the single braves quickly took advantage of their proud status as blooded warriors, and they began to pay court to the maidens of the tribe. Only Escumbuit seemed strangely detached and unimpressed with his celebrity. The elders, especially the grandmothers who had known Assacumbuit from birth, gossiped about his demeanor; a wise elder summarized their collective thought: *the memory of the white man's treachery at Pemaquid holds him captive. He can only be set free by taking Chubb's scalp*. In the meantime, the French had learned a great deal about events in Boston from returning prisoners and from neutral traders who did business with the English. It did not take long for the news of Chubb's release from prison to reach the Pigwacket council.

With the signing of the peace treaty, Chubb was discharged from the military and returned to his wife in Andover, Massachusetts. It was not long before the news of Chubb's whereabouts found its way to the Pigwacket Council in Fryeburg, Maine. Their scouts confirmed this information. The small scouting parties of Indians that operated along the frontier were constantly on the alert for an opportunity to kidnap unwary English woodsmen or farmers. They knew that the Andover militia was patrolling the south shore of the Merrimack River every day. Although there was unanimous agreement in the Pigwacket council that Chubb must die, the elders counseled patience. As one elder wisely put it, *the bear is easier taken in his winter den. When raccoon (trickster) sleeps in warm den—that is time for raid*! Escumbuit heeded the counsel of the Pigwacket elders, and he waited patiently for the time when deep snow made it impossible for the Andover militia to patrol the Merrimack River. When the patrols stopped, Escumbuit and thirty Pigwacket warrior headed south for a lethal rendezvous with Pasco Chubb. As Chubb tended his fireplace enjoying the novelty of home cooking and unaccustomed leisure, Escumbuit and his thirty warriors were making their rendezvous with Joseph, the Wampanoag Indian who had agreed to lead them to their prey.

On the night of February 21, 1698, Escumbuit and his warriors camped on the north bank of the Merrimack River near the present boundary of Lawrence and Methuen, Massachusetts. Directly across the river lay the unsuspecting Andover settlement (presently North Andover). They were clothed in their traditional winter outfits. The ankle-high moose hide moccasins had inner buckskin liners for warmth. Their leggings and shirts were made out of deerskin, and they were robed in a variety of furs to shield them from the intense winter cold. In addition to the ubiquitous musket, each warrior carried parched corn, pemmican and tobacco in a leather pouch. Another pouch held fire-making equipment and musket balls. A powder horn was slung over the shoulder, and each warrior carried a tomahawk and a scalping knife at his waist. As night fell, they built a few small fires using a small knoll to shield the light of their fires from the far shore. Then, like a pack of Alaskan sled dogs, they burrowed into the snow and rested.

Across the river residents added logs to the fire and smothered the wicks in their lamps, or they sought the comfort of goose down comforters and foot warmers. It had been the coldest winter on record with the most snow that anyone could remember. The militia, having found it impossible to walk in the hip-deep snow, had suspended their patrols. Indian activity along the frontier had quieted down after the signing of the peace treaty, and folks were allowing themselves to think that the worse Indian depredations were behind them. Memories of the unreasoned terror that had swept the population in the 1690s, and the traumas of the climactic witch trials, were beginning to fade. Their normal cautious instincts were unduly lulled by the comfortable feeling that the harsh winter was their friend until the militia resumed its patrol in the spring.

It was still dark when Escumbuit roused his warriors. They moved to the fires that had been rekindled with dry wood, and they chewed on pemmican and parched corn from their personal stores. Small birch bark containers were opened, and the warriors applied war paint to each other's faces using the light of the flames. When they saw Escumbuit strap on his snowshoes and pick up his musket and war club, they murmured their approval and they were ready. The strong northwest wind of the previous day was gone, and the reflection of moonlight from the snow illuminated a surreal scene. While Escumbuit conferred with their guide, the warriors stood patiently in the bright moonlight, their breath forming clouds of steam in the frigid air. As they formed up and marched in a long line across the frozen Merrimack, the shuffle and crunch of their snowshoes in the dry powder snow was the only audible sound. Anyone on the far side of the river could have seen the dark line of fur-clad warriors coming across the ice...but the far shore was silent!

When they reached Chubb's house, Escumbuit and ten warriors concealed themselves behind his barn. The remaining warriors followed the guide to the home of Colonel Bradstreet,[36] who was the commander of the Andover militia. After posting ten warriors there, Joseph led the third assault team to a nearby farm where they awaited Escumbuit's signal. Six years earlier, the town had been paralyzed by the irresponsible accusations made by teenage children against imagined witches in the town. During that era, the hysteria that began in Salem had reached epidemic proportions in Andover. Once again, through no fault of their own, calamity was to be their bedfellow. The whole town was endangered by the vengeance that stalked Pasco Chubb.

The sound of a rooster crowing spurred Escumbuit to action. The war cries and yelps of the warriors merged with the echoing report of his musket, and the Pigwacket assault began. They used a log as a battering ram to burst through the back door, and a musket ball felled Chubb before he could reach his musket. The former Hannah Faulkner's loyalty to her husband did not help her; she shared her husband's fate. The only solace in regard to the death of Pasco Chubb and his wife was that they were not tortured. After taking the scalps of Chubb and his wife Hannah, the Indians rapidly stripped the house of loot, leaving the bodies to burn after setting a fire with coals from the stove.

In the meantime, the other two parties were creating havoc elsewhere in the town. Two more houses were burned, they killed two other people, and they destroyed the town records. They took pulpit cushions from the church, and they burned them outside. A barn containing a large store of corn was

---

[36]Authors' note: Bradstreet and his wife had previously treated the Wampanaug Indian Joseph kindly. He was not above sharing any loot from the raid, but he insisted that Bradstreet and his wife not be harmed.

burned with more than twenty head of cattle inside. After invading the Bradstreet home, they killed Major Wade who was visiting from Mystic, Connecticut. Although the Indians killed Wade and looted their home, Bradstreet and his wife were spared. Anticipating a counter attack from the local militia, the Indians took off on snowshoes carrying as much loot as possible. The lightening fast execution of the attack and the apparent disinterest in prisoners indicated that they had already accomplished what they set out to do—Pasco Chubb was dead.[37] The Pigwacket withdrawal soon took them out of the reach of any possibility of retaliation by a militia that was not equipped with snowshoes. They headed east along the Merrimack River, and went north in the vicinity of Haverhill where they encountered two men out walking with their two sons. The Indians killed and scalped Jonathan Haines and Samuel Ladd and took the two boys captive. The Haines boy managed to escape from the Indians as he had done after being captured on a previous occasion. Near Haverhill, they invaded the farm of Timothy Johnson, and they killed his nineteen-year-old daughter Penelope. After this final depredation, Escumbuit and his thirty warriors continued north taking Samuel Ladd with them. This 1698 surprise raid on Andover was the last recorded Indian attack on the town. As a result of that raid, the town built two blockhouses along the river, and the militia was provided with snowshoes from that point forward.

Chief Escumbuit continued to lead Pigwacket war parties in raids against English frontier settlements for the next eight years. After his second expedition against the rebuilt fort at St. John's Newfoundland in 1706, Escumbuit had the singular honor of being invited to France where King Louis 14th knighted him. In his *History of the Indian Wars*, the New Hampshire militiaman, Samuel Penhallow, harshly denounced the famous Pigwacket sachem in the following passage:

---

[37]Historical Sketches of Andover by Sarah Loring Bailey, p. 131; "All facts indicate that it was a deliberate act of Indian revenge. The attack was led by the fierce and implacable foe of the whites, Assacumbuit."

> Of the Indians that was ever known since King Philip, never any appear'd so cruel and inhumane as Assacambuit, that insulting monster, who by the encouragement of the French went over to Paris, and being introduced to the King, lifted up his hand and in the most arrogant manner imaginable, saying "This hand of mine has slain one hundred and fifty of your enemies within the Territories of New England and Canada. Which bold and impudent speech was so pleasing to that Bloody Monarch, that he forthwith Knighted him, and order'd eight livres a day to be paid to him during life; so at his return, to exert sovereignty over the rest of his brethren, by murdering one and stabbing another, which so exasperated those of their relations, that they sought revenge, and would instantly have executed it, but that he fled his country and never return'd after.[38]

The rich interior of the Saco Valley had fired the imagination of land-hungry settlers from the very beginning. Tentative early explorations of the lower Saco had revealed many thousands of acres of untilled rich meadowland. For many years historians have tried to tie the linguistic roots of the name Saco to the Abenaki language. The name is actually derived from a map of the coastline made in 1525 by the Spanish explorer Esteban Gomez. He named the bay at the mouth of the river *Bahia de Saco* (Bay of the Sack). The distinctive profile of Biddeford Pool at the south end of the bay resembles the outline of a sack. The famous navigator Verazano sailing north-

---

[38]*Abenaki Warrior*; *The Life and Times of Chief Escumbuit*, 1998, by Alfred E Kayworth. This historical novel is a complete chronicle of the remarkable career of Escumbuit, a.k.a. Assacumbuit and Nescambiouit. The renowned Pigwacket sachem that was excoriated by Penhallow was enthusiastically praised by the French historian Charlevoix as a brave man who performed prodigies of valor at Haverhill, MA in 1708 wielding the saber presented to him by King Louis 14th. *Abenaki Warrior* tells of his discovery of a silver mine and relates the fascinating story of the hero's welcome he and the Sieur de Montigny received from the French aristocracy during their visit to Paris.

east from Portsmouth in 1524 saw "*high mountains within the land*." In clear weather early explorers used the gleaming peaks of *Crystal Hills* (The White Mountains) to fix their position at sea. On a cloudless day the mountains appeared as a bright cloud on the distant horizon. The lure of the mountains proved irresistible to explorers, and in 1642, several groups made trips into the interior. One expedition traveled up the Saco River in birch-bark canoes. They reported finding an Indian village ninety miles up river that was actually only 60 miles from the coast by land. They were obviously describing the Pigwacket village that was located at the base of the great 30-mile loop in the river.

The decade beginning in 1660 brought a curious alliance between the Indians of the interior and the white settlers on the coast. Before the onset of King Philip's war in 1775, the Indians were more fearful of Mohawk raids from the west than they were of the English presence close by. They made arrangements with the English to build a fort on Ossipee Lake that the Indians planned to use as a refuge from their Mohawk enemies. It was a substantial structure built of vertical logs fourteen feet high with bastions at the corners that allowed the defenders to direct crossfire on attackers. When the Abenaki Indians sided with King Philips in 1775, the English planned an expedition to Ossipee to destroy the fort that they suddenly perceived as a threat to their security. Their paranoia continued even after the death of King Philip. On November 1, 1676, Captain Hawthorne marched to Ossipee with 130 volunteers and 40 Iroquois Indians to destroy the fort. While a portion of his force was demolishing the fort, a separate detachment entered the Pigwacket Valley through its western portal in search of Indians. The war party of one hundred Indians that had been spotted at Ossipee Lake shortly before Hawthorne arrived vanished when the large English force appeared. This was the Pigwacket strategy for the next fifty years.

In June of 1703, Governor Dudley held a *Brotherhood Conference* in Casco, Maine with all the Abenaki tribes. Despite solemn pledges of peace and brotherhood by the Indians, the conference was sabotaged by the insidious intrigue of French emissaries who exploited the Indian distrust of the English. The French further strengthened their relationships with the Abenakis by persuading many to migrate to refuge villages they had established for them at Becancour and St. Francis.

As a result of prodding by the French, scarcely six weeks after the conference, the Abenakis launched devastating raids against the coastal settlements. The new outbreak in hostilities continued for the next ten years. French Jesuit Historian, Charlevoix made the following analysis to rationalize the unaccountable hostility of the Abenakis, who had attacked without warning after signing a pledge of brotherhood at Casco:

> They committed some trifling ravages, and killed about three hundred men, but the essential point was to engage the Abenakis in such a manner that to retreat would be impossible.

This frank admission of French strategy with regards to their Indian allies by the King's own historian reveals the Indian dilemma. The English were systematically driving them from their ancestral lands. They were being cynically used as mercenaries by the French, and in the face of the ever-increasing strength of the French and the English, their ability to resist was growing weaker by the day. Their only hope was to use the forest survival skills of their ancestors. *Mother Earth* was still their trusted ally, and the forest was still their friend. In August two English expeditions into Pigwacket territory were launched from Casco. By simultaneously invading Pigwacket Valley through the western and eastern portals to the valley, the duel expeditions hoped to trap the Pigwackets between the two forces, but again, the Pigwackets' ability to fade into and blend with the forest saved them.

Colonel March had a little more success when he returned to the valley in October with three hundred and sixty men. The expedition killed six Indians and returned with six captives. It had to be highly frustrating for the English to mount three expeditions and have such meager results to show for their efforts. It was at this point that Massachusetts began to offer a bounty of 40 pounds for Indian scalps. The scalp hunting expeditions continued into the winter of 1703-04 when Major Winthrop Hilton and Captain John Gilman of Exeter, and Captains Chesley and Davis of Oyster River led separate companies of men on missions to Pigwacket country. During the same winter, Captain John Tyng of Dunstable received 200 pounds for scalps he had taken in the valley. The English kept the pressure on the Pigwackets in 1708 with an expedition of two hundred and seventy men under Captain Hilton, and there were additional missions by Captains Gilman and Cass in 1710. In the winter of 1723, Captain Sayward led an expedition into the White Mountains that returned empty handed. In November of 1724, an expedition of fifty-two men under Captain Samuel Wheelright decided to return after getting within ten miles of their goal; they cited illness and general discontent among the men as their reason for giving up their quest. Captain John Lovewell was leading his first expedition through that same general area in that time period, but the two expeditions did not meet.

There were several good reasons why all of the scalp-hunting missions were launched during the winter months. The English had learned through experience that it was much more difficult for the Indians to hide in the bare winter forest, and the frozen terrain made it easier for the raiders to follow direct routes over the frozen ponds and swamps that were in their line of march. In addition, the lack of cover neutralized much of the Indian ability to launch devastating attacks from concealed positions. There was a more practical reason for the winter raids however. In the agrarian society of the period, most of the scalp hunters were farmers that were looking for something to do during the idle winter months. It is unlikely they could have been persuaded to leave their farms during spring planting, or during the haying season. The size of the scalp hunting parties and the frequency of their occurrence demonstrates how the balance of power was beginning to tilt heavily in favor of the

English. In contrast, Indian raids against the English settlements were becoming sporadic and ineffective. In August of 1724, Chief Wahwa[39] and twenty Pigwacket warriors attempted a raid on Kennebunkport, but the settlement appeared too heavily defended, and they were obliged to return to their village. The two adversaries seemed to have attained a standoff of sorts. The Indians were learning that their small war parties were increasingly ineffective against well-defended English settlements, and the English were unable to locate the Indians with their large scalp hunting expeditions. The semi-nomadic lifestyle of the Indians served them well in these difficult times. With a few minutes warning, an entire village of men, women and children could gather their personal belongings and be up the river in their canoes, or safely hidden in the woods. Once in the forest, they were able to use natural materials to fashion crude wigwams to shelter them. The objective student of history must admire the Indian's ability to confine the battle to the wilderness where his native bush fighting skills gave him an advantage over his white adversary. At ease in his natural element, it was easier for him to follow his natural instincts. His spiritual guardian (manatou) could signal him to fight—or he could vanish to live and fight another day.

In spite of his being knighted by King Louis 14th in the Palace of Versailles in 1707, the fame of the Pigwacket Chief Escumbuit never approached the cult status of the legendary Chief Paugus who led eighty Pigwacket warriors into battle at Saco Pond in 1725. In the century that followed the historic fight with Lovewell's scalp hunters, Paugus was celebrated in song and verse, and countless historians attempted to describe everything about him, from the manner of his dress, to his musket and his famous duel with Chamberlain. Two hundred and seventy six years after the epic battle, there are still public reminders; there is a Paugus Hall in Fryeburg, and *Mount Paugus* with its companions *Whiteface, Passaconaway* and *Cho-*

---

[39]Authors' note: Chief Wahwa (The broad shouldered) was with Paugus and Adeawando the following year in the epic fight between Lovewell's scalp hunters and the Pigwacket Indians.

corua continue to guard the western portal to the Pigwacket Valley. Each year millions of tourists enjoy scenic Paugus Bay, which is located between Laconia and Meredith on Lake Winnipesaukee. In 1975, a Paugus Day, celebrating the 250th anniversary of the fight was observed in Fryeburg.

As successive historians returned to the fight, the original story began to accumulate substance and detail that were not part of the original account. The liberal interpretation of the facts by poets and songwriters also helped to establish myths that eventually became part of the folklore surrounding the event. The Reverend Symmes of Bradford actually persuaded three survivors of the fight to sign a statement that the fight occurred on Saturday the 8th instead of the true date, Sunday the 9th. In regard to the Pigwacket leader, it required sixteen years of study by an exceptional researcher named Fannie Hardy Eckstorm[40] to uncover the unvarnished facts about who Paugus really was. Her meticulous research over many years established beyond a reasonable doubt that Paugus was not a Pigwacket Indian—he was a Mohawk—from a small band called the *Scaticook*. The strange circumstances that caused the legendary Paugus to become a Scaticook Indian, and how he, a Mohawk, came to be a Pigwacket war chief is a fascinating story. Although the disclosure of his true identity casts doubt on the accuracy of ballads and poems, and contradicts the writings of eminent historians like Penhallow and Parkman, the facts of his true identity are in some ways more interesting than traditional folklore.

The onset of King Philip's War in 1675 had a great unsettling effect among many of the Indian tribes who were not di-

---

[40]Cold River Chronicle, by David A Crouse; October 1999: Born in 1865, Fannie Hardy was educated at Abbot Academy in Andover and was a graduate of Smith College. She was a published author of several books and was married to the Reverend Jacob A. Eckstorm. Her favorite subjects were life in the Maine woods, birds, and the customs of local Indian tribes. She spent sixteen years researching the events surrounding the 1725 fight at Saco Pond, and during the late 1930s her findings were published in a few magazine articles. She challenged many of the accepted myths about the fight at Saco Pond.

rectly involved in the conflict. Rather than become involved in a conflict in which they had no personal stake, many small bands of Indians sought refuge with other tribes they perceived to be neutral. Paugus was a member of a band of Penacook Indians who fled to Albany, New York to become voluntary wards of a Mohawk tribe known as the Scaticook Indians. Having paid tribute to the fierce Mohawks for years, the Penacook Indians, who felt threatened by both the English *and* the Mohawks, chose the latter as their protectors. As wards of the Scaticook Indians, the English authorities in Albany considered this small band of Penacooks to be friendly Indians. Paugus was an English simplification of his Indian name, *Paucanaulemet.*

After King Philip's War ended in 1676, Paugus and the other displaced Penacook Indians often returned to the Merrimack River Valley to hunt and to visit their relatives and friends. Paugus had learned his English through frequent contacts with the English both in Albany and Dunstable. In the *History of Hudson, NH,* published in 1913, the author Kimball Webster related a fascinating anecdote about Paugus and Webster's ancestor, Mrs. Ann Hills.

> During an interval of peace on the frontier, Paugus was a frequent visitor to the Hills Garrison that was located in Hudson, NH[41] Ann Hills often fed him when he came by the garrison hungry. Paugus returned her kindness by bringing her select cuts of bear steak or by performing helpful chores around the garrison. It was through an unfortunate combination of English arrogance and blunders that Ann Hills' "kindly Paugus" became *the scourge of Dunstable* and the fierce War Chief of the Pigwacket Indians.

---

[41]Authors' note: The Hills Garrison was situated on the east side of the Merrimack River on the present Route 3. A stone marker behind 189 Webster Street in Hudson marks the site. Lovewell and his 46 scalp hunters spent the first night of their expedition to Pigwacket at the Hills Garrison.

Early in 1722, a band of thirty Scaticook Indians returned to the Merrimack Valley to hunt and to visit relatives and friends. During this period small parties of Abenaki and mission Indians from Canada were harassing Dunstable. Nervous about the presence of Indians on their border, the English captured the peaceful band of Scaticook hunters and took them to Boston where they were lodged in prison. Paugus, his wife and three children were among this group of prisoners. The mixed nature of the Indian band should have clued the English that they were not hostile. In October of that year, a Mohawk delegation came to Boston for a conference with the English. The English were hoping that the Mohawks would intercede with the Abenaki on their behalf to cease their hostile acts. The Mohawks agreed to send one of their chiefs to Norridgewalk to talk to the radical Jesuit Sebastian Rale and Chief OBombazine. The English released Paugus from prison in order to act as an interpreter between the Mohawk Chief and the Norridgewalk who spoke different Indian dialects. Paugus was trilingual; besides his native Algonquian dialect, he could speak some English and he had learned to speak the Iroquois dialect as a ward of the Mohawk Indians in Albany. The Mohawks warned Paugus that they would personally settle accounts with him if he tried to escape. After finding the Norridgewalk village abandoned, the Mohawk chief with Paugus in tow returned to Boston where Paugus was again jailed. This is very likely the point at which Paugus became alienated from both the English and the Mohawks. At another British/Mohawk conference in September in the following year, the Mohawk delegation petitioned the English saying to them; "*You have several of our nephews in your prison. We desire that the doors may be open and that they may be delivered unto us.*" Six days later Governor Dummer announced the "*Consent of the Court for delivery of prisoners Paucanaulemet and his family to go back with the Mohawks to Scaticook where they belong.*" So, after almost two years in prison, Paugus was a free man. After the English had imprisoned him and his family unjustly for almost two years, and having been virtually abandoned by his Mohawk masters, the embittered Paugus had no intention of returning to the Scaticook in Albany. At another conference held the following year in Albany, a September 17, 1724 letter from the Boston Indian Commission was read which stated:

> That many of the Scaticooks had been at war against us, and that Paucanaulemet, who had been set at liberty at their desire was gone to Canada; and we heard that he was gone to war.

His unwarranted imprisonment by the British, and the Mohawk intransigence in obtaining his freedom served to alienate Paugus from the English *and* the Mohawks. Nursing a deep hatred for the English, he ignored his promise to return to the Scaticook in Albany, and instead, he headed for Canada where he fell in with the fierce *French Mohawks* at the Saint Louis Mission near Montreal. They were the *Caughnawaga Indians,* also called the *Maquas,* that Jesuit missionaries had successfully converted to Catholicism.[42] The kindly Indian Paugus, who had brought choice cuts of bear meat to Ann Hills at her family garrison house, eventually became known as *The Scourge of Dunstable* and renowned for his cruel treatment of prisoners. The war party of "French Mohawks" who took Blanchard and Cross prisoner on September 4, 1724, and killed nine of the ten Dunstable man rescue party, was led by Paugus a.k.a. Paucanaulemet.

After the shattering defeat of the Norridgewalk Indians on August 16, 1724, it was Vaudreuil who initiated the events that would ultimately make the Paugus legend possible. In Vaudreuil's eagerness to avenge the destruction of the Norridgewalk village and the death of Sebastian Rale, he sent Pau-

---

[42]Authors' note: *The Last of the Mohicans* by John Fenimore Cooper. The fierce, cruel enemy of the Mohicans described in the book and the movie were the same *Maquas* who are described here. Like many religious converts they were renowned for their cruelty and the zeal with which they pursued their new religion.

gus south to incite the Pigwacket warriors against the English. The legendary Paugus who shares the historic limelight with John Lovewell was not even a Pigwacket Indian. As succeeding pages will reveal, the fight at Saco Pond on May 9, 1725 may never have taken place if Paucanaulemet a.k.a. Paugus had not come to Pigwacket Valley nursing a personal vendetta against the English.

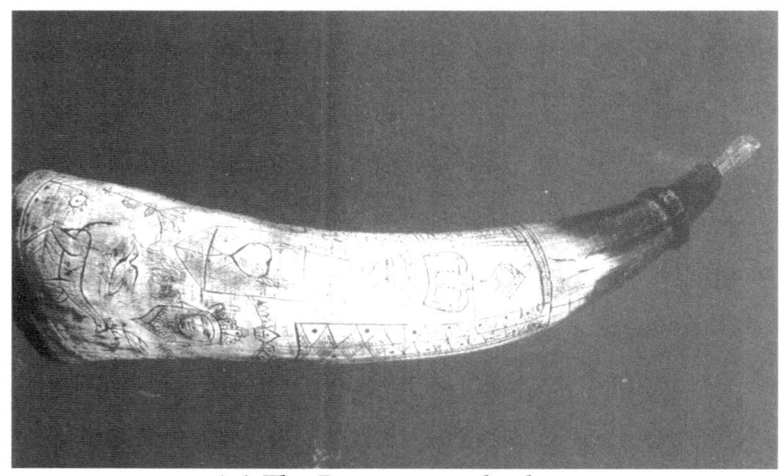

4-1 The Paugus powder horn

4-2 The modern Saco River

CHAPTER 5

THE FIGHT

What time the noble Lovewell came,
With fifty men from Dunstable,
The cruel Pequ'at tribe to tame,
With arms and bloodshed terrible
--The ballad: *Lovewell's Fight*

As John Lovewell was preparing for his final scalp-hunting raid in the spring of 1725, there were rumors about that the Penobscot Indians were ready to talk peace. The rumors had begun to circulate soon after the incendiary Sebastian Rale was killed in an English attack on Norridgewalk that ended with the survivors of the raid fleeing to the French missionary village in Odanak. The Penobscot Indians were still a formidable force, but similar punitive raids on their village near Bangor, Maine were frustrated by their elusive tactics. At the approach of a superior English force, they dispersed into the forest leaving an empty village to the scalp hunters. Despite their elusiveness and their remarkable ability to adapt to changing conditions, the lives of the Indians were made miserable by increasing white forays into their territory. Their entire existence was controlled by the cycle of their food gathering activities. Failure to man their *naamkeeks* (fishing stations) could result in empty caches of dried salmon for their use during the long cold winter. Any disruption of their gardens could mean there would be no dried squash for their stews and no maize for the women to grind in their stone mortars. Although the Indians were avoiding destruction by employing these tactics, the constant English pressure was taking a heavy toll on their traditional way of life.

The overwhelming victory at Norridgewalk had buoyed the spirit of the Massachusetts Colony, and Governor Dudley decided to seize the initiative and put out a peace feeler to the French Governor in Quebec. Communications between belligerents was a tedious process during that era. In the absence of telephones, telex, facsimile machines, and email, authorities had to communicate with each other through the exchange of letters delivered by ship, or carried overland by couriers. The correspondence between Governor Dudley of Massachusetts and Governor Vaudreuil of New France consumed five months in time, and the exchange of letters produced no immediate results. Dudley initiated the correspondence in a letter dated September 15, 1724 after learning that Vaudreuil had publicly declared that the Abenaki Indians were French allies. He challenged the French governor's claim in the following passage:

> As they are the subjects of his Britannic Majesty, they cannot be your allies, except through me, his representative. You have instigated them to fall on our people in the most outrageous manner. I have seen your commission to Sebastian Rale. But for your protection and incitements they would have made peace long ago.

Given the accusatory tone of the letter, it is little wonder that Vaudreuil decided to match Dudley's belligerence in a letter dated October 29, 1724. After admitting that he had given safe conduct to Sebastian Rale, he went on the offensive:

> You will have to answer to your King for his (Rale's) murder. It would have been strange if I had abandoned our Indians to please you. I cannot help taking the part of our allies. You have brought your troubles upon yourself. I advise you to pull down all the forts you have built on the Abenaki lands since the Peace of Utrecht. If you do so, I will be your mediator with the

> Norridgewalks. As to the murder of Rale, I leave that to be settled between the two Crowns.

Dudley didn't back off an inch in his January 19, 1725 reply to Vaudreuil. He branded Rale as an incendiary, and he added other complaints about Indian atrocities against the English:

> Instead of preaching peace, love and friendship agreeable to the Christian religion, Rale was an incendiary as appears by many letters I have by me. He has once and again appeared at the head of a great many Indians threatening and insulting us. If such a disturber of the peace has been killed in the heat of action, nobody is to blame but himself. I have much more to complain that Mr. Willard, minister of Rutland, who is innocent of all that is charged against Rale, and who always confined him self to preaching the Gospel, was slain and scalped by your Indians, and his scalp carried in triumph to Quebec.

Governor Dudley closed his letter declaring that, in the interest of promoting peace, he was sending Colonel Samuel Baxter and Colonel William Dudley to personally deliver his letter to the governor. An envoy named Williams of New Hampshire was assigned to go with them. In mid-winter the three set out on foot for Canada crossing the frozen ice of Lake Champlain in late January 1725. In the same time period that Lovewell was tracking down ten Abenaki Indians near Wakefield, NH, these three men were embarked on a peace mission to Canada. Governor Vaudreuil received them cordially, and they were made comfortable during their stay. They managed to ransom sixteen prisoners that were controlled by the French, but Vaudreuil denied that he had anything to do with inciting the Indians against the English settlements. The three envoys claimed to have no authority to negotiate with the Indians, but after some persuasion by Vaudreuil, the English agreed to meet with a group of Indian chiefs. At length a meeting was held on May 22, 1725, but the wily Vaudreuil, who effectively sabotaged the meeting before it ever took place, deceived the English envoys. The French Governor later wrote:

> Being satisfied that nothing was more opposed to our interests than a peace between the Abenakis and the English, I thought that I would sound the chiefs before they spoke to the English and insinuate to them everything that I had to say.

From the onset the meeting between the English envoys and the chiefs was a farce. Instead of asking for peace, the Indians demanded that the English demolish all the forts they had built in Abenaki territory, and they asked to be reimbursed for the destruction of their church at Norridgewalk and for the death of Sebastian Rale. Even worse, Vaudreuil assigned the Jesuit La Chasse to act as interpreter for the opposing sides. He was the Jesuit who had written the sympathetic obituary about the life and times of Father Sebastian Rale. Using his advantage as an interpreter to interject his own militant point of view, La Chasse effectively kept the two sides at odds with each other. The meeting was a complete failure. Having effectively sabotaged the meeting, Vaudreuil concluded the diplomatic mission with a nice flourish. He graciously furnished the three envoys and the sixteen captives with a military guard to escort them out of French territory during their long overland journey to Albany, New York.

At the same time these negotiations were going on in Quebec, John Lovewell and his company of scalp hunters were enjoying a tumultuous reception in Boston, where they paraded through the streets displaying the scalps of the ten Indians they had massacred near Wakefield, NH. Lovewell and his men had been hiking on snowshoes since the 29th of January, and they had traveled from Dunstable, Massachusetts to a point north of Lake Winnipesaukee. After tracking down and killing 10 Indians near Wakefield, NH, they finished their long trek by boarding a sloop at Great Bay that conveyed them to Boston. After their arrival in Boston on the 10th of March, they were received as conquering heroes, and the citizens of Boston, as well as Governor Dudley and his Council entertained them. It was mid-March before the tired warriors got back to Dunstable, where Lovewell paid them their share of the scalp bounty money. He told them they were free to return to their families. After six weeks subsisting out of knapsacks, and after traveling on snowshoes through bitter ice and snow, the men sorely needed a rest, and no one expressed regret that the company was being disbanded. They looked forward to the receptions they would receive in towns like Billerica, Dunstable, Haverhill, Londonderry, Tyngsboro and Chelmsford. There were plenty of postponed chores to attend to, and it would soon be time to turn out the horses and the plow.

Homecoming for John Lovewell, his brother-in-law Josiah Farwell, and Jonathan Robbins was quite different. Although they looked forward to spending some time with their respective families, the three men were already thinking about a new expedition that they hoped to complete before spring plowing. Lovewell had the council's approval to mount a new raid with up to fifty men, but he realized that it would be difficult to raise a new company so close to spring planting. Fame and notoriety have a narcotic effect on most men, and Lovewell the farmer and bush fighter, was beginning to enjoy his newfound popularity. The journal of his second raid revealed the type of man he was. He was not a showman. He was a plainspoken bush fighter who did not take any chances with the welfare of his men, but he was not immune to the heady effects of celebrity. Behind his quiet exterior, the thought lurked.... *they loved my last raid, but they haven't seen anything yet!* News of his new expedition spread to the towns of the Merrimack Valley on the legs of the disbanded men.... *Lovewell is heading north again!*

Despite Lovewell's misgiving about the lateness of the season for scalp hunting, the volunteers began to come in. As before, the human grapevine of relatives and friends quickly spread the word about the new expedition. The potential danger of being killed by the Indians was now being downplayed. By now, everyone was familiar with Lovewell's skill as an Indian fighter, and it was favorably noted that he had not lost a single man in his two previous raids. In this relaxed atmosphere, brothers, cousins, brothers-in-law, and mutual friends eagerly signed on, looking forward to an all-male adventure in the woods with close friends and relatives. As one might expect, it was the parents, wives, and girlfriends of the volunteers who expressed misgivings and counseled caution. The volunteers eased their fears by talking down the risk and by reminding their concerned relatives of the bounty money. One of the most notable among those who volunteered was a young man whose background was unique.

Jonathan Frye was two years out of Harvard where he had been a divinity student. He lived with his family in Andover, and he was currently a graduate theology student. He was twenty years old when he signed on as Lovewell's chaplain. Because the name Frye figures prominently in the battle, as well as in the aftermath, a short profile of the family best fits the narrative at this juncture. Jonathan's parents, Captain James Frye and Lydia (Osgood) Frye, were affluent residents of Andover that were well connected to the founding families and the ecclesiastic hierarchy of the town. Captain Frye was a man who was very much aware of his respected status in the community, and he expected his son to conform to certain high family standards. In other words, although he was twenty years old and a college graduate, Jonathan's parents still ran his life.

Jonathan was in love with thirteen-year old Susanna Rogers, and his parents vigorously opposed any idea of marriage; they cited the girl's limited education and her modest dowry as reasons for their opposition.[43] To Jonathan, the 100-

---

[43]Authors' note: Reverend Symmes, a close friend of the Frye family, had been involuntarily dismissed as pastor of a Boxford church, and Susanna Roger's father replaced him. The dismissal and replacement created hostility between the parishioners of Symmes' new church in Bradford and his former church. In the chapter that relates the aftermath of the fight at Saco

pound bounty for scalps offered a way out of the impasse with his parents. Hidden behind his apparent eagerness to serve the spiritual needs of Lovewell's raiders, lay the more urgent motive to collect bounty money to finance his wedding to Susanna Rogers. Historians reported that young Frye joined the expedition fully outfitted with a musket and scalping knife, and that he quickly earned the reputation among his companions as being willing and able to use both weapons effectively. Compared to the interwoven family connections that characterized the other volunteers, Jonathan Frye was definitely an outsider.

A man he was of comely form
Polished and brave, well learned and kind;
Old Harvard's learned walls he left,
Far in the wilds a grave to find.

Curiously, except for Lovewell's lieutenants Farewell and Robbins, not a single member of the previous expeditions volunteered for the new mission. It is possible that the new foray came too soon on the heels of the exhausting snowshoe trek that ended with the massacre of ten sleeping Indians at Lovell Lake in Sanbornville, NH. Among the volunteers was Benjamin Hassell of Dunstable, whose grandparents had been killed by Indians in 1691. He seemed a logical member of the new company being related to John Lovewell, and presumably having a score to settle with the Indians. Unfortunately, he was destined to dishonor his family name by his later conduct. The most controversial player in the drama at Saco Pond was John Chamberlain of Groton. The dispute over his role during the fight and in the aftermath has never been fully resolved. At thirty-nine years, Seth Wyman of Woburn appeared too old to be a scalp hunter. He came from one of the original Woburn families, and he had a wife and five children at home. His official rank as ensign indicated that he was responsible for keeping a journal of the expedition, but unlike Benjamin Hassell,

---

Pond, Symmes is revealed as conspiring to alter the official account of the battle in order to protect the reputation of Jonathan Frye and his family.

when all seemed lost at Saco Pond, Wyman rose to the challenge and rallied the company. When he signed on as a volunteer, Solomon Keyes of Chelmsford had no idea that his miraculous escape from almost certain death would make him famous. Lovewell's men, with the exception of Hassell and a ten-man reserve force, served with honor. From the forty-six-man roster, a caprice of destiny selected the handful of men who would be remembered for their actions at Saco Pond. They were, John Lovewell, Josiah Farwell, Solomon Keyes, Jonathan Robbins, Jonathan Frye, John Chamberlain, Seth Wyman, and Benjamin Hassell.

When gone my Mary think of me,
And pray to God that I may be
Such as one ought that lives for thee,
And come at last in victory

There was a festive air to the gathering of the forty-six men who met with John Lovewell by the Merrimack River on the 16th of April in 1725. Some came to the rendezvous by wagons or carriages driven by friends or family. They were a formidable looking group dressed in their frontier outfits. Carrying long muskets, they resembled a gathering of woodsman assembling for a deer hunt. In addition to a powder horn, each man had a hatchet slung from his shoulder as well as a leather bag of musket balls at the waist. Their knapsacks carried the bare necessities for living in the field…bread, dried meat or fish, blankets, and rain gear. Although they had an intimate knowledge of the Indian trails they planned to follow, Lovewell and his officers carried magnetic compasses. They stood together…. bathed in the admiration of their peers…. proud yet uncomfortable with the attention…. eager to be off.

Finally—in a welter of advice, jest, exhortations and tears—they were on their way. There was a confident air about these men. As they marched feeling the weight of the hatchet under their arm and the lead shot at the waist, there was sensuality to the smooth, solid weight of the musket in their hand.

Their personal appearance, as well as the comfortable feeling of serving with close friends and relatives conveyed a sense of pride; the experience of serving with Lovewell and his lieutenants imparted an aura of irresistible power.

They were not long on their way when a minor incident interrupted their comfortable thoughts. The stragglers caught up to the leaders who were gathered about Toby, the Mohawk Indian. Instead of having eased with the marching, the nagging pain in Toby's leg had worsened to the point that he was unable to maintain the pace. After a short conference, John Lovewell decided that Toby must go back while it was still safe to travel alone. After consoling the reluctant Toby, the company proceeded north with little more thought to the loss of their Indian guide.[44] In the vicinity of Contoocook (Boscawen), there was another casualty. William Cummings of Dunstable was unable to continue the march when an old leg wound from a previous Indian encounter disabled him. He required assistance to make it home, so his kinsman, Josiah Cummings, went with him. Although this new casualty did not dampen the spirit of the men, there was some joking comment about the expedition being jinxed.

After passing the long winter inside dark cramped quarters with little to relieve the tedium of sleeping, eating and stoking the fire, the fresh air and blue sky were an exhilarating experience for the scouts. The streams they crossed were running swift with the spring melt down of snow, and the men entertained themselves by noting the different species of returned

---

[44]Authors' note: Toby's full name and the particulars of his life are not given in the dozens of historic accounts of Lovewell's raid. This omission goes directly to the heart of the rift between the Indians and the English. Historians' indifference to the Indian is typical of the low regard the English had for the aboriginal inhabitants of their adopted land. By treating aboriginal people of the world as faceless, sub-humans, the so-called civilized people of the world sowed the seeds of resentment and anarchy. When this faceless minority eventually rebelled, the civilized world asked—"why do they hate us so?" To give due credit to the English, however, Toby was later given a share of the land grants awarded to the survivors of Lovewell's party.

birds as they marched. It was wonderful to be alive on a spring day, bound together with their relatives and friends by a common bond. As they continued north, Lovewell exercised his customary caution by sending out advance parties to scout out Indians signs on their fore trail. On two occasions he rested his main party, and he dispatched a scouting party on their back trail to make sure the enemy was not stalking them. They had followed the ancient *Mou-Ro-Mak Trail* to Concord that gave way to the *Merrimack Trail* that brought them to the juncture of the Winnipesaukee and the Pemigewassit Rivers north of Franklin, N.H. From there, they followed the *Winnipesaukee Trail* to the great lake. They then trekked almost due east on the old *Ossipee Trail* (U.S. Route 25) between *Cusumpe Pond* (Squam Lake) on their left shoulder and Lake Winnipesaukee to their right. The march from Contoocook to Ossipee went routinely, but when they arrived at Ossipee Lake, Lovewell was faced with a difficult command decision. Benjamin Kidder of Nutfield (Londonderry) became so ill that it was impossible for him to continue. Knowing that he was only one-day march from the Pigwacket Valley, Lovewell made a wise decision. He assigned the men to cut logs to construct a small hut inside of a vertical log stockade. He left the expedition surgeon to tend Kidder's needs, and he assigned Sergeant Nathaniel Woods of Dunstable and seven men to guard the fort. The expedition now began to resemble an assault on Mount Everest where the final climb to the summit is made by a small elite group of men from an advanced base. The stark difference lay in the fact that Lovewell intended to assault the Pigwacket Indians in their own village *with a force reduced to only thirty-four men*. It was at this juncture that a subtle change in the mood of the men began to appear. One can imagine what the private thoughts of the men might have been: *what next? After starting out with 46 men, we are reduced to 43, and we now have to go into Indian country with only 34!*

After the three-day delay at Ossipee, Lovewell was ready for the final march on the Pigwacket stronghold. He ordered the men to lighten their packs, directing them to leave a major portion of their food at the fort. At this point, one has to begin to question Lovewell's strategy. Why, at this critical juncture, did he elect to include the young chaplain Jonathan Frye in the final assault party? Would it not have been wise to bring the surgeon along to treat any casualties they might incur? Why did he not direct Frye to stay with the sick patient and bring another scalp hunter in his place? A logical response to these questions is that Lovewell made the choice based on his personal evaluation of Frye's potential as a bush fighter. He had noted how the Harvard educated Frye had won the acceptance of the other men during the march. The youngster had openly acknowledged that his real motive for joining the expedition was to share in the bounty money. The men had become fond of their scalp-hunting chaplain, and Lovewell, who was intrigued by the notion, decided.... why not.... we can use another bush fighter.

On Saturday the 8th of May, the thirty-four men took their departure from the Ossipee fort marching north along the relatively flat contour of the present Route 16.

A succeeding chapter will reveal how the dates were critical to Reverend Symmes' scheme to alter the dates to suit his own designs.[45] The names of the thirty four men who made the final march and took part in the fight follow:

Asten, Abiel,	Haverhill
Ayer, Ebenezer,	Haverhill
Barron. Elias	Groton
Chamberlain, John	Groton
Davis, Eleazer,	Concord
Davis, Josiah	Concord
Farrah, Jacob	Concord

---

[45] The New England Quarterly September 1936 article by Fanny Hardy Eckstorm; The article contains compelling circumstantial evidence that the Reverend Symmes of Bradford made a concerted effort to change the official date of the fight at Saco Pond from Sunday the 9th to Saturday the 8th. Having carefully examined the evidence, the authors decided to use Eckstorm's calendar of events.

Farrah, Joseph	Concord
Farwell, Josiah, Lieut.	Dunstable
Frye, Jonathan, Chap.	Andover
Fullam, Jacob, Serg.	Weston
Gilson, Joseph,	Groton
Harwood, Jne, Ensign	Dunstable
Hassell, Benjamin, Corp.	Dunstable
Jefts, John	Groton
Johnson, Ichabod	Woburn
Johnson, Josiah	Woburn
Johnson, Noah, Serg.	Dunstable
Jones, Josiah	Concord
Keyes, Solomon	Billerica
Kittredge, Jonathan	Billerica
Lakin, Isaac	Groton
Linkfield, Edward, Corp.	Nutfield(Deerfield)
Lovewell, John, Capt.	Dunstable
Melvin, Daniel	Concord
Melvin, Eleazer	Concord
Robbins, Jona. Ensign	Dunstable
Richardson, Thomas, Corp.	Woburn
Richardson, Timothy	Woburn
Usher, Robert	Dunstable
Whiting, Samuel	Dunstable
Woods, Daniel	Groton
Woods, Thomas, Ensign	Groton
Wyman, Seth	Woburn

The ancient *Sokoki Trail* they traveled led them north along the western shore of Silver Lake and near the modern town of Madison. From there their trail followed the modern Route 113 to Conway. It was a traditional trail that followed the course of the Pigwacket stream to its juncture with the Saco River. In their march, small streams swollen with the spring runoff of snow connected a series of ponds; these slowed their progress requiring them to make frequent detours. The trees along the march had not yet emerged from their winter sleep, and the grandeur of the northern skyline was breathtaking; it was if they were parading at the feet of giants! On their left shoulder, the morning sun illuminated lingering drifts of snow on a procession of mountain peaks. The anonymous mountains of that era are known today as, *Whiteface, Passaconaway, Paugus and Chocorua.* The tenuous line of men moving slowly amidst fallen trees and gurgling brooks appeared out of context; yet they continued to move steadily northward towards an inexorable destiny.

In spite of their apprehension, there were no fresh signs of Indians as they entered Pigwacket Valley through the western portal. Lovewell, sure of his ground, led them to a ford on the Saco River that they crossed without incident. At that point they were just north of Stark Hill and less than a mile south of the Indian village stockade; there was neither smoke nor sound to signal an Indian presence. The troop stayed in place while a small force went to scout the village. Being already late in the day, Lovewell chose the most secure site that he could think of to bivouac for the night. They encamped on the north shore of Saco Pond on the east bank of a small brook that entered the pond from southeast of the Pigwacket village. The extensive pitch pine barren they camped in was relatively free of vegetation, and with the pond at their back, the perimeter of their camp was clear in all directions

At this point, it is important to orient the reader to the physical layout of Saco Pond in relation to the Indian Village and the Saco River. An illustrative map is provided at the end of the chapter to aid this understanding. The map shows the Saco making a meandering thirty-mile loop to the north passing close to its starting point on its return. The Indian village and Saco Pond were both located inside this narrow area. The main Indian village was situated approximately where the Fryeburg fair ground is located today. In addition to being an important source for fish and waterfowl, the Indians used 2-1/2 miles long Saco Pond as a short cut to their village from the river. An important landmark for the original inhabitants was *Pigwacket Hill* known today as *Jockey Cap*. The Indian meaning of Pigwacket was "*at the punched up through hill*". Indians coming down the Saco River from Conway used the familiar landmark to locate the carryover into Saco Pond. That carry-over eliminated the river's loop to the north, and for the Indians at Conway, the shortcut reduced their canoe trips to the coast by thirty-two miles.

The march from Ossipee and the prolonged tension of being in the enemy's stronghold had tired the men, and after Lovewell assigned guards for the night, the off duty men welcomed the chance to catch up on their sleep. During the night, the guards thought they heard Indians prowling about the campsite. The sounds kept the company in a high state of alert throughout the night, but with the coming of daylight, they concluded that the noise came from moose browsing in the small brook that entered the pond near their bivouac. Without a formal field kitchen to prepare a morning meal for the men, they were left to fend for themselves as best as they could. It was the Sabbath, and with tension from the previous night rapidly subsiding on a beautiful Sabbath morning, Jonathan Frye called the men for morning prayers. As the men slowly assembled under the high green canopy of the pitch pines, Mother Earth's creatures were reacting to the ranger's intrusion on their domain. Chipmunks darted for their holes, and squirrels scurried up nearby trees. A squadron of ducks flew south towards a distant shore, and overhead, a kingfisher circled looking for his morning meal. By now, the men had become fond of Frye. They were amused by his youthful exuberance, and they sympathized with the dilemma he faced with his domineering father. As the brothers, cousins, and close friends listened to their young spiritual leader by the shore of the forest girded pond, with the blue bowl of *The Creator's* sky overhead, the thought must have occurred to some.... *this a wonderful day to be alive!*

Suddenly, the magical moment was shattered by the distant echoing crash of a musket! They hastened to the shore of the pond where they immediately identified the source of the sound. From their position on the north shore of Saco Pond, they saw a solitary figure standing on a point of land that jutted out from the eastern shore of the pond. What had appeared to be a rest day for the men was quickly forgotten, and they instinctively gathered about Lovewell, ready for immediate action. After Lovewell got them quieted down, he calmly laid out the options. He cautioned them that Indian scouts could have caused the sounds of the previous night. He warned them that the lone Indian on the point could be a deliberate ruse staged to lead them into an ambush. Lovewell seemed to be suffering one of his rare moments of indecision as he shared his thoughts with the Rangers, and in a subtle way, he appeared to be asking them to help him make a decision. After a spirited discussion, his men were later credited with making the following bold statement:

> The men generally and boldly answered, "We came to see the enemy; we have all along prayed God we might find them; and we had rather trust Providence with our lives, yes, die for our country, than try to return without seeing them, if we might, and be called cowards for our pains."[46]

There is nothing in the historic record that reveals what actually took place in that animated discussion among the men, but there is little doubt that Lovewell was worried that they might be falling into an ambush. But we do know that in the aftermath of the fight some of the survivors claimed that Jonathan Frye was at the forefront of those urging Lovewell to go after the lone Indian. Possibly distracted by his own personal doubts about the wisdom of the decision, John Lovewell then issued an order that ultimately proved to be catastrophic. He

---

[46]Narrative of the Great Fight, by Reverend Mr. Symmes; 1725: the Reverend Symmes of Bradford wrote the first official report of the fight. Symmes' inspirational version of the men's response to Lovewell was repeated verbatim by countless succeeding historical accounts of the fight. Fannie Hardy Eckstorm suggested that the actual author of this statement might have been Jonathan Frye.

ordered the men to lighten their load by leaving their blanket rolls and knapsacks in a pile on the ground. For some inexplicable reason, in those risky circumstances, Lovewell decided to leave the bulk of their food and supplies unguarded! This was the same man who routinely sent out scouting parties to reconnoiter the trail ahead, and who periodically dispatched scouts on his back trail to avoid being ambushed. The journal of his 2nd expedition reveals how differently he reacted in almost identical circumstances. On the 16th of February, hot on the trail of an Indian raiding party, he made the following notation in his personal journal:

> We traveled 6 miles and came upon the tracks of Indians, and *we left 16 men with our packs* and the rest pursued the tracks till dark that night and staid there all night, and on the 17th we followed their tracks till about 8 o'clock.

Historians in the wake of the ensuing action universally criticized this fateful decision by Lovewell. Having ordered the scouts to leave their packs in plain sight, Lovewell and his men headed along the north shore to investigate the lone figure on the east shore of the pond. When they reached a brook that entered the northeast corner of the pond, they had to detour around a swamp that was fed by the waters of that brook.[47] After gaining the ground on the east side of the swamp they went south along the east shore of the pond. The pitch pine plain was now behind them, and they began to move more cautiously through the brush and thickets that lay in their path. Their knapsacks now lay in a pile approximately 1-½ miles to the rear.

Suddenly, an Indian emerged from the brush less than thirty yards ahead! Although he was startled by the encounter,

---

[47] Authors' note: This brook now bears the name *Fight Brook*. As the brook nears the pond it spreads out into a broad swampy area. Several visits to the actual site of the battle by the authors were essential to an accurate portrayal of the events of May 9, 1725.

he reacted first. He dropped one musket and a pair of ducks from his left hand, and he swung a second musket to his shoulder and fired in a single fluid motion. Frye and Wyman returned the Indian's fire in almost the same instant, but Frye missed while Wyman's ball found the Indian's heart dropping him instantly. The entire action took less than five seconds at a range of less than thirty yards, and as the black powder smoke drifted over the scene, there were three forms on the ground. Samuel Whiting was badly wounded by beaver shot from the Indian volley, and a few pellets had found Captain Lovewell's mid section as well. Although the shot had probably pierced his intestines, Lovewell declared he could manage without assistance. A curious incident occurred at this point. Despite Whiting and Lovewell's injuries, the brief skirmish seemed to rule out any immediate threat of an ambush, and the men turned their attention to who should take the Indian scalp. Even though the chaplain's shot had missed the mark, the men all wanted him to have the scalp. Whether it was the novelty of having a scalp hunting chaplain, or whether they were simply fond of him is uncertain, but the general sentiment was, "*Let the chaplain have it.*" With Seth Wyman's acquiescence, they all urged Jonathan to go take his scalp. The twenty-year old Frye was torn by conflicting emotions.... he was eager to take the scalp, but in the moment of realizing his dream, he didn't know how to do it. One of the scouts perceiving his discomfit said, "*Let's go, I'll give you a hand.*" He walked to the still form and rolled the Indian on his face, and then talked Frye through the procedure. He showed him how to raise the brave's head by holding the hair with his left hand, and then he instructed him to make a cut across the forehead with his scalping knife. A strong jerk with his left hand peeled the scalp to the back of the head, and with a second upward stroke of his knife, he cut it free at the nape and showed it to the troop. At that moment Captain Lovewell reminded them that they needed to go back to retrieve their packs, and the men slowly began to retrace the trail that would take them back to their equipment.

Throughout history man has sought spiritual support in time of battle. It is not uncommon for men on both sides of the line of battle to be assured by their leaders that God favors their cause. And in the wake of battles, military leaders often credit victory or defeat to ethereal approval—or disapproval. The strange confluence of events that decided the circumstances in which Lovewell's scalp hunters would meet Paugus and his Pigwacket warriors were almost metaphysical in nature. A single musket report, a headlong pursuit, and Lovewell's brief lapse of judgment needed only a catalyst to complete the recipe for mayhem.... and the *Karma* of Paugus provided that catalyst. It was almost as if the actions of Paugus and his warriors were programmed to arrive at the precise moment needed to seize the advantage.

While Lovewell and his men had been building their fort at Ossipee, Paugus and eighty warriors had been down the Saco in their canoes planning to attack the coastal settlements and to bring back some captives. The large war party of Pigwacket Indians had been sighted in the Scarboro and Kennebunkport areas, but when the local militias mustered to meet the challenge, Paugus decided to return to Pigwacket Valley to await a better opportunity. The disconsolate warriors were forced to return to the Saco River and begin the long paddle back to their village. When they had started out on their raid, their sachem *Adeawando,* who was wary of a possible attack on their village, had instructed the elders, women, and children to set up a temporary fishing camp near the Saco Pond outlet. The salmon, shad, and sturgeon were just beginning their spring spawning run, and the women and elders were kept busy netting and spearing fish and drying the split halves on wooden racks over slow burning fires. With the war party on the coast, and the rest of the village fishing at the south end of Saco Pond, the Indian village was empty!

The returning war party had been paddling all night, and the Saco Pond outlet presented a welcome sight to the weary braves. Although the sun had not yet cleared the eastern horizon, there was already activity around the temporary camp where the women, children, and elders had stayed during the absence of the war party. In spite of the failed raid, the women and children were happy to have their braves return home safely. The elders and women told the returning braves that they would break down their temporary camp, and that they planned to follow them to the village in their own canoes. After subsisting for many days on parched corn and pemmican, the braves eagerly looked forward to the warm meal that the women planned to prepare at the village. A honking flight of ducks along the eastern shore of the pond gave one young brave an idea. He gave up his place in one of the canoes, and he began to walk up the east shore of the pond towards a small cove guarded by a point of land; it was a favorite place to hunt ducks. He took along a spare musket loaded with birdshot. The other members of the war party dallied; they checked on the catch of fish, and they visited their families. After paying their respects to the elders, they embarked in their canoes, and they began the 2-1/2 mile paddle up the west shore of the pond.

All the players were now in place for a diabolical sequence of events. Any minor quirk of fate could have thrown the advantage either way in the events that followed. What if the lone Indian had not decided to go duck hunting? What if Lovewell had left ten men to guard the packs? What if the war party had not returned at that precise time? Notwithstanding the myriad "what if" possibilities, one is left only to analyze what did happen and to wonder how the drama unfolded the way it did. To follow the movement of the players, it helps to envision Saco Pond as a 2-1/2 mile by ¾ mile rectangle with its long axis upright and leaning slightly to the west. When the lone Indian fired his musket midway up the eastern shore of the pond, the scalp hunters were at prayer with Jonathan Frye on the north shore of the pond. The main war party was either still at the temporary camp at the south end of the pond, or the warriors were just beginning to paddle up the pond. As Lovewell and his men began walking east to investigate the gunshot, the small flotilla of Indian canoes was coming up the west side of the pond headed toward a beach at the northwest corner of the pond—behind Lovewell and his scouts! By the time Paugus and his men heard the exchange of shots that killed the duck hunter, the warriors had already found tracks that led to the pile of blanket rolls and packs. One can only imagine the flow of adrenaline experienced by Paugus and his warriors as they stood by that pile of unguarded packs. Was this an omen from *The Great Spirit?* For a long moment they stood transfixed.... it was Chief Wahwa who spoke the first words:

> Behold—*Kchi Niwaskwa* (The Great Spirit) makes big medicine for his people. From high in the clouds of *Agiochook* (Mount Washington) he sends us a sign. We must heed his magic—this day we do not hide in the forest—this day our warriors will do the scalp dance to celebrate a great victory!

A collective *Aho* punctuated Wahwa's statement, and all heads turned to Adeawando and Paugus. With a broad sweep of his arm to indicate the pile of packs, Paugus spoke slowly.... his distain for the English apparent:

> Witness the arrogance of the English.... they claim *N'da Kinna* (Our Land) as their own.... that which only the *Great Master of Life* can grant. As the lynx marks the forest with his urine, the English flaunt their packs. Our *French Father* sent Paugus to the Pigwacket...now *Kchi Niwaskwa* sends us an omen.... Death to the English!

For a people who routinely consulted native sorcerers for spiritual guidance, the signs were unmistakable. It was as if the English were deliberately challenging the Pigwacket warriors to fight; it took strong medicine to cause the English to make this fatal error. The invitation to take English scalps was clearly powerful medicine by *Kchi Niwaskwa* and his helper *Glooscap*. The excitement of the discovery displaced the disappointment of their failed raid as they eagerly listened to Paugus—no one challenged him. The scalp hunters were only thirty-four and they were eighty, and the terrain invited an assault from ambush that would overwhelm the English. After one or two volleys from close range, they would run at the survivors and finish them off with war clubs and tomahawks. Accordingly, Paugus directed them to hide the packs behind the bank of the brook that entered the pond about 150 yards west of the packs. Since there was little cover close to the pile of packs, he had to devise another plan. He placed Chief Adeawando and Chief Wahwa with 40 warriors behind a slight ridge that winter ice had pushed up at the edge of the pond. They were diagonally behind the site of the packs. Paugus and the rest of the braves concealed themselves below the bank of the small brook on the other side of the packs. The Paugus instructions were specific. The warriors concealed at the shore of the pond were to wait until the English had passed their position. They were to run at the scouts from the rear causing them to turn to meet the charge. Simultaneously Paugus and his forty braves would overwhelm them by attacking them from the opposite side. He planned to wipe them out in the first assault, or the English might even ask for quarter. The conditions were not ideal for a typical Indian ambush; the musket range from their concealed positions was too great to be effective. They would have to charge at the English from front and rear to close the range. This of course would expose them to counter fire. Once the fight began, scattered pine trees would be the only available cover for both sides. Given the conditions, it was the best strategy Paugus could devise.

By the time Lovewell and the rangers got back to the pitch pine plain, it was almost mid-morning. Relieved of the weight of their muskets, both Whiting and Lovewell managed to keep up with the others. The previous tension among the rangers had dissipated in the exhilaration that came from the taking of their first scalp. Many of the men were beginning to accept the reality that the single scalp might be the only trophy of the expedition. The warmth of the sun on their shoulders promised a fine day, and the men began to speculate whether Lovewell and

Whiting's wounds would force them to abandon the expedition. As they headed back to their packs, their eyes were drawn to the sparkling waters of the pond on their left, and the uniformity of the pitch pine plain failed to alert them to the impending Indian ambush. Only when they approached the small brook where Paugus and his men lay waiting did they realize that their packs were gone. In that brief instant of panic when the heart seems to sink to the bowels.... Paugus triggered his ambush:

> *Anon there eighty Indian rose,*
> *Who'd hide themselves in ambush dread;*
> *Their knives they shook, their guns they aimed,*
> *The famous Paugus at their head.*

The sudden appearance of eighty howling warriors running at them from front and rear must have been a terrifying experience for Lovewell and his men. In the few seconds before the free-for-all began, it appeared as though they would surely be overwhelmed. Survivors of the fight claim that the English and the Indians were only a few rods (less than 50 feet) from each other when they opened fire. Both sides fired at least two volleys before they began to scatter and take cover behind the trunks of nearby pine trees. From this inadequate cover, they continued to fire at exposed body parts from close range. With the exception of one man, the English resolutely stood their ground and fought back. Benjamin Hassell of Dunstable panicked when he saw Lovewell and others fall. Seeing a chance to escape, and believing that all was lost, he ran for the protection of the fort in Ossipee. The effect of his desertion is covered in succeeding pages. Lovewell was hit in the first volley, but he somehow managed to fire his musket twice as he lay dying. With fading vision, and his lifeblood seeping through the pine needles into the sandy soil, one can scarcely imagine what his final despairing thoughts might have been.... *why didn't I leave a guard.... how did they get behind us?* At 10 o'clock on the morning of May 9th, the essence of John Lovewell's being departed his earthly form.

> *Fight on! Fight on! Brave Lovewell said;*
> *Fight on while Heaven shall give you breath!*
> *An Indian ball then pierced him through,*
> *And Lovewell closed his eyes in death.*

Sergeant Jacob Fullam killed one of the charging Indians with his first shot. With practiced skill he dropped the butt of his musket to the ground, poured powder down the barrel, and rammed home a lead ball on top of a cotton wad; he then cradled the musket in his left forearm as he poured powder into the flash pan and pulled back the flint. Directly in front of him a Pigwacket warrior was just finishing the same drill. From dueling distance, with the deadly dexterity of trained killers, they fired simultaneously and both fell dead. Besides Lovewell and Fullam, Ensign Harwood, John Jefts, Jonathan Kittridge, Daniel Woods, Ichabod Johnson, Thomas Woods and Josiah Davis lay dead. Lt. Jonathan Robbins, Lt. Josiah Farwell and Robert Usher, though seriously wounded, were still able to fall back with the others. Although stunned by the assault of the screaming Indians from front and rear, Lovewell's men had managed to kill at least nine of the Indians. Despite his superior force, Paugus and his warriors had not overwhelmed the scouts. The fight raged on with the English and Indians continuing to reload and fire at each other from behind the meager protection of individual pine trees. The point blank range and the inadequate cover provided many targets, and the casualties continued to rise, particularly among the Indians. One can only imagine the fright of having to concentrate on reloading a musket with an enemy trying to shoot at you from behind a tree—less than 20 yards away!

Presently the scouts could see that the Indians were trying to surround them, and they began a fighting retreat toward the pond giving up ground slowly in the direction of Fight Brook. As they continued to retreat, they gave up the ground that held the bodies of their dead, but the fight was so intense that the Indians were unable to take any scalps. The English were trying to reach a place near the shore where winter ice had pushed up a small barrier of rocks and earth. With Lovewell gone and both of his lieutenants wounded, the English were fighting without a leader. It was Seth Wyman, with a wife and five children at home in Woburn, who rallied the men to the new defensive position. Their situation was desperate. If they tried to hold their position by the shore, the Indians could easily overrun them. Their only option was to continue their retreat—but to where?

Alternating spring freshets and summer drought had created a broad swamp at the mouth of Fight Brook, that depending upon the season, varied from a shallow water-filled cove to a muddy swamp. Also, the eroding action of spring floods had built up a long sandbar that ran parallel to the shore towards the English defensive position. The only access to this sandy peninsula lay directly behind them. The sixty to one hundred foot wide peninsula ran all the way back to Fight Brook.... some three hundred yards. Framed by high swamp grass and rushes where it met the water, the wide sand bar held scattered pine trees and a few fallen pines that might serve as breastworks. If Wyman and his men could get to the fallen trees, the swamp would protect their right flank. In the early afternoon Wyman and his men gradually worked their way onto the peninsula where some of them managed to reach the protection of two fallen pine trees. With their packs, blankets and rations gone, and with more than a third of their company dead or wounded and nowhere to retreat, they appeared to be at the end of their tether.

Paugus and his warriors were intent on annihilating the English, but their aggressive frontal assault was costing them many casualties. As the Indians attacked, they howled like wolves and enraged cougars hoping to intimidate the English, and the English responded with their own huzzahs, jeers and insults. Wyman called out to his companions saying that the day might still be theirs if they continued to fight with courage.

The continuing reckless Indian attack was unaccountable. Out of the dozens of historical accounts about the fight, there has never been a logical reason advanced to explain why the Pigwacket warriors continued to attack in these circumstances. The Indians were past masters at using the forest and the natural terrain to surprise their enemies. The answer may be that they simply refused to believe that they could not overwhelm the small English force with their superior numbers. In his *History of Hudson, NH* written by Kimball Webster in 1913, he succinctly summarized the situation:

> Had the Indians known their advantage, they could easily have destroyed the whole company. If, instead of immediate attack, they had quietly seated themselves at the only approach to the peninsula, hunger would have done its work, and not a man of Lovewell's gallant band could have escaped. But the Indians could not brook delay, and confident of success from superior numbers, they continued the attack, firing at any one of the little band who happened to expose a part of his body.

About the middle of the afternoon, the tempo of the battle began to subside, and the Indians drew back in the pines for a powwow. In the center of a circle, the medicine man, Wahwa, performed a dance setting the cadence with his turtle shell rattle. The rest of the warriors danced around him chanting and striking the ground with musket butts to simulate the beat of drums. Adeawando and Paugus had both survived to this point, and they joined the dance as well. They appealed to *Kchi Niwaskwa* and his helper *Glooscap* seeking their magic for victory over the white men. They knew the English were weak and cornered, but their chant appealed for help to overrun the whites, or to influence them to ask for terms. While the idea of breaking off the fight for a powwow may seem bizarre by modern standards, it was no different than if Frye had called a prayer meeting in the middle of the fight had he been given the opportunity. Truly bizarre is the concept of one side praying help from *God* while the opposing side was chanting and dancing an appeal to *Kchi Niwaskwa* as if *The Creator* were some sort of celestial referee—a perfect example of man's folly.

> *Good Heavens! They dance the Powwow dance!*
> *What horrid yells the forest fill!*
> *The grim bear crouches to his den,*
> *The Eagle seeks the distant hill.*

Although they were incredulous of the temporary respite, the intrepid Seth Wyman perceived an opportunity, and he stole forward to the pine plain and slowly worked his way towards the powwow. Taking careful aim, he fired his musket and killed the central figure in the dance circle, and in the confusion that followed his shot; he crouched and quickly ran back to his former position. The death of their chief medicine man, Wahwa, was a psychological blow to the Pigwackets, but Adeawando and Paugus rallied them quickly, and they skillfully deflected their shock and anger at the English. Like Lovewell before them, Adeawando and Paugus had committed a major battlefield blunder. Why did they not post at least one lookout to report any unusual movement by the English? After this setback, why did Paugus and Adeawando not make the wise decision to let hunger deliver the English to them? For some unaccountable reason, they did exactly the opposite!

The battle resumed with renewed ferocity with a great clamor of howls, barking sounds, and feline screeches by the Indians designed to scare the defenders into submission. Seth Wyman, now fully in command, cheered his men on despite the overwhelming numerical superiority of the Indians. A number of Indians, who managed to gain the peninsula, were close enough to exchange verbal threats and insults. Some of them waved short lengths of rope as if to offer quarter. In response, Wyman defiantly shouted that they would only accept quarter at the point of their muskets.

After being wounded for the third time, Solomon Keyes of Billerica was no longer able to reload his musket. He crawled over and told Seth Wyman that he was a dead man, declaring that the Indians would not have his scalp if he could help it. In a desperate attempt to conceal himself from the Indians, he crawled to the pond where he providentially found a birch bark canoe. He somehow managed to roll his body into the light craft, and he pushed the canoe away from shore to be carried out into the pond by a light breeze. The outcome of his desperate action is revisited in succeeding pages. Jonathan Robbins was wounded again as was Jacob Farrar. At about that same time, chaplain Jonathan Frye was badly wounded. Unable to move, his voice continued to be audible to the other men as he prayed for their ultimate triumph. The marathon struggle wore on into the late afternoon, and the combatants sensed that night would soon be upon them.

He prays kind heaven to grant success,
Brave Lovewell's men to guide and bless,
And when they've shed their heart blood true
To raise them all to happiness.

One of the most storied legends of colonial history occurred at this crucial point in the fight. Having managed to move onto the peninsula, Chief Paugus had worked his way to a position within talking distance of John Chamberlain of Groton. They knew each other well from frequent contacts during kinder times. Now the two were trading insults and shots at close range. They were taking pot shots at any small target the other offered from behind the narrow trunks of their respective trees. Thinking to have the other at a slight disadvantage, they raised their muskets to fire only to have each musket flash in the pan (misfire). According to folklore, they agreed to go down to the brook to clean out their guns. Motivated by some strange code of honor, the Indians and the scouts allowed the pair safe passage to go to the edge of the brook-fed swamp to finish their personal duel. In recharging the muskets, the ball of

Paugus was small enough to roll down the barrel. Chamberlain had to force his larger ball down with his ramrod. Sensing the advantage, Paugus began to raise his gun to fire saying, "*Me kill you quick.*" Chamberlain retorted, "*Maybe not*"—slammed the butt of his gun on the ground to seat the ball and shot Paugus dead. According to the theory, the design of his gun enabled him to force enough powder through the touchhole to prime his gun.[48]

T'was Paugus led the Pequa't tribe;
As runs the fox would Paugus run;
As howls the wolf would he howl—
A huge bearskin had Paugus on.

But Chamberlain of Dunstable,
(One whom a savage ne'er shall slay—)
Met Paugus by the waterside,
And shot him dead upon that day.

The Indians appeared dispirited with the loss of their war chief, and the intensity of their fire turned sporadic as shadows lengthened and darkness gradually enveloped the tragic scene. As the Pigwacket Indians drew back onto the pitch pine plain, the scouts hugged the ground, some of them no doubt wondering if they would ever see home and family again. The long terror of being hunted by an implacable foe had taken a heavy toll; they were exhausted physically and mentally. The chaotic din of battle was now muted, replaced by a chorus of night frogs from the swamp.... not a single sound came from the Indian attackers. Presently they arrived at the incredible conclusion that the Indians were gone—they were actually gone! The Pigwackets had left the field of battle!

Under Seth Wyman's direction, they began to explore their position to assess their situation. They found a total of twenty

---

[48]Authors' note: Controversy over this particular episode as well as the follow-up story about how Paugus' son sought to avenge his father's death are discussed fully in a later chapter.

men on the peninsula. They discovered the prostrate form of Jacob Farrar by the pond close to death. Robert Usher and Jonathan Robbins were mortally wounded and unable to move. Robbins accepted his fate with great courage. He asked one of the men to charge his musket commenting, "The Indians will come in the morning to scalp me and I'll kill another of 'em if I can." After loading Robbins musket, the twenty survivors of the fight walked off the peninsula leaving the three mortally wounded men behind. The eleven badly wounded were, Lieut. Farwell, Jonathan Frye, Sergeant Johnson, Timothy Richardson, Josiah Johnson, Samuel Whiting, Elias Barron, John Chamberlain, Isaac Lakin, Eleazer Davis, and Josiah Jones. The remaining nine men, some of whom were slightly wounded, were Ensign Wyman, Edward Linkfield, Thomas Richardson, Daniel and Eleazer Melvin, Ebenezer Ayer, Abiel Asten, Joseph Farrar, and Joseph Gilson.

Shortly before midnight the twenty survivors began to retrace the trail to their advanced base at Ossipee where they expected to find provisions and a surgeon to attend the wounded. It is difficult enough in daylight for an experienced woodsman to make his way through the snarls, pitfalls, and fallen trees of an untracked wilderness. To do so in the darkness was well nigh impossible, even for the strongest. But the need to put the nightmare of Saco Pond behind them drove them to accomplish the impossible. They had traveled less than two miles before they discovered that Jonathan Frye, Josiah Farwell, Josiah Jones, and Eleazer Davis were unable to go on. All four had serious wounds, and despite the fear of being left behind, their legs would carry them no further. The troop gathered about the men and made the only logical decision. They concluded that the terrain was too difficult for them to carry the four men on litters. Each man knew in his heart that the situation had come down to individual survival—it was every man for himself. They reasoned logically that there were ten men and a surgeon only a day's march away who could come to their aid. The four men were somewhat comforted by the assurances that help would soon be on its way. They told them to stay in place and wait to be rescued. As the four lay in pain with only their canteens of water to sustain them, and with all their senses attuned to the fading sounds of the retreating company, one can only imagine what despairing thoughts filled their minds.... alone in darkness and silence.

According to historical accounts of the battle, the Pigwacket war party came out of the fight with far more casualties than the English. In contrast to the outpouring of Anglo literature about the fight, there were no written chronicles of the fight by Native Americans. Aside from "telling beads" and pictographs, the Abenaki Indians had no written language to record their history. Notwithstanding this lack of a written language, the pre-contact Indians did have an effective way of preserving their history. They were noted for the detail and accuracy of their oral history.[49] While the idea of maintaining a history through its repeated retelling may seem suspect to certain people, native oral histories are often more accurate than written histories. It all depends on the dedication of the *Keeper* of the historical record. One has only to do research on conventional books written by different authors about a particular historic event to find contradictions and errors. These inconsistencies bring to mind the old admonition—don't believe everything you read!

It is a rare privilege to examine any historic event of the French and Indians Wars that is a true representation of the na-

---

[49]*The Walking People*, by Paula Underwood; Ms. Underwood, an Oneida Indian descendant, was chosen by her father and grandmother to be the official "keeper" of the history of her people. As a young girl she spent many years committing this history to memory. Her 750-page manuscript tells the story of her people's 10,000-year journey from Asia to the East Coast of America. Al Kayworth used material from *The Walking People* in his book, *Legends of the Pond*. As a result of the friendship growing out of that collaboration, in the spring of 2000, Ms. Underwood, together with her manager and an indigenous Hawaiian descendant, visited Al Kayworth on tiny Escumbuit Island in Derry NH. Ms. Underwood passed away unexpectedly at her home in California later in that same year.

tive point of view. It is a special privilege to relive the fight at Saco Pond through the mind and memory of a Native American descendant, albeit many generations removed from the original *N'datlogit* (Storyteller). The oral history offered here not only agrees with English accounts of the event, but it contains compelling clues that support its accuracy. Mrs. Marilyn Jones of Norway, Maine gave a handwritten copy of the oral history of her own family to the D.A.R., which in turn passed on her letter to the Fryeburg Historical Society.[50]

This is the story of my many times great-grandmother who was a full-blooded Indian princess. She was the daughter of a full-blooded Penobscot Indian Chief named Powak of the Abenaki Indians. This story is in the princess' own words:

> *Many moons ago, me know like two moons, my father, Powak, one of the big chief of Penobscot Nation, want peace with white man. Call council of all chiefs. Council send Powak from council to Pegwacket Tribe up by big Saco to talk peace with tribe. Powak take me and Little Elk (brave me promised to).*
>
> *After many suns we come to Saco Pond. We look see Pegwacket (punched up thru Hill) great rock craig.*
>
> *Soon we come to village of Pegwacket Tribe. Many hogans with stockade around. We stay with tribe to talk peace.*
>
> *Paugus, a big chief from another land came here to get Pegwackets to raid white settlements. He take all young braves in raiding party.*

---

[50]Authors' note: During a research visit to the Fryeburg Historical Society, the authors were shown a copy of Mrs. Jones letter. Marilyn Jones is a member of the *Daughters of The American Revolution*. She plans to carry on the tradition of passing on the oral history to her daughters, Wanda Jones Ryerson and Vicky Jones MacDonald as well as grandsons Zachary Ryerson and Charles (Chuck) MacDonald.

Old men, squaws, papoose go fishing down Saco Pond.

On way back we hear many gunfire near head of pond. We put canoe into shore and find war party fight with whites. We warned to circle battle and go to village.

Powak and Little Elk stay with war party.

Paugus tell Powak he come on packs of white men. He count packs and know he has many more braves than whites so he attacks.

We circle and head for village. Whites are scalp hunters!

Long after moon is up, braves come to village only few. Say Paugus is killed, Powak is killed, Little Elk is killed.

They are to move to Canada so me go with them. It is many suns back to my people. Me not make alone.

Me get to Canada, and me find trader. After many suns we start on trail for my people.

We get here, want to stay, build cabin so we stay. We have papoose maiden.

The information that the Penobscot Chief Powak was on a mission to try to persuade the Pigwackets to join in proposed peace talks with the English is very significant. As a later chapter will reveal, the Penobscot Indians were angling for peace talks at that particular time. The English were prodding their Penobscot contacts to bring other hostiles like the Norridgewalk and the Pigwacket Indians into the talks, and the Penobscot negotiators assured the English that they spoke for those tribes. The Penobscot Indians did eventually broker a peace treaty between the English and the Abenaki Indians of Maine in late 1725. Powak and Little Elk did not go down river with the Pigwacket war party. They apparently stayed with the fishing party at the outlet of the pond, and they came up the pond with the women and elders and joined the fight after it got started. It is also true that the surviving Pigwacket warriors and their families went to the French Mission Village on the St.

Francis River. The Penobscot "princess" had no other option than to go with them. She apparently met a *voyageur* or *coureur-de-bois* (forest trader) in Canada. The pair returned to Maine where they had a baby girl. All of the other details of her story jibe with the known facts. The part of the oral history that states that *only a few* warriors returning to the village confirms English estimates that no more than twenty Pigwacket warriors survived the fight.

Like the Penobscot "princess" whose life was changed by the battle, the survivors still faced many hardships after its conclusion. Some early historians seized upon the notion that the Indians withdrawal from the field was a clear admission of defeat. Others lamented Lovewell's "defeat" at the hands of the Pigwacket Indians. Although twenty rangers walked off the battlefield unassisted, not all of them made it home. There is sorrow and tragedy in their individual stories as well as examples of courage that honor the human spirit. On that lovely spring day, the most optimistic plans of Indian and white man went terribly awry at Saco Pond. There were no victors among the warriors—red or white—who walked away from that bloody fight. The red and white men who fought there seemed to acknowledge the folly of their actions by not taking the scalps of the fallen. Saco Pond was renamed Lovewell Pond to honor the famous bush fighter Lovewell, and all signs of the battle have long since faded. In his 1919 book, *Pigwacket,* George Hill Evans wrote a moving epitaph to the men—red and white—who, on a warm spring day in 1725, gave their lives on the north shore of Saco Pond:

> *The beautiful sheet of storied water that bears the name of Lovewell still holds in its crystal depth the blue bowl of the sky, and the predatory kingfisher still drops like a plummet from the outthrust branches of the guardian pines. Somewhere in its golden sands still lie peacefully together the moldering bones of red and white foeman.*
>
> --*Pigwacket, 1919,* by George Hill Evans

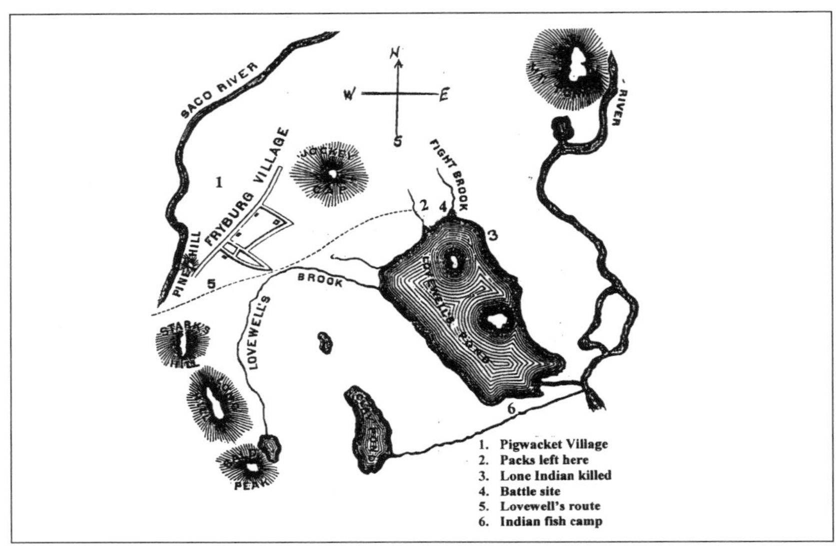

5-1 Battle site, Lovewell Pond

5-2 The site of the battle

CHAPTER 6

THE WAY HOME

Sleep, soldiers of merit, sleep, gallant of yore,
The hatchet is fallen, the struggle is o'er.
While the fir tree is green and the wind rolls a wave,
The tear drop shall brighten the turf of the brave.

Throughout the long day the sounds of the battle had carried clearly to the waiting elders, women, and children inside the Indian stockade. Buoyed by the report that they had an overwhelming advantage in manpower, they had gone to the village in late morning to await the return of their victorious braves. They were familiar enough with the terrain to know that the scalp hunters were trapped. As the afternoon wore on, however, their confidence gradually turned to alarm, and they began to gather in small groups inside the stockade for mutual comfort. By late afternoon, all of their plans for a victory celebration were forgotten, and a pall of gloom enveloped them. Some suggested sending young boy runners to check the progress of the fight, but the elders advised against it, saying that such action would not be well received by the warriors, and that it might well prove a fatal distraction. The ebb and rise of the volume of gunfire in the warm spring air tied each person emotionally to the fight. The occasional crescendos of gunfire seemed to signal a climax, only to fade to scattered shots as the day wore on. It was late afternoon, with the sun slipping below the horizon, when the battle sounds gradually gave way to an ominous silence.

Shortly after sunset, the wounded warriors began to slip through the main gate of the stockade. It soon became apparent to the gathering women and elders that the fight had not gone well for their braves. Still, they would not know for sure until the main body of men returned to the village. There was no weeping among the Indian women. The stoicism of the braves had its effect on the mothers, the wives, and the children. That is not to say that they did not grieve.... like the braves, they had learned to grieve silently. Throughout the long night, the woman and elders were busy tending to the needs of the many wounded warriors. When they were finally able to pause to tally the dead and wounded, they were stunned at the magnitude of their casualties. In spite of their best efforts, eighteen mortally wounded warriors had died at the village, and it was certain that there would be many invalids among the survivors. Because of the confusion and the darkness, Adeawando had been unable to calculate the Indian casualties at the pond. As wounded braves continued to expire during the night, he prepared himself to accept the bad news with the stoic dignity of a sachem. Thus, when elders told him that only twenty-two braves had survived the battle, his face remained impassive. He quietly asked them to pass the word to the villagers of a general council meeting the following day.

The next morning they removed their dead from the battlefield, and they buried them in the traditional way. For some obscure reason they did not bury Paugus, Powak and Little Elk with the Pigwacket warriors. It may have had something to do with their tribal origins; Paugus was a Scaticook and Powak and Little Elk were Penobscot Indians. These three were buried in a common grave on the field of battle; the English later uncovered their burial site. The location of the Pigwacket burials remained secret. Although he was shattered by the outcome of the battle, Adeawando continued to provide leadership. As a sachem and elder statesman of the tribe, his wise consul had been brushed aside in the headlong rush to follow Paugus on the warpath. Through twenty years he had placed his totem on English treaties, and his long experience and clarity of purpose were vital to the broken tribe. He dispatched three scouts to shadow the retreating scalp-hunters, to make sure that there was no English reserve force heading for the village. He then retired to his wigwam to smoke his pipe and to plan his address to his people. That evening, as tribal members joined the ritual council circle, the immensity of their loss struck them. The small representation of young vital braves in the circle was powerful evidence of their loss. It was a council circle made up of women and elders. After discussing some of the immediate needs of the tribe, the talking stick was passed to Chief Adeawando. Holding the ritual talking stick outstretched before him, their attention was commanded by his firm—aho! While he held the ceremonial talking stick, Adeawando knew there would be no interruptions:

> Hear me speak my people! I.... your sachem Adeawando.... through countless moons I have sat with the English to talk of peace many times. Always there were those who counseled against peace with the white man. Much of what they said about the white men is true; he does not keep the promise of his treaties. Our young warriors point to those betrayals and cry out for revenge. The cycle of war and peace with the white man is like the returning snows of winter. And always our young warriors swear revenge.... but their young eyes do not see what my old eyes have seen.
>
> I have seen the English settlements in flames, and I have seen hundreds of their women and children taken to Canada. We have taken the scalps of hundreds of their men; we have destroyed their cattle and their gardens. Yet.... out of the dust of their defeat.... they rise and multiply like the mushroom in the forest. We made our most powerful medicine against them.... but their sorcery was greater. When Paugus came from our French father to talk war with our young braves they listened only to him. Our young warriors would not heed the counsel of their sachem.... Adeawando!
>
> Now Paugus is gone; Wahwa is gone, and many of our young braves are gone.... gone forever! Our Penobscot brothers came to our village to talk peace; they too fell under the spell of Paugus.... now they lie with him!

> I....I, Adeawando ask you.... will you now heed the counsel of one who knows the white man well? Like the bitter potions of our medicine makers, my counsel is bitter.... there is no revenge in my plan for your survival. Yet, we have no choice; we must abandon our home and go to live with our French brothers. It is bitter medicine that we can never return to the sacred land of our ancestors.... for the English will surely destroy us. For those who seek revenge.... let them join the war parties of our mission brothers. For the rest.... if *Kchi Niwaskwa* wills it.... we will find peace with our French brothers.

The oratory was muted as the talking stick moved around the council circle; it was apparent that the tribal members were resigned to Adeawando's vision of their future. The handful of surviving warriors gazed into the council fire with the vacant stare of men who knew they had visited death's threshold. As the talking stick reached their hand, most voiced their acceptance with a simple "Aho" as they passed on the ritual symbol of authority. Light from the council fire illuminated somber faces.... faces displaying the look of a people planning a trip into the unknown.

In the following days, with the remarkable adaptability innate to semi-nomadic people, the remnants of the ancient race known in earlier times as the Sokoki left their village in Pigwacket Valley for the last time and began the long trek to the French Mission Village of St. Francis. Along the shore of Saco Pond, the bodies of Lovewell and his men lay scattered about the sandy peninsula exposed to the elements and forest scavengers. There was something in the ethic of the Pigwacket Indian that inhibited him from taking the scalps of the fallen English.

The heroic way to take a scalp was in the heat of the battle amidst gunfire, smoke, and the screams of dying men. To take the scalp in the midst of chaos; to hold it aloft and yelp the scalping cry was the mark of a man and a true warrior. To take these scalps would be like a vulture feeding on carrion. But there was an inbred instinct for revenge built into the Indian warrior psyche. Among the scores of Pigwackets making the long trek to Canada, there were many young males who had not yet gone on their *vision quest* to seek their spiritual guardian (*manatou*). These pre-pubescent youths dreamed of the brave deeds they would perform against the English in future war parties sent from Canada. But not all of the Pigwacket people were bent on revenge. There was a small silent minority that was tired of everything associated with raids, war parties, and scalp dances. This small group of people yearned for a way out of the endless cycle of war with the whites. The trail they cut for themselves would eventually find them serving with Colonial forces against the British in the *Revolutionary War;* their story is an interesting sidelight of the chapter entitled, *The Aftermath.*

In the meantime the English survivors were making a desperate bid to reach safety. Although Benjamin Hassell's headlong flight had not decided the outcome of the battle, his subsequent actions proved to be disastrous for the survivors. The terrified deserter managed to make his way to Ossipee in the middle of the night, arriving at the fort early the following morning. His precipitous arrival and his graphic account of the attack were comparable to a man shouting fire in a packed theater. It is entirely possible that Hassell truly believed every detail of his account of the ambush. His subsequent conduct on returning to Dunstable suggests that he actually believed that Lovewell's entire company had been annihilated. In all fairness, one must at least try to understand his actions in light of *his* perception of the action. In a blur of charging Indians, musket fire, and war cries he had seen a third of his company fall about him at the very beginning of the fight. Abruptly, with eighty howling warriors running at him from two directions, his self-survival instinct emerged, and he panicked and ran for his life with only a fleeting look back to see if he was being followed. Unfortunately his panic spread to the Ossipee contingent, and they immediately prepared to head for home. Sergeant Nathaniel Woods ordered them to stay and wait for possible survivors, but after hearing Hassell's terrifying tale, they would have none of it. Before heading for home, they left a bag of bread and another sack of pork together with a brief message written on a piece of birch bark. The message advised that they were returning to Dunstable because they believed Hassell's eyewitness report that Lovewell and his men had been wiped out. There is nothing like fear to lighten a man's load and give wings to his feet.... and these men were frightened!

Leaving early on the morning of the 10,Th they arrived in Dunstable in the late evening of the 11th.... marching two days and one night without rest! The New England Historical and Genealogical Register of 1909 contained a very interesting passage in regards to these men:

> It was one hundred and thirty-one years after the fight at Pigwacket before the name of Benjamin Hassell, intentionally omitted by Symmes, and the names of the ten men left at the fort, as members of the historical company were made known. The names first appeared in Chandler's Manchester, 1856.

In the blizzard of publicity generated by the fight, the press and the public labeled these men cowards. Yet, in fairness, one must try to view their actions on the basis of their perception of the situation as described to them by Benjamin Hassell. The terrified Hassell had described an ambush in which eighty Indians had ambushed and overwhelmed thirty-four rangers. One can see how they might conclude that Lovewell and his men were annihilated. They had no idea that Wyman and nineteen survivors of the battle were desperately seeking their help. Had the critics of the day analyzed the facts carefully, they might have posed a hypothetical question to themselves: *being one of the ten reserve, how would I have reacted had I been told that Lovewell and thirty-three men had been wiped out by eighty Indians, who might be headed in my direction?* They had none of the intelligence that could have helped them make the right decision; they knew nothing of the plight of Frye, Farwell,

Davis and Jones, and they certainly did not know that the Indians were no longer a credible threat. They knew only what they had been told by the terrified Hassell. Although these men later received their share of the land grants awarded to Lovewell's men, their names were not published until 1856. The passage of time eventually blurred the controversy over their actions, and they managed to live normal lives.

After telling Frye, Farwell, Davis and Jones that help would be arriving from Ossipee, Seth Wyman and the remaining survivors of the fight traveled in darkness stumbling over rocks, fallen trees, and brush until dawn. Early in the morning, after forcing their way through thick brush, they realized that they were leaving tracks that a child could follow. They decided to split into three smaller parties in order to minimize their trail and to confuse any pursuit. The three groups were breaking their own trail through difficult terrain. The pace of each man was governed by his physical condition and the strength of his will to reach the fort. Under these circumstances they often lost sight of one another being guided only by the sound of bodies crashing through underbrush ahead of them. Elias Barron of Groton was part of the group that spotted a small scouting party of Indians shadowing them. These Indians were very likely the braves sent out by Adeawando to scout their retreat. The rangers had no way of knowing that the fighting strength of the Indians was exhausted, so the sighting of the Indians renewed their determination to reach the fort. The wounded Elias Barron became separated from his small group; with each man intent on his own survival, it is understandable how it could happen. An empty gun case by the side of the Great Ossipee River was later identified to be his. In the aftermath, his friends and relatives could only speculate over what his fate might have been. Had he drowned crossing the river, or in his wandering, did he simply leave his gun case and die alone in the wilderness?

All three groups managed to find their way back to the fort in Ossipee without any further losses. The Indian scouting party, which had showed no inclination to attack, had simply vanished. The starving scouts, having survived the battle and the difficult night march through the wilderness, then suffered another psychological blow—the fort was empty! They were greatly refreshed by the pork and bread that had been left by the departed scouts, but Wyman reminded them that they had a long march ahead and that other survivors might be headed for the fort. No one was more astonished than Seth Wyman when an apparition appeared outside the stockade; it was the thrice-wounded Solomon Keyes whom they all thought was dead! At the height of the battle, after receiving his third wound, he had managed to roll into an abandoned canoe and set himself adrift. When the wind-driven canoe finally grounded itself on the west shore of the pond, Keyes found that he had enough strength to travel, and he set out alone towards the fort. His indomitable will to live drove him to complete the trek to the fort, despite his multiple wounds and his exhausted condition.

Seth Wyman and the fifteen rangers who managed to return to Dunstable were not subjected to the critical scrutiny of Hassell and the ten men that had arrived late at night on the 11th. In regards to Wyman's group, it should be noted that having found the fort at Ossipee empty, they too were eager to insure their personal safety. They immediately set a course for home with little thought for the four gravely wounded men they had left on their back trail. Like the others, these men must be judged on the basis of what they knew about the physical condition of Jonathan Frye, Josiah Farwell, Eleazer Davis and Josiah Jones. They had already decided that they were unable to carry the four on litters and they knew they would be hard pressed to make it home without food. Historical accounts tell us that the four wounded men did urge the others to go on without them. It simply came down to a matter of survival. Having made the decision to leave the mortally wounded Robert Usher and Jonathan Robbins at the battle site, they were forced to make the same cruel judgment when the four men were unable to continue. Once they found the fort abandoned, they were sure that the four were doomed.... so they left them.

The tattered remnant of Lovewell's party traveled light on their return journey. Besides the clothes they wore, they had only their muskets, powder horns and leather shot pouches to encumber them. Somewhere along the way it became apparent that three of the wounded men could not keep up. Seth Wyman elected to stay with these men until they got back to Dunstable. The stronger survivors came into Dunstable the 13th of May at night. By the time Seth Wyman arrived with the three survivors on the 15th, his public reputation was already beginning to build. The four told a harrowing story of going without food for four days. Their enforced fast ended after they caught and roasted two mouse squirrels that they declared to be a "tasty morsel." After that they managed to kill some partridge and other game that sustained them during the remainder of their trip. During the four days after the return of the survivors, as mounted couriers were shuttling between Dunstable and Boston, sensational news reports of the fight covered the entire gamut from disaster to glorious victory—a thesis for later analysis.

At this point, the particulars of the engagement and the aftermath were only partially complete. Only a few miles from the scene of the battle, four wounded men lay waiting to be rescued. They all had grievous wounds, but young Jonathan Frye was in the worse condition. After waiting three long days with no food to sustain them, they knew they could wait no longer. Weak from starvation, they managed to travel several more miles enduring the pain and the stench of their putrefied wounds as best as they could. When Jonathan Frye sank to the ground that final time, his companions knew he would never rise again. By all accounts, Jonathan's final earthly moments were heroic; the twenty-year old chaplain confided his belief that he was dying, urging them to abandon him. To Davis, he pleaded that if it pleased God to carry him safely home, he asked him to tell his father that he expected to be in eternity within a few hours, and that he was not afraid to die. By these acts, the young chaplain demonstrated why he was beloved by the men in Lovewell's company, and why they all wanted him to have the Indian scalp. The young Harvard student, a bible-toting outsider, proved that he was not only an apostle of God, but that he was a man's man. The body of Jonathan Frye and the expedition journal he was keeping were never found:

Come hither, Farwell, said young Frye;
You see that I'm about to die
Now for the love I bear for you,
When cold in death my bones shall lie;

Go thou and see my parents dear;
And tell them you stood by me here;
Console them when they cry, alas!
And wipe away the falling tear,

Lieutenant Farwell took his hand,
His arm around his neck he threw,
And said "brave Chaplain I could wish
That heaven had made me die for you."

The Chaplain on kind Farwell's breast,
Bloody and languishing he fell;
Nor after this said more, but this,
"I love thee soldier; fare thee well!"

One hundred years after the fight at Saco Pond, men were reciting lines like these around a hundred campfires in the New England woods. Until the Revolutionary War began, no other event captured the imagination of the American public like the storied deeds of Lovewell, Paugus, Chamberlain, Wyman and Jonathan Frye. Oddly, the details of the remaining three men's incredible struggle for survival were never celebrated in song and verse, as were the others. Nevertheless, *their* story is a tribute to the human spirit, and to their determination to survive in the most difficult circumstances.

Despite the hunger and the stench of their maggot-infested wounds, the three men slowly pushed towards the fort. After becoming separated from his two companions in the vicinity of the Ossipee River, Josiah Jones made a desperate choice. Instead of trying to cross the river and push on towards the fort at Ossipee, he decided to follow the course of the Saco River to the coast. In his condition, the outlook for his survival was bleak. He was already starving; he had lost his thumb, and worse of all, he had a gut wound that had severed his intestines. Indeed, it was possible to reach civilization by following the Saco to the coast, but the winding river was a route best traveled by canoe. In his starving condition, he sampled everything that he thought might sustain him; roots, ferns, and even tree bark. What he managed to chew and keep down emerged from his severed intestine and came out of the wound in his side. In spite of all this he persisted, and incredibly, after fourteen days in the woods, he arrived at Biddeford on the 23rd of May! Filthy, emaciated, and near death, his astonishing will delivered him against all the odds! There, under the kind care of a frontier surgeon and caring women, Josiah Jones was nursed back to health.

After Josiah Jones became separated from them, Eleazer Davis and Josiah Farwell continued their painful march towards the fort. Their progress was agonizingly slow. They had only a few roots and water to sustain them. On one occasion Davis caught a fish and broiled it and was somewhat refreshed by it. Farwell, steadily growing weaker, was only able to pick at his portion. On the 15th day of their ordeal, Farwell was unable to continue. The near escape from death the previous year had not fazed Farwell; he had been the sole survivor of the ten-man massacre at Thornton's Ferry. A brother-in-law to Lovewell, Farwell was an equal to Lovewell as a bush fighter, but the man whose brushes with death might have earned him the tribute of *Fortunes Favorite* had reached the end of his endurance. After slowing his pace for days to accommodate the failing Farwell, Eleazer Davis had to make the soul-wrenching decision to proceed alone—he arrived at the fort the following day. After eating the pork and bread he found inside the fort, he was greatly strengthened. Thus refreshed, he made it to

Berwick in two days, and then to Portsmouth where Samuel Penhallow, the New Hampshire militiaman and historian, interviewed him. The death of his companion Farwell affected Davis deeply; he later spoke of the melancholy and desolation he experienced after being obliged to leave the dying lieutenant. The ordeal of Davis was an epic eighteen-day test of human courage and endurance. There is no doubt that, had Josiah Farwell's wound been less severe, that the heroic companions would have walked into Berwick side by side on May 27th .

The staggered return of the survivors over a sixteen-day period contributed greatly to the suspense and confusion that followed the first news of the event. In order to understand the succession of events that followed, it is helpful to recap the return of the survivors in the proper sequence:

May 11 th at night: The return of Hassell and the 10-man rear guard.
May 13 th at night: 12 survivors of the fight returned
May 15th Ensign Wyman arrived with 3 wounded survivors.
May 23rd Josiah Jones arrived in Biddeford, Maine
May 27th Eleazer Davis arrived in Berwick, Maine

The commander of the local militia, Colonel Tyng, debriefed Benjamin Hassell on the morning of the 12th. Anticipating the criticism that he knew was certain to come, Hassell arrived at his meeting with Tyng bearing a short written account that was designed to justify his conduct. Although his report did not specifically declare that Lovewell and his men were dead, he offered no hope that there would be additional survivors.

Dunstable, May 11, 1725—To His Honor ye Governor Dummer

An information from Capt. Lovewell's Company, at Ossipee Pond a man being sick we left nine men with him. We made a fort there and sent out scouts, discovered tracks and then marched to Saweco River (Saco River), discovered more tracks; then coming to Pigwacket, found where some Indians went into canoes, then marched and see one

Injun; kild him, and returning two miles; thare we ware shot upon, Capt. Lovewell wounded, and none returned but I, & ye ten men, and we and no more are yet come to Dunstable.

—Benj. Hassell, corp.

Colonel Tyng forwarded Hassell's report to Governor Dum-mer together with his own cover letter. In his own letter, he not only stated that the fight took place *on the 9th*, but he made a point of including Sergeant Nathaniel Wood's message that described the circumstances of the withdrawal of the rear guard at the fort. At the time he wrote the letter, Tyng apparently held out no hope that there were any survivors of the actual fight.

May it please your honor.

Upon hearing the news early this morning, this twelfth instant, and Benj. Hassell gave me this account: That *on the ninth* of this instant, about nine or ten in the morning, Capt. Lovewell saw an Indian on the opposite side of Sawco Pond, and then they immediately left their packs and went about two miles before they came to him; they coming within about five or six rods before the saw the Indian, and the Indian made the first shot at them, and wounded Capt. Lovewell & Sam' Whiting, and they immediately killed the Indian, & returning back to their packs came within forty or fifty rods of them; the Indians Waylaid them under the banks of a little Brook Capt. Lovewell's men being between the brook and the Pond, it being a Pine Plain, the Indians fired upon them both in the front and the rear, shouting & running towards them.

Capt. Lovewell fell at the first Volue the Indians shott, and Groand; this man being clost by him, and then he saw several of Capt. Lovewell's men get behind trees. Upon this, seeing such a great number of Indians, thought it best to go to some men they had left with a sick man at the Fort they had made, about thirty miles back, by Ossipee Pond, and he got to the Fort the next morning about nine of oclock

Your Hon. Most Humble Servant.

And if your Honor thinks fitt,
I will march up to the place.

Eleazer Tyng

Sargent Nathl. Wood Desired me to aquaint your Honor, that he was left with the nine men at the fort, and upon Hassells coming to the Fort, the men would stay no longer; Woods both desired & commanded them to stay, but could not prevail with them, & then he made the best of his way home.

The small packet of letters traveled to Boston via a mounted courier and was delivered to Governor Dummer on the afternoon of the 12th. He in turn replied in kind to Colonel Tyng in Dunstable, and he dispatched another courier to Portsmouth, New Hampshire with a second letter to his Lieutenant Governor, Colonel Wentworth. He appeared to have recognized the misconduct of the men who had returned at night on the 11th, but he too seemed to hold no hope for the return of additional survivors. As mounted couriers galloped toward Dunstable and Portsmouth, NH on the 13th the first actual survivors of the fight were approaching Dunstable on the *Mo-Ro-Mac Trail* near the Amoskeag Falls. Due to the complete absence of electronic communications, Governor Dummer's letters did not reflect this latest development—there were survivors!

Boston, May 13th, 1725(Gov. Dummer's letter
to Col. Wentworth)

Sir I have just time to inform you, that one of Capt. Lovewell's men is run from him & left him engaged with the Indians at Pigwacket *last Lord's Day,* & saw they were overpowered by numbers, & that he saw Capt. Lovewell fall & heard him groan, & that he himself was cut off from the company by the Indians passing between them. I have ordered out Capt Tyng with forty men to make the best of his way to Ossipee & Pigwacket in quest of the Enemy, & Capt. White to follow him with his company of Volunteers, & I must pray that you will act in concert with us in the affair, & send from New Hampshire a party of men upon the same ground. For if the enemy are such strength as to defeat Lovewell, they will thereupon be upon our frontiers in great Numbers.

It is of the greatest importance that something be done vigorously, & expeditiously on this occasion.

Wm. Dummer

In his reply to Colonel Tyng, the governor authorized him to undertake an immediate search and destroy expedition to Pigwacket, and he assured Tyng of reinforcements for his town. It is interesting to note that, after branding Hassell and the rear guard cowards, he suggests that Hassell might be used as a guide (if it be necessary):

To Col. Tyng; May 13th

Sir, This morning I rec'd ye account of Indians Engaging Capt. Lovewell at Pigwacket, I have not time to make any observations on the management of Hassell, & the men at the Fort who have so cowardly deserted their commander & fellow soldiers in their Danger. Your readiness to go out forthwith after the enemy is well accepted & approved of by me, and the Council; accordingly I direct you to make up a body of forty Effective Men well armed and provided,

(If you think so many necessary), & proceed without delay to Ossipee & Pigwacket & the country thereabout, & make careful search for the Enemy in order to kill & destroy such as may be found there, and at the place of the Engagement with Capt. Lovewell. Endeavor what you can to find the bodies of the Indians or English that may have been slain, and you are hereby empowered to draw out of Capt. Willard's Company twelve men to join you, & he is accordingly ordered to detail them & send them to your rendezvous forthwith.

If you find it necessary, you are hereby Authorized and empowered to impress out of the various Towns in your Regiment, twelve or fifteen men for this service if you cannot enlist ye necessary number.

Capt. White is ordered to follow you as soon as he can possibly get the men ready & I have written to Lieut. Gov. Wentworth that a party may be sent from that Government to Pigwacket as soon as may be.

I depend upon your acting in the matter with the utmost diligence & vigour, you must take your Lt. Blanchard with you in this march—Take two or three sufficient Pilots (& if it be necessary) take Hassell who left the company—I would have you go without your full complement than to make any delay.

Wm. Dummer

This exchange of letters was taken from a book published in 1865 by Frederic Kidder. The book entitled, *Expeditions of Captain John Lovewell*, is only one of dozens of books and articles written about the marathon battle that came to be known simply as.... *The Fight.* These and other official correspondence about *The Fight* are no doubt still preserved somewhere in the official archives of the State of Massachusetts.

It is evident from the official correspondence of the period that the political hierarchy had no idea how badly the Pigwacket Indians had been hurt in the engagement with Lovewell and his men. John Lovewell's reputation as a bush fighter had reached such proportions that, in the public eye, his defeat could only come from vastly superior forces. And in the immediate aftermath of the fight, people *did* write and talk about Lovewell's defeat. But early Colonial America had its share of spin-masters as well. Succeeding pages will describe how one man sought to alter the facts of the battle in order to protect the reputation of influential friends. The official overreaction to the death of the renowned Lovewell was predictable. As Governor Dummer stated in his letter to Lt. Governor Wentworth, "If the enemy is of such strength as to defeat Capt. Lovewell, they will be upon our frontiers in great numbers."

Lieutenant Gov. John Wentworth of New Hampshire, reacting quickly to Governor Dummer's request, assembled fifty-two men who marched up to Ossipee along the general line of the present Route 16. Wentworth posted a letter to Dummer dated May 23rd in which he revealed that the company had found no signs of Lovewell or his men. The body of the letter reveals that the expedition didn't penetrate beyond the fort in Ossipee. Whether through lack of proper intelligence, or lack of purpose is not clear, but Wentworth's explanation for the ineffective performance points to the latter. According to the official report, the day before they reached the fort at Ossipee Pond, they encountered the trail of a large body of Indians...."much larger than ours." At the abandoned fort the next day, they found some abandoned provisions and "*a writing on a piece of bark, that the men that went out were all lost*." That same day they heard several Indians and the barking of their dogs. Fearing they had been discovered by the Indians, and unable to make contact with the expedition out of Dunstable, they "*thought it advisable to return least they meet the same fate*." It is obvious that the Indian defeat of the mighty Lovewell had a chilling effect on the psyche of these men.

Wentworth replied to Governor Dummer as follows; "You may depend Sir, that they (The Indians) will be down on some of your frontier Towns very soon," and he proposed that Dummer raise another one hundred men to bolster his own fifty-two-man company and the eighty-seven men under Tyng's command. It is obvious that Wentworth was not aware that the Pigwacket Indians were already on their way to Canada.

Colonel Tyng left Dunstable on the 17th with eighty-seven men. A letter from Governor Dummer dated May 19th to Colonel Flagg ordered him to send twelve men from his command to Dunstable as reinforcements for the garrisons of Joseph Bloghead, Nathaniel Hill, John Taylor and John Lovewell. With the assurance that his own community would be protected, Colonel Tyng and his eighty-seven-man company marched for Pigwacket. After initially agreeing to act as a guide for the new company, Benjamin Hassell dropped out at the last moment citing personal illness. The former member of Lovewell's party who went in his place was never identified.

Unlike the expedition out of Portsmouth, NH, the Dunstable men were ready for action. It took brave men to venture into Pigwacket Valley on the heels of Lovewell's defeat. When they reached the Pigwacket Valley and reconnoitered the village and the surrounding area, it was apparent that the Indians were gone. The canoes were gone, there were no food stores, and there were no signs of Indians in the area.

They had little difficulty finding the battle site, and they began the melancholy task of burying the dead. They buried Lovewell and his men where they had fallen under the pitch pines on the sandy peninsula by the shore of Saco Pond. In the course of their search for the bodies, the men discovered what appeared to be a fresh burial mound. Opening the ground on Colonel Tyng's orders, they uncovered the bodies of three Indians. As they examined the bodies closely, they noted that the face of one of the buried warriors was tattooed. Knowing of the Mohawk fondness for facial tattoos, they concluded that it was the body of the famous Paugus—*The Oak*. They had discovered no other Indian burial sites during their investigation, and in spite of their curiosity, they were unable to explain why two unidentified warriors were buried with Paugus. They knew nothing of the Penobscot Chief Powak and Little Elk and their decision to join their Abenaki brothers in battle.

Through an ironic twist of fate, these three warriors were consigned to share that sacred ground with their white foes. One can only hope that they agreed to share the sacramental pipe in the afterworld.... renouncing the hatchet. Mother Earth cradled them in the physical world at the verge of a forest-girded pond, under the blue bowl of *The Creator's* sky. Here.... the earthly forms of Little Elk, Powak, and Paugus.... lay close to the remains of John Lovewell, Jonathan Robbins, John Harwood and Robert Usher of Dunstable; Jacob Fullam of Weston; Jacob Farrar and Josiah Davis of Concord; Thomas Woods, David Woods, and John Jefts of Groton; Ichabod Johnson of Woburn; and Jonathan Kittridge of Billerica.

Although there were to be no earthly tomorrows for these men, they had been a part of an epic event, and their exploits at Saco Pond would be celebrated in song and verse by succeeding generations of New England people.

Ah! Many a wife shall rend her hair,
And many a child cry "woe is me!
When messengers the news shall bear,
Of Lovewell dear bought victory.

With footsteps slow shall travelers go
Where Lovewell's Pond shines clear and bright;
And mark the place where those are laid
Who fell in Lovewell's bloody fight.

Old men shall shake their head and say,
"Sad was the hour and terrible,
Where Lovewell's brave 'gainst Paugus went,
With fifty men from Dunstable.

--The ballad of Lovewell's Fight

By His HONOUR

SPENCER PHIPS, Esq;

Lieutenant-Governour and Commander in Chief, in and over His Majesty's Province of the Massachusetts-Bay in New-England.

A PROCLAMATION.

WHEREAS the Tribe of Penobscot Indians have repeatedly in a perfidious Manner acted contrary to their solemn Submission unto His Majesty long since made and frequently renewed;

I have therefore, at the Desire of the House of Representatives, with the Advice of His Majesty's Council, thought fit to issue this Proclamation, and to declare the Penobscot Tribe of Indians to be Enemies, Rebels and Traitors to His Majesty King GEORGE the Second: And I do hereby require His Majesty's Subjects of this Province to embrace all Opportunities of pursuing, captivating, killing and destroying all and every of the aforesaid Indians.

AND WHEREAS the General Court of this Province have voted that a Bounty or Encouragement be granted and allowed to be paid out of the Publick Treasury to the marching Forces that shall have been employed for the Defence of the Eastern and Western Frontiers, from the [illegible] to the [illegible] of this Instant November;

I have thought fit to publish the same; and I do hereby Promise, That there shall be paid out of the Province-Treasury to all and any of the said Forces, over and above their Bounty upon Inlistment, their Wages and Subsistence, the Premiums or Bounty following, viz.

For every Male Penobscot Indian above the Age of Twelve Years, that shall be taken within the Time aforesaid and brought to Boston, Fifty Pounds.

For every Scalp of a Male Penobscot Indian above the Age aforesaid, brought in as Evidence of their being killed as aforesaid, Forty Pounds.

For every Female Penobscot Indian taken and brought in as aforesaid, and for every Male Indian Prisoner under the Age of Twelve Years, taken and brought in as aforesaid, Twenty-five Pounds.

For every Scalp of such Female Indian or Male Indian under the Age of Twelve Years, that shall be killed and brought in as Evidence of their being killed as aforesaid, Twenty Pounds.

Given at the Council-Chamber in Boston, this Third Day of November [illegible], and in the Twenty-ninth Year of the Reign of our Sovereign Lord GEORGE the Second, by the Grace of GOD of Great-Britain, France and Ireland, KING, Defender of the Faith, &c.

By His Honour's Command,
J. Willard, Secr.

S. Phips.

GOD Save the KING.

BOSTON: Printed by John Draper, Printer to His Honour the Lieutenant-Governour and Council. [illegible]

6-1 1754 Bounty Notice

CHAPTER 7

AFTERMATH

The bugle is silent; the war whoop is dead;
'There's a murmur of waters and wood in their stead.
And the raven and owl chant a symphony drear,
From the dark waving pines o'er the combatant's bier

--Thomas C. Upham
New Hampshire Poet

Lovewell's defeat at Saco Pond caused great consternation in Boston and in the frontier settlements. Lt. Gov. John Wentworth's dire prediction of stepped up Indian attacks was echoed by others who called for new punitive raids against the enemy by large expeditions. Poor intelligence about the strength of the Indians, and an inefficient communication system, prevented them from knowing the truth—the native power was broken! Newspapers of that period were single sheet tabloids about events that were sometimes weeks old. *The Gazette*, *The New England Courant* and the *News Letter* were all published in Boston as weeklies. On May 17th the *Gazette* printed the first story of *Lovewell's Fight*—six days after Hassell's return! The follow-up reports in *The New England Courant* and the *News Letter* appeared to be direct copies of the *Gazette* story. All three newspapers reported that Lovewell's fight had taken place on the *8th of May!* And, as if to make it very clear, the actual wording was: *on Saturday the 8th Instant!* —The story details, the phrasing, and the punctuation were identical in all three news reports. It was obvious that the same person had written all three. Those who read the official correspondence and the news accounts of the fight made no effort to set the record straight, though it is possible that they either didn't read the news accounts, or they failed to note the discrepancy. In the meantime, every piece of official correspondence marked the date as *Sunday the 9,th* and in some cases, *The Lord's Day,* while the incorrect date printed by the newspapers went unchallenged.

This strange discrepancy between the official records and the news reports would have gone unchallenged were it not for the dogged efforts of a remarkable woman named Fanny Hardy Eckstorm. The September 1936 issue of the *New England Quarterly* contained an article written by Eckstorm in which she demolished many of the traditional myths about *The Fight.* Her dogged search for the truth, and the logic of her conclusions, marks her as a woman who would have been a first rate investigative journalist. Her 1936 article made a compelling case in which she accused the Bradford Parson Thomas Symmes of conspiring to alter the official record in order to accommodate his friends. As to the public officials who kept silent in the face of the lie, she accused them of being co-conspirators in the deception. She provided convincing evidence that all three news reports were verbatim copies of a story written and hand delivered to them by Parson Symmes. By modern standards, Symmes' efforts to spin the news to protect the reputation of close friends might seem like a harmless deception, but it was his curious sense of right and wrong that is surprising. To Symmes there was nothing wrong in Jonathan Frye hunting Indians scalps. There were stock companies formed in that era for that purpose, and there were clergymen who owned shares in such syndicates. To Parson Symmes, there was a much more urgent motive to shield Frye's prominent parents from public humiliation and criticism—*it was the shame of taking scalps on the Sabbath!*

There was more to the relationship between Symmes and the Frye family than their church affiliation. Both families had ties to the Stevens family through marriage. An Andover antiquarian named Charlotte Helen Abbot researched the biographies and genealogies of all three families and she concluded that Jonathan had been one of Parson Symmes' pupils. Eckstorm claimed that certain members of the clan asked Symmes to alter the public record to put young Jonathan Frye's role in the best possible light. Symmes went to work at the earliest possible opportunity to interview some of the survivors. His *Memoirs of the Late Fight at Piggwacket* was published as an addendum to a sermon he gave on the affair. He explained in the preface that he was writing the account "*in response to the requests of some persons who I am firstly obliged to gratify.*" As it turned out Symmes' *Memoirs* became the official account of the battle. Penhallow, Kidder and others used it to write their own versions without checking for inaccuracies. Fanny Hardy Eckstorm minced no words in her review of Reverend Symmes' *Memoirs:*

> The Historical Memoirs of the *Late Fight at Piggwacket* is not by any means the unbiased account that every one has long supposed it to be, for the clerical author was doing his best to cover up something which he did not wish the public to know. The real object of the *Memoirs* was to show what a brave, pious, and admirable young man was Chaplain Jonathan Frye, and (by tacit contrast), how false was the report that he went scalp hunting for money on the Sabbath.
>
> For such was the unkind rumor. Survivors of the fight, who indiscreetly told the truth, must have been responsible for it. Just because, so it was whispered, a young chaplain needed scalp money to marry, against the wishes of his family, a girl not yet fourteen years old, he stirred up undisciplined volunteers in such a fashion that, against the judgment of Captain Lovewell and his experienced scouts, the whole troop went off after one lone Indian who had been seen at a distance by the pickets while the rest of the troop were having devotional exercises on a Sunday morning. As a result of this goose chase they were ambushed by Indians twice their own number.
>
> The shame did not lie in the young man's disobedience of parental authority, although he was not yet

> twenty-one, nor in his seeking scalp money, which other clergymen saw no harm in doing. The shame was to have hunted scalps on Sunday. Nor would popular feeling run high against the chaplain who was dead, but rather against his purse-proud family and a miserly, arrogant, besotted old father, who had driven his only son out to his death.

Eckstorm offers a great deal of evidence to support her claim of a conspiracy that was designed to hide the true facts behind the fight at Saco Pond. Parson Symmes left no stone unturned in his efforts to suppress the truth. He arranged a meeting with three survivors of the fight, and he read his *Memoir* to them instead of letting them read it themselves. Symmes sorely needed their endorsement for his doctored account, so he worded their signed affidavit of his *Memoir* in a way that would enable them to deny complicity if his *Memoir* was ever challenged by others. The three men agreed to the *substance* of what had been read to them, but they could not attest to every particular article and circumstance.... like the correct date!

AN ATTESTATION

> We whose names are hereunto Subscribed, having had the Preceding Narrative carefully Read to us (though we can't each of us indeed Attest to every particular Article and Circumstance in it) yet we can and do Aver that the substance of it is True, and are well Satisfied in the Truth of the whole.
>
> Seth Wyman
> Ebenezer Ayer
> Abiel Asten

These three men fought in the same battle! If the details were incorrect, why couldn't they set the record straight in Symmes' presence? Eckstorm correctly branded the signed affidavit a farce. Near the conclusion of her article, Eckstorm figuratively put the final nail in Parson Symmes coffin by adding a final bit of proof. Six months after the fight, Thomas Symmes died from uncontrollable bleeding from the nose. He was only 47 years old. At his memorial service on October 30, 1725, the printed program had an advertisement by Samuel Gerrish, the publisher of Symmes' book. To put it crassly, the publisher of Symmes' *Memoir*, was trying to peddle Symmes' book— *Historical Memoirs of the late Fight with the Indians at Piggwacket, May 9, 1725 by the late Reverend Mr. Thomas Symmes*—at Symmes' own memorial service!

In her article, Eckstorm jumped on this final tidbit with relish; *this let the cat out of the bag. The fight occurred on Sunday, and everybody knew it; as soon as Symmes was dead it was openly acknowledged.* The Abbot Academy and Vassar graduate, Fanny Hardy Eckstorm, never published her expose in book form. Despite authoring several published works about Maine, her report on Lovewell's fight was never published. The New England Quarterly published articles written by Eckstorm on the subject, and the public library in Bangor, Maine has a microfiche of her work.

There has never been an historical event as important as Lovewell's fight that didn't involve a certain amount of finger pointing and second-guessing. To conclude that the excessive zeal of his 20-year-old chaplain caused Lovewell to make his fatal error requires a stretch of the imagination. It is an unlikely scenario to accept that Lovewell set aside his faith in his trusted lieutenants and the experienced men of his company.

Viewed through the lens of our present day morality, Parson Symmes' scheming seems ludicrous, but those were different times. The clergy of that period were a powerful force in the community, and few people dared to defy their edicts in regards to what was considered proper conduct on the Lord's Day. Also, for men like Symmes and his associates, hubris was a powerful motivator.

With Lovewell gone, the public needed a new hero, and Seth Wyman fit the role perfectly. The story of his calm courage at Saco Pond spread quickly throughout the community, and Governor Dummer lost no time in acknowledging his deeds. He invited Seth Wyman to Boston where he presented him with a silver-hilted sword, and commissioned him a captain. Edward Linkfield was made an ensign in the same ceremony, and the Boston Council voted the sum of 1,500 pounds to be paid to the widows and children of the dead rangers. By early summer, Wyman was preparing to lead a new expedition to Pigwacket with a force of men that had been raised in Lancaster by Captain John White. White had previously served under Lovewell on his second expedition, and he had also been with Colonel Tyng when they buried Lovewell and his fallen comrades at Saco Pond. Governor Dummer and the Council knew very little about the condition of the Indians at Pigwacket, and they were anxious to learn what they might expect from the Indians in the coming winter season.

Wyman arrived near Lake Winnipesaukee with his troop in July. The exceedingly hot weather may have contributed to the contamination of their food supply, and almost the entire company was stricken with dysentery that was called the *Bloody Flux* in those days. The effects of the sickness so debilitated the troop that they were obliged to go home. When they finally made it home on August 5,th the entire company was still suffering from what one might guess was a form of salmonella. A number of men died from the effects of the illness. Among the victims were Wyman and White who both died shortly after their return. At Saco Pond Wyman had rallied the besieged scouts with his stirring cry, "*The day will yet be your own if your courage do not fail.*" To die in his own bed due to something as commonplace as food poisoning did not fit Wyman's image, but the manner of his death did not dim the memory of his shining hour at Saco Pond.

In the immediate aftermath of *The Fight,* there was no hint that the legendary duel between Paugus and Chamberlain had actually occurred! Parson Symmes' *Memoir* made no mention of the incident, nor did Samuel Penhallow in his *History of the Indians Wars*. The Paugus-Chamberlain tradition got its impetus in 1799 in Fryeburg, Maine—74 years after the actual battle! In that year a printer named Elijah Russell published a story in connection with his edition of Reverend Thomas Symmes' "*Memoir of the Fight at Piggwacket*:" Russell's version of the Paugus-Chamberlain duel was related as follows:

> Several of the Indians, particularly Paugus their chief, were well known to Lovewell's men, and frequently conversed with each other during the engagement. In the course of the battle Paugus and John Chamberlain discoursed familiarly with each other; their guns had become foul from frequent firing; they washed their guns at the pond, and the latter assured Paugus that he should kill him; Paugus also menaced him, and bid defiance to his insinuations. When they had prepared their guns, they loaded and discharged them, and Paugus fell.

In the ensuing years, the episode was repeated in many books and articles by various authors. In the process, the story gained additional details that tended to heighten the drama of the encounter. Some versions described Paugus using a ramrod to seat his ball, giving Chamberlain the advantage, and in one version, Chamberlain gained a slight advantage by firing his ramrod through Paugus' heart. Even their brief remarks to each other varied with individual writers. To confuse the issue even further, there were people who claimed that Paugus was actually killed by Seth Wyman. Their evidence was based on the lyrics of the *Song of Lovewell's Fight* that was widely circulated beginning in 1725. The lyrics of this song, written by an unknown author, contained the following lines:

> *And yet our valiant Englishmen in fight were ne're dismayed,*
> *But still they kept their motion, and Wyman a Captain made,*
> *Who shot the old chief Paugus which did the foe defeat;*
> *Then set his men in order and brought off the retreat.*

It was not only the volume of arguments that were published pro and con about the Paugus-Chamberlain folklore, but it was the intensity of the debate that confused the issue. In 1898

George W. Chamberlain of the Maine Historical Society prepared a scholarly paper on the controversy for the Maine Historical Society. Although his evidence was circumstantial, he made a convincing case for his ancestor. The John Chamberlain who served with Lovewell had a cousin named Captain John Chamberlain who was a prominent landowner near the Souhegan Falls. He was married to Hannah Farwell, the daughter of Josiah Farwell. Throughout his life, his friends and neighbors called him *Souhegan John* to distinguish him from his famous cousin, who after the fight, was called *Paugus John.* Why was the John Chamberlain of Lovewell's Fight called *Paugus John* from 1725 until his death in 1754—forty-four years before Elijah Russell's story was published? It could only occur because the story of his duel with Paugus was in circulation seventy-four-years before Elijah Russell published his story. If anyone knew the details of Lovewell's fight, it would be Souhegan John's wife Hannah whose father was killed in the battle, as was her uncle John Lovewell. Is it not reasonable to assume that she knew that Paugus John was so called because he shot Paugus? At a minimum, the 1898 analysis by George W. Chamberlain proves that the story of the Paugus-Chamberlain duel did not originate with Elijah Russell in 1799. We know that the legend began at least seventy years earlier. The following argument by the Chamberlain descendant that contradicts the claim that Wyman killed Paugus is equally convincing:

> "Why did not Wyman's neighbors accord that act (the killing of Paugus) to their own townsman who had received praise from the newspapers and a captains commission from the Commonwealth—but to John Chamberlain, a private? Why did not Sarah Wyman, the widow of Seth Wyman, in her petition to the Great and General Court in 1726, in giving the particulars of her husband's military record, incidentally refer to his Paugus combat if the ballad story were true?"

After weighing the fourteen scholarly pages of evidence presented in George W. Chamberlain's pamphlet against the contrary data of Eckstorm and others, the modern arbitrator, confronted with more than two hundred and seventy five years of tradition, is inclined to agree with the Paugus-Chamberlain tradition—it is simply too good a story to be discredited on circumstantial evidence. For the aficionados of the Chamberlain legend, however, there are other questions about the aftermath of the Paugus-Chamberlain duel. Those who insist that Chamberlain killed Paugus also tend to believe that Paugus's son did try to kill Chamberlain. In his report to the Maine Historical Society, George Chamberlain declined to challenge the critics of the other Chamberlain legends that had surfaced by 1898:

> "It is not claimed, however, that the other traditions relating to Chamberlain and the son of Paugus, and growing out of this one, are true; but the bottom fact that John Chamberlain shot the old Chief Paugus on the shore of Lovewell's Pond on that memorable May 8th,[51] 1725 must, in my opinion, await a more critical investigation before the honor can be consistently denied him."

Part of the folklore in connection with the Paugus-Chamberlain duel is the story of how Paugus' son traveled to Groton some years after *The Fight* to revenge his father's death. Through the years the folklore continued to accumulate new details like a snowball rolling down the side of a hill. There *is* a lot of evidence to show that the Indians were powerfully motivated by revenge. It appeared to be part of the code of behavior taught to young Indian braves as they were approaching manhood. Experience tells us that the code of taking revenge against enemies and wrongdoers is not unique to the Indians; one has only to take note of what goes on in the Mid-

---

[51]Authors' note: Note the incorrect date. Fanny Hardy Eckstorm did not write her expose on Parson Symmes's subterfuge until 1936, 38-years after Chamberlain's report to the Maine Historical Society.

dle East today to realize that the revenge motive runs deep in modern society among certain people.

John Chamberlain was the son of Thomas and Elizabeth Chamberlain of Chelmsford, where he was born March 29, 1692. The elder Chamberlain was a carpenter and miller who moved his family to Groton in 1699. He bought a mill situated on fifty acres of land "*at Baddacook by Browne Loafe Brooke, near Cow-pond Medow in Groton*". The man who would later be known as "Paugus John," lived at this farm from 1699 to 1729. At a town meeting in 1706, the townspeople designated Thomas Chamberlain's mill a garrison house to be used by the townspeople during Indian attacks. A fourteen-year-old lad at the time, John Chamberlain grew up virtually cradled by military tradition and frontier folklore. Although he had not been with Lovewell on his previous expeditions, he already had earned a formidable reputation as a fighter. Prior to his service with Lovewell, he was known to have had considerable contact with Indians during peaceful times. Charles James Fox, in his *History of the old Township of Dunstable,"*1846 related the following story about him:

> An Indian once called on Chamberlain at his sawmill, intending to way-lay him on his return homeward at nightfall, through the forest. It was time of peace, but Chamberlain suspected the character of his pretended friend, and the motive of his visit. While engaged in his work, he invited the Indian to examine the wheel pit, and seizing the opportunity, knocked him on the head with a handspike with no compunction.

It would appear from this story by Fox that Chamberlain had already earned a reputation as a man not to be trifled with, and it also bolsters the tradition that Chamberlain had dealings with Indians prior to his service with Lovewell. This in turn supports the legend that he knew Paugus prior to the fight at Fryeburg. It is the following story that captured the imagination of thousands, and has become an integral part of the folklore and legend of the period. Samuel A Green, M. D. described the famous sequel to the Paugus-Chamberlain duel in a book entitled *Groton during The Indian Wars, 1883:*

> The son of Paugus, after it had become a time of peace, went to Dunstable (Groton), to revenge his father's death, with the death of Chamberlain—He did not go directly to Chamberlain's but to the house of a neighbor, where he tarried several days, upon some pretended business, that his design might not be discovered; his errand was however suspected, and a hint given to Chamberlain—who cut a port-hole above his door, through which he very early one morning discovered an Indian behind his wood-pile, lying with his gun pointed directly to the door; and it was supposed that the same musket which had conveyed the means of death to the bosom of the great Paugus, also proved fatal to his son, as he was not afterwards heard of.
>
> It was also reported that Chamberlain (who was a stout and a courageous man, and who used to say that he was not to be killed by an Indian), that he was once fired at by an Indian, as he was at work in the saw mill at night; he was in a stooping position, and did not discover the Indian til he fired, who was so near him that he immediately knocked him down with a crowbar, with which he was setting his log.[52]

In spite of the massacre of the Norridgewalk Indians in 1724, and the devastating losses of the Pigwackets at Saco

---

[52]Authors' note: A great deal of early American folklore is built around legendary heroes who killed scores of Native Americans "with no compunction." Precisely because the Indians had no written language to record their own history, many early Americans wrote them off as sub-human. Can we not assume that they had some legitimate grievances against the whites? One can understand the hate that drove Paugus' son, but in regard to the two other nameless Indians, we never learn why they wanted to kill Chamberlain. Is it not reasonable to assume that Chamberlain may have wronged them in some way?

Pond in early 1725, the frontier settlements remained a dangerous place to live for early Americans. The powerful Penobscot tribe had consistently frustrated English attempts to destroy them by fading into the forest whenever the enemy came after them with superior force, but the relentless English pressure disrupted the whole rhythm of their semi-nomadic existence. Although they were unable to mount their earlier massive raids against the English, they continued to conduct a guerilla war against them. Reluctant to abandon their ancestral home and go to Canada, they fought on knowing in their hearts that they were doomed. After the English massacre of the Norridgewalk, the Penobscots began to send their emissaries to the other tribes in Eastern Maine to talk peace. The mission of Chief Powak together with his daughter and Little Elk to the upper Saco River were part of that search for peace. The Penobscot accepted the untimely death of their two braves, Powak and Little Elk philosophically. They understood that when the Pigwacket warriors ambushed the scalp hunters at Saco Pond, that there was no way the two Penobscot warriors could avoid the fight without being branded cowards. But the war had gone on long enough, and the Penobscot Indians were seeking a way out of the endless carnage. In those days, however, the procedure of arranging a truce was a long, tedious process.

During this period, there were Indian and French captives languishing in Boston prisons, as well as English men, women and children in Canada. In the summer of 1725, the English made a curious deal with two Indians they held in Boston. An Indian called Soccalexis was being held as a hostage to guarantee a previous agreement, and the other Indian, Nebine, was a prisoner. The authorities granted paroles to the pair with an odd provision that they had to return to Boston after visiting the Penobscot Indians and other Eastern Maine tribes. The English appeared to be sending out a peace feeler. After conferring with the council, the two paroled Indians found the Penobscot generally disposed to a new treaty of pacification. Then, after visiting some of the smaller tribes in Eastern Maine and finding them equally disposed to peace, the two Indians returned to Boston to report their findings to the English. Upon hearing the encouraging news, the authorities immediately put together an exploratory commission that was empowered to advance the peace process. The commission, which consisted of Colonel Walton of New Hampshire and Colonel Stoddard and a Mr. Wainwright of Massachusetts, went to Fort St. George in the company of Soccalexis and Nebine. After arriving at the English fort on July 2, 1725, the two Indians went out of the fort to deliver a message to the Penobscot chiefs, advising them that the three Englishmen had arrived.

Six days later the Penobscot chiefs appeared some distance from the fort carrying a truce flag. Captain Bean, an interpreter, went out to meet them. They gave him a letter from the Penobscot Sagamore Winnenimmit written in French that congratulated the English on coming on a design of peace. The letter further stated that the Penobscot elders earnestly desired to treat about peace providing they might do it safely, "*being under some fear and jealousy*." Their fear was well justified by an earlier episode during which the English had attempted to capture some of their members while treating under a truce flag. In the ensuing melee one of the Englishmen was killed and another was wounded. After being assured of peaceful English intentions, the Penobscot delegation asked the English party to wait until they rounded up their braves, who they said were out hunting.

After five days, seven more Indians came within a quarter mile of the fort bearing a truce flag. The English refused to go outside the fort to treat with them saying that they were only there to hear what the Indians might have to offer, but they added that the Indians would suffer no bodily harm if they did agree to come to the fort. The Indians eventually agreed to meet with them providing the English guaranteed their safety in the name of God. Presently, the Indians sent thirteen representatives into the English fort that was located near Bangor, Maine.

After the first formal exchange of compliments that assured their peaceful intentions, the English immediately put the

Indians on the defensive demanding to know—what the Indians had to offer— and why they were making war on the English. The Indians replied that they were making war because of English encroachment on their lands "*so far west as Cape Nawagen*" where they said two of their braves had been beaten to death by the English. The English replied that they had bought the land in question, and that they were prepared to show the deeds as proof. They acknowledged the beating death of the two braves, but they countered the Indian complaint by arguing that the Indians were supposed to make claims for such atrocities through official channels—not by going to war! The Penobscot chiefs, who seemed bent on peace at any price, told the English that they desired peace, and they promised to restrain their young braves from any further hostile acts. After Loran and Abenquid signed an agreement that called for a *Secession of Hostilities,* the meeting was adjourned. Surprisingly, the two chiefs agreed to accompany the three Englishmen to Boston to help further the quest for a treaty.

A careful examination of the numerous negotiations between the English and the Indians reveals certain recurring inequities. The treaties usually referred to "*the agreement and submission*" of the Eastern Abenaki Indians or whatever other tribe was involved. The language in the following submission treaty is typical:

> Whereas the several tribes of the Eastern Indians, viz. The Penobscot, Norridgewalk, Pigwacket and other tribes inhabiting his Majesties Territories of New England and Nova Scotia; HAVE contrary to the several treaties they have solemnly entered into with the said Governments, made an open Rupture, and have continued some years in Acts of Hostility against the Subjects of his Majesty KING GEORGE within the said Governments; they being now sensible of the Miseries and Troubles they have involved themselves in, and being desirous to be restored to his Majesty's Grace and Favour, and to live in Peace with all his Majesty's Gov-

> ernments of the Massachusetts Bay, New Hampshire and Nova Scotia, and that all former Acts of Injury be forgotten; HAVE concluded to make AND WE DO by these presents in the Name and Behalf of the said Tribes, MAKE our Submission unto His most Excellent Majesty GEORGE by the Grace Of God of Great Britain, France and Ireland, King Defender of the Faith, in as full and ample manner as any of our Predecessors have heretofore done.

The so-called treaties consisted mostly of Indian confessions of past sins and their solemn pledges to never do it again. Usually, the only commitment made by the English involved promises to build trading posts near the Indians that would provide trade goods at reasonable prices. Indian leaders affixed their totems to countless treaties having little understanding of the long-term implications. Many Indian leaders were either bribed or duped into selling large tracts of land to the English, while others succumbed to greed and sold their sacred lands for trinkets or rum. The inevitable disillusionment came when the English began to move onto these lands. That is when the trouble began. The historic record of their negotiations with the English suggests that the Indians were out of their league dealing with the English. They were like a bunch of grammar school kids trying to day-trade stocks with the pros; it was like stealing candy from a baby!

New Hampshire militiaman Samuel Penhallow, a contemporary and partisan historian of the period, was considered an authority on the Indian wars. In his *History of the Indians Wars* he describes how Loran and Abenquid were "friendly entertained" in Boston and were then transported back to Fort St. George in a vessel especially consigned to their convenience. The two chiefs left with a promise to return to Boston with other chiefs within forty days. Penhallow disclosed details of the debate that took place in the Boston Council during that 40-day delay. Certain members of the Council complained that the English were too eager for peace, and that they were conceding too much to the Indians. Others suggested that since they now knew the location of the Indian gardens and fishing places, that they should go and destroy their crops and disrupt their fisheries in order to make them more malleable to English demands. It appeared that diehards on the Council were not satisfied with the mere subjugation of the Indians; they were looking for an unconditional surrender.

In the meantime, the Penobscot chiefs were not having much success enforcing their end of the *Secession of Hostilities* agreement. The inability of the elders to control their militant young braves fit the historic pattern of their dealings with the whites. The native custom of training their young men to endure hardship, to scorn fear and to exalt valor, was a severe handicap during peace negotiations. There were always defiant warriors or renegade bands eager to bolster their reputation by performing bravely in raids against the English; these renegades were a constant hindrance to the peace process. Penhallow, whose writings reveal great bias towards the Indians wrote,

> Although the Penobscot Indians seemed guarantee for the other tribes, yet as we knew them treacherous, we could put no confidence in them, but rather lay ourselves open unto a snare, and become the more secure! Something like this according fell out; for on September 15th a party of them fell on some of Cocheco (Dover) while at work in the field, where they slew one, scalped another, cut off the head of a third, and carried a fourth captive; all which belonged to the family of the Evans.

There is a second account of this raid attributed to Belknap in a footnote of the Penhallow book. His graphic description is included here to show why the English hated the Indians. To understand the depth of their anger, one must take into account the fact that, by 1725, they had been living with Indian atrocities for fifty years.

> Belknap p. 80; The Indians had come down to Cocheco with a design to take the family of Hanson again. When they had come near the house, they observed some people at work in a neighboring field, by which it was necessary for them to pass, both in going and returning. This obliged them to alter their purpose and conceal themselves in a barn, till they were ready to attack them. Two women passed by the barn while they were in it, and had just reached the garrison as the guns were fired. They shot Benjamin Evans dead on the spot; wounded William Evans and cut his throat. John Evans received a slight wound in the breast, which bleeding plentifully, deceived them, and thinking him dead, they stripped and scalped him. He bore the painful operation without discovering any signs of life, though all the time in his perfect senses, and continued in the feigned appearance of death, till they turned him over, and struck him several blows with their guns, and left him for dead. After they were gone off, he rose and walked, naked and bloody, towards the garrison; but on meeting his friends by the way, dropped fainting on the ground, and being covered with a blanket, was conveyed to the house. He recovered and lived fifty years. A pursuit was made after the enemy, but they got off undiscovered, carrying with them Benjamin Evans, Jr. a lad of 13, to Canada, whence he was afterwards redeemed.

In other actions beginning a few days later, Indians attacked a garrison in North Yarmouth where, after being repulsed, they killed some cattle in the field before withdrawing. At Mowsum and at Damaris Cove east of Kennebec, they burned shallops owned by Stephen Hunuel and Alexander Soaper. They carried five men and a boy captive to Winnipesaukee where they killed one of the men and took the others to Canada. Since this raid took place two leagues within the cease-fire line, the Penobscot put the blame for the raid on the

St. Francis Indians. At the same time, the English had several search and destroy companies out at Ameriscoggin, Rockamagog and Norridgewalk. There were arguments about whether these areas were within the line that the Penobscot had agreed to, but as charges and counter charges went back and forth, the war continued unrestrained. On September 28, 1725, Captain Dwight sent out a six-man scouting party from Fort Dummer. They stopped to rest before heading back to the fort. The first hint of danger came with the sound of fourteen Indians running straight at them. The Indians killed two and took three captives, and one man later managed to escape.

The forty-day window given the Penobscots to bring the other tribes in for a parley had long expired, and the English were beginning to fear that the peace initiative by the Penobscots had been a ruse to cover their malicious intentions. Nevertheless, early in November, several Penobscot chiefs finally showed up in Falmouth (Portland) to negotiate the details of the treaty. They were Sauguaaram (Loron), Arexus, Francois-Xaviar, and Meganumba. Over the course of the next month, they negotiated a treaty that was called *The Submission and Agreement of the Representatives of the Eastern Indians.* On December 15, 1725, the treaty was executed in the presence of The General Assembly in Boston. The four Indian chiefs signed the official document by rendering line drawings of their clan totems on the treaty. For Sauguaaram alias Loron it was a beaver, and Arexus drew the crude outline of a bird in flight. Francois-Xavier made the outline of a turtle, and Meganumba drew a representation of a lobster for his signature. The treaty gave the English the right to freely develop the lands for which they had legal title, and it gave the Indians the right to live, hunt and fish on their own lands. A glaring defect in the treaty was that other hostile tribes such as the Norridgewalk, the Pigwacket, the Kennebec, and smaller tribes like the Anasaguntacook did not sign it. Notwithstanding the Penobscot assurances that their signatures guaranteed the compliance of the other tribes, the treaty was a document based on blind faith, particularly by the English. An additional provision inserted by the English called for the Penobscot Indians to send their young warriors to fight alongside English militiamen against those tribes who refused to abide by the terms of the treaty. In setting the date for the ratification of the treaty well forward into May of the following year, the English were allowing plenty of time for the Penobscot Indians to persuade the other tribes to join them in the ratification of the treaty. After a great deal of posturing and negotiation, Wenemovet arrived in Falmouth on the 30th of July, 1726, and the ratification of the treaty was concluded on August 6, 1726. The Penobscot Indians represented all the Eastern Tribes in signing the document. When the Lt. Governor asked Wenemovet why the other tribes were not present, he replied that the Penobscot had full power to act for the others including the Anasaguntacook and the St. Francis Indians. The exiled tribes sent two belts of wampum to the conference via the Penobscots. One was a gift to the Penobscots as a token of their appreciation for being included in the treaty, and the English Governor accepted the other wampum belt at the ratification treaty.

After the conference, a series of meetings was held with the Indians to discuss matters of mutual concern. The Indians made an urgent request of the English governor asking him to issue an order to all offshore vessels as well as all taverns that would prevent them from selling liquors to their young braves. The governor assured them that he sympathized with their request, and that he would do as they asked. At one juncture in the conference, the Lt. Governor told the Indians, "*Tomorrow is the Lord's Day, on which we do no business*" Loron, who was their principal speaker, responded readily saying, "*Tomorrow is our Sabbath Day; we also keep the Day.*"

Optimism about the treaty was fueled by the high hopes of the participants. Penhallow expressed wonder that so small a number of Indians should be able to distress a country so large and populous to the degree that he had related in his book. He put the cost of the three-year war at 250,000 pounds, and he estimated that at least one third of the Indian population had been destroyed. He expressed reservations that the peace treaty in itself was a guarantee of peace, warning that the greatest difficulty would be to support it and maintain it. He spoke of the importance of trading houses for the Indians. He prayed that they might be well regulated by the government, and that under God, they might be the means of tranquility, "*especially if the government can also prevail with them to receive the ministry for their instruction in the principles of the true religion.*" In reality, even the renowned Jesuits had been unable to eliminate native spiritual traditions. For Penhallow to hope that the Indians might renounce Catholicism *and* their native spirituality in order to embrace the Protestants faith was a forlorn hope.

The Lovewell survivors lost no time in petitioning the General Court to ask for compensation in consideration for their hazardous duty with Lovewell. Many of the petitions came from the dependents of men who had lost their lives. The requests for monetary assistance were invariably modest requests for help that were readily granted by the Governor, the Council and the State Representatives. Typical examples of these petitions are included with the profiles of Lovewell's men that are part of a later chapter. There were also petitions by groups of individuals who sought grants of land from the government as payment for their hazardous duty fighting the Indians. In their enthusiasm to reward the heroes of Lovewell's Fight with land grants, officials of the state sowed the seeds for a land controversy that came back to haunt them for more than twenty years. The voluminous details of the long legal wrangle between Massachusetts and New Hampshire over the *Penacook Grant*, the *Suncook Grant* and *Bow Township* go far beyond the scope of this book Nevertheless, a cursory examination of how the conflict evolved, and how it was ultimately resolved in 1741 by an English court, provides a fascinating glimpse into 18th Century power politics.

In 1725 Massachusetts approved a petition for a new township called Penacook; the location of the grant was of great concern to New Hampshire. The new grant, that was six miles wide, lay astraddle the Merrimack River beginning at the Contoocook River. This large block of territory extended south on both sides of the Merrimack for about nine miles. In 1727 David Melvin and William Ayer submitted another petition for themselves and other Lovewell men that sought to extend the Penacook grant further south to form an additional six-square-mile grant that was called Suncook. In 1728 Massachusetts approved the Suncook Grant even though the Penacook Grant had already been challenged by New Hampshire. The combined Penacook and Suncook grants extended from the Contoocook River in the north to the present town of Hooksett in the south. By the time the Suncook Grant was approved, Massachusetts and New Hampshire were already embroiled in an earlier legal battle over the ownership of the land covered by the Penacook Grant. Adding the Suncook Grant to the Penacook Grant merely turned up the intensity of the legal rhetoric. When the Penacook grantees had begun to run boundary lines in 1726, a committee sent by New Hampshire arrived to remonstrate with them and to inform them that the land was theirs, and that they intended to keep it. Despite this notice by New Hampshire, the Massachusetts committee and the grantees went forward with their plans, and they proceeded to divide and settle the Penacook Grant that same year.

In March of 1727, New Hampshire made its own grant to more than one hundred individual residents of Stratham and adjoining towns. The new *Township of Bow* covered eighty-one square miles in a nine-miles square tract. The footprint of this tract overlaid virtually all of the land within the Penacook and Suncook grants. This was an "in-your-face" move by the State of New Hampshire. The so-called *Bow Controversy* that followed was a boon to the solicitors of both Massachusetts and New Hampshire; their legal briefs filled the archives of both states with their mind numbing details.

A liberal interpretation of the original charter of the Massachusetts Bay Colony was at the root of the entire controversy. Early explorers of the New England coastline had only a rudimentary knowledge of the interior. In their explorations of the Merrimack River, they had failed to go beyond the Pawtucket Falls in Lowell. Consequently, early crude maps by the earliest cartographers depicted the Merrimack River originating from due west of its outlet to the ocean. They didn't know that the river made a right turn at Lowell and went due north. The original grantor of the Massachusetts charter drew its outline based on this incorrect geographical assumption. Nevertheless, Massachusetts lawyers continued to argue that the boundary between Massachusetts and New Hampshire began three miles north of the "black rocks" at the mouth of the Merrimack and that the boundary ran parallel to the river all the way up to the fork of the river above Franklin, NH and thence to a rock in the Piscataqua River. They claimed that the line ran due west from that rock to the province of New York. The lawyers insisted that Massachusetts owned all the land south of that imaginary line. After many failed attempts to resolve the dispute by representatives of the various American provinces, the matter was finally taken up by the King of England and his council in 1741. The controversy had finally been taken out of the provincial courts, and was turned over to "unbiased" arbitrators in England. The proceedings before the English court turned out to be a disaster for Massachusetts. A wily English agent for New Hampshire named Tomlinson, and the oratory of an English solicitor named Parris, proved to be the undoing of Massachusetts' ambitions. Parris described Massachusetts in scathing terms: it was *a vast, opulent, overgrown province*, and New Hampshire *was the poor, little, loyal, distressed province, ready to be devoured, and the King's own property and possession to be swallowed up by the boundless rapacity of the charter government"* Massachusetts didn't have a chance!

The British court declared the boundary between Massachusetts and New Hampshire to run as follows. Beginning three miles north of the black rocks at the mouth of the Merrimack, it followed the course of the Merrimack River to a point three miles due north of the Pawtucket Falls in Lowell. From that point the line ran west in a straight line to the Province of New York. The strip of land fourteen miles wide and fifty miles long that New Hampshire gained in the settlement was far more than she had argued for, and the controversy over the

Bow Township evaporated! The previously disputed land now lay within the province of New Hampshire. Having been split into two parts by the new boundary line, that portion of Dunstable that lay north of the line eventually became Nashua, NH. In 1759 sixty families from the former townships of Suncook, Bow and Buck-street were incorporated into the new town of Pembroke, N H. To compensate the Indian fighters for the loss of their township, Massachusetts made a new grant of land just north of Fryeburg, Maine that they named New Suncook. The New Suncook grant eventfully became known as Lovell, Maine.

The marathon battle between Lovewell's scalp hunters and the Paugus-led Pigwacket warriors proved to be a turning point in the First People's long struggle to hold on to their ancestral lands. Like the Norridgewalk, the Pigwacket Indians were left virtually defenseless by their latest encounter with the English. Unlike the early days when the frontier settlement lived in fear of their attacks, the Indians found themselves hard pressed to defend their villages, and now they were forced to flee their ancestral homes and seek refuge in Canada. And while Indian attacks would never again be launched from Pigwacket Valley, it was not yet the end of an era. In the broad historical context, the era of the Indians wars did not end until the *Treaty of Paris* in 1763. Other landmarks in the decline of French influence in Canada were the capture of the Louisbourg fort in 1758, Rogers' raid on the Saint Francis Indians in 1759, and the surrender of Quebec and Montreal to the British. Under the terms of the *Treaty of Paris*, France ceded all of its possessions in Canada and the West Indies to Great Britain.

For almost two score years Pigwacket Valley lay unclaimed by man; it reverted to a habitat for Mother Earth's creatures. The stockade surrounding the Indian village crumbled and moldered, and the interval cornfields lay fallow, the stray seeds of the maize and squash picked clean by foraging birds and animals. There were a few nostalgic visits by homesick Pigwacket Indians, but they did not linger. The event that marked the beginning of a new era in the valley was the arrival of white settlers to the valley in 1762. In that year Massachusetts made a grant to General Joseph Frye, who had a distinguished record as an Indian fighter in the French and Indian War and as a soldier in the Revolutionary War. Pigwacket was renamed Fryeburg to honor General Joseph Frye, the nephew of Chaplain Jonathan Frye.

In 1762 the general together with his friends and military associates established the first white settlement in the valley. Among the first settlers who made the difficult trek into the valley with General Frye were Nathaniel Smith, John Evans, Major Samuel Osgood, Squire Moses Ames, Jedediah Spring, Captain Timothy Walker, Colonel David Page, David Evans, Squire Nathaniel Merrill and Lieutenant Caleb Swan.

News of the remote valley and its rich farmland soon attracted others, and beginning in 1764, a group of pioneers arrived to settle the town of Conway, New Hampshire. Among the first pioneers who made the long trek from Concord, New Hampshire, were James and Benjamin Osgood, John Dolloff, Ebenezer Burbank, and Daniel Foster. Early efforts to farm the interval land along the Saco were often frustrated by devastating floods. The so-called "freshets" were caused by the spring runoff of melting snow in the mountains to the north and west of the valley. It was a problem that surely must have plagued the Indians during their long reign in the area. In 1812 a three-mile canal connecting several small ponds was dug to bypass thirty miles of the "old course" of the river. Today the "old course" exists as a mere shadow of its former self, an insignificant vestige that meanders through West Fryeburg, Fish Street and Fryeburg Harbor.

In the modern era, the Pigwacket name eventually faded to obsolescence. In its place, one often sees the name Pequawket displayed about the area. Fanny Hardy Eckstorm wrote that John Farmer initiated the spelling change when he edited a second edition of Belknap's work. According to her, the linguistics expert W. R. Gerard gave the meaning of Pequawket as "*a hole in the ground*," as opposed to Pigwacket that means "*punched up through ground.*"

Today the Conway-Fryeburg region is a favorite all-season destination for tourists and a variety of sports enthusiasts. The area has many quaint "Bed and Breakfast" establishments that seek to accommodate visiting skiers, canoeists, golfers, hikers, rock climbers, foliage lovers, and people who simply want to relax in the warm camaraderie of a small town atmosphere. Fryeburg Academy, that was chartered in 1792, is still widely known for it academic excellence. The renowned Fryeburg Fair, which was incorporated in 1851, is a yearly diversion for thousands of people. The fair grounds occupy the same general area where the Pigwacket Indian village once stood.

For the student of history, there are still reminders of the ancient race of people who lived in the area. The sweeping fields of corn one sees along the Saco River remind us of Indian women, their papoose strapped to cradle boards, tending the *Three Sisters* (corn, squash and beans) in these same fields. The small flotillas of canoes and kayaks on the river recall ancient scenes when fragile birch bark canoes plied these same waters, their high swept bows and their graceful lines skimming the surface like wind blown leaves in October. One can imagine a brave pointing with his paddle to the silhouette of Jockey Cap, thrust boldly into the blue sky and exclaiming.... Aho, Pigwacket! We are home!

CAPTAIN LOVEWELL'S WAR

Was fought between 1722 and 1725 against several tribes of eastern Indians. The principal campaigns took place in the Ossipee region and led to the eventual withdrawal of the Indians to the north. Commemorated in Colonial literature by "The Ballad of Lovewell's Fight."

7-1 Memorial Plaque, Ossipee, New Hampshire

7-2 Groton Historical Society stone
Memorial plaque, Ossipee, New Hampshire

CHAPTER 8

PROFILES AND BALLADS

They mind us of primeval years,
Of Indian war whoop, death and tears
--Caverly

The epic fight at Saco Pond profoundly moved the people of New England. Over the course of a single long day, all the pent up frustrations of troubled people, both red and white, had been vented in a way that gripped the public imagination. The episode contained all the elements of an epic—courage, heroism, endurance, inspiration and tragedy. The Yale historian, Francis Parkman, made the observation that Lovewell's Fight was long as famous in New England as Chevy Chase on the Scottish border. It is not surprising that the vivid images invoked by the fight inspired a series of poems and ballads that almost every child could recite, at least in part, in the 1800s.

For the survivors and their descendants, there was a justifiable pride in being able to say, *I was with Lovewell at Saco Pond,* or *my grandfather fought with Lovewell in Fryeburg.* An earlier chapter listed the names of the handful of men who seemed destined to share center stage on that fateful day. Because of the importance of the event, however, no single actor in the drama should be overlooked. Therefore, all forty-seven of the men in Lovewell's original company are listed here together with brief profiles. The names appear in the same order as their listing in the *New England Historical and Genealogical Register of 1909*. The listing sequence is a useful key for the reader. In the order named, the first 12 were killed and buried at the battle site; numbers 13 to 15 died during the retreat; 16-24 were wounded, but survived; 25 to 34 fought in the battle, but were not wounded; 35-44 were in the reserve force at the Ossipee fort; and 45-47 dropped out during the march to Pigwacket.

1. Captain John Lovewell, son of John and Anna (Hassell) Lovewell and grandson of John and Elizabeth (Sylvester) Lovewell was born in Dunstable October 24, 1691. The second marriage of his widow Hannah to Benjamin Smith of Merrimack came sometime after 1728. Lovewell's three surviving children were raised in Merrimack, New Hampshire. His wife's petition stated that she was unable to repay debts her husband had incurred recruiting his men without selling his estate. The court subsequently voted to give Colonel E Tyng the sum of 50 pounds to pay off Lovewell's debts. The total value of Lovewell's estate was valued at 444 pounds, 5 shillings, 6 pence.
2. Lieutenant Jonathan Robbins, the son of George and Alice Robbins, was born in Chelmsford November 19, 1686. He moved to Dunstable in 1710 and received his commission in 1724. He was with Lovewell on all three of his expeditions. After his marriage to Margaret Lund, daughter of Thomas Lund, they had five children. He is remembered for his heroic dying plea; to be left alone on the field of battle with a loaded gun in case the Indians came for his scalp. In 1729 his widow Margaret married William Shattuck of Groton. Their son Job Shattuck performed conspicuous service during the Revolution and was involved in Shay's Rebellion. She received a share of the 1500-pound payment to dependants. Robbins estate was valued at 50 pounds, 19 shillings.
3. John Harwood, son of William and Esther (Perry) Harwood, was born at Concord May 28, 1699. His family subsequently moved to Dunstable. He was listed as an ensign in Lovewell's third expedition. According to the NEHAGR (New England Historical and Genealogical

Register) there is no record of his marriage. He was killed in the initial onslaught. Several stanzas in the *Ballad of Lovewell* are devoted to his relationship with his wife and infant child.

4. Jacob Fullam was the only son of Major Francis and Sarah (Livermore) Fullam. He was born in Weston November 19, 1693. He was listed as a sergeant in the company. He was married in 1716 to Tabitha Whitney, daughter of Jonathan and Sarah (Hapgood) Whitney. He died on the field of battle after fighting bravely alongside Captain Lovewell. His widow married a second time in 1726 to George Parkhurst of Weston, and after his death, she married Samuel Hunt of Weston in 1736.
5. Robert Usher, the son of Robert and Sarah (Blanchard) Usher, was born in Dunstable in 1700. He was the maternal grandson of Deacon John Blanchard. He was mortally wounded in the fight and was left with Robbins on the field of battle when the survivors left. Colonel Tyng's men later buried him.
6. Jacob Farrar, the son of Jacob and Susannah (Reddit) Farrar, was born in Concord on October 23, 1693. He was married in 1714 to Sarah, the daughter of Josiah Wood by whom he had five children. He was mortally wounded in the fight and died about midnight on the field of battle. His widow's second marriage was to David Parlin of Concord in 1726. His brother Joseph survived the battle.
7. Josiah Davis, the son of Ebenezer and Dinah Davis was born February 24, 1705 in Concord. He was killed in the fight and was later buried on the field of battle. His badly wounded brother Eleazar Davis had to abandon the dying Farwell in the woods the day before reaching the fort at Ossipee. The brother Eleazer survived the fight.
8. Daniel Woods, the son of Nathaniel and Eleanor Woods, was born in Groton August 10, 1696. He was

not married. He was a brother of the Nathaniel Woods who was left in command of the fort in Ossipee. He was killed on the field of battle as was his cousin Thomas Woods.

9. Thomas Woods, the son of Thomas and Hannah (Whitney) Woods was born in Groton November 25, 1705. He was the youngest man in the company.
10. John Jefts, the son of John and Lydia Jefts, was born at Billerica December 19, 1696. He was one of the men who were killed in the first stage of the battle. His body was later found and buried by Colonel Tyng's men.
11. Ichabod Johnson, the son of Captain Edward and Sarah (Walker) Johnson was born in Woburn April 22, 1703. He was a cousin of Noah Johnson and of Josiah Johnson. He was killed and buried on the field of battle.
12. Jonathan Kittredge, the son of Dr. John and Hannah (French) Kittredge, was born in Billerica January 10, 1696. He was not married.
13. Lieutenant Josiah Farwell, the son of Henry and Susannah (Richardson) Farwell, was born in Chelmsford August 27, 1698. He was the sole survivor of the massacre at Thornton's Ferry in 1724. He was a member of all three Lovewell expeditions. He married Hannah Lovewell, a sister of Captain John Lovewell. Their daughter Hannah married "Souhegan John" Chamberlain, cousin of "Paugus John" Chamberlain. Eleazer Davis was forced to leave him within a day march to the Ossipee fort. His friends located his body by means of a handkerchief he had tied to a sapling. They buried his remains in the forest.
14. Jonathan Frye, the son of Captain James and Lydia (Osgood) Frye, was born in Andover in 1705 and graduated from Harvard College in 1723. He was chaplain of the company and took the first scalp. After fighting bravely in the engagement, he was wounded and died on the march to the Ossipee fort.

15. Elias Barron, the son of Ellis and Sarah (Ingersoll) Barron, was born in 1695. He married Priscilla Wilson by whom he had four children. He was seriously wounded in the fight and lost his way on the march to the Ossipee fort. His gun case was recovered on the bank of the Ossipee River, but his body was never recovered. His wife married a second time in 1729 to Jonathan Mead.
16. Noah Johnson, the son of William and Esther (Gardner) Johnson, was born in Woburn on February 2, 1699. He moved to Dunstable and enlisted from that town. He was severely wounded in the engagement and later received a pension. He was the only grantee of the New Suncook Township to move there. He revisited the site of the battle when he was 80 years old and he pointed out where various companions had died. His son Noah was a lieutenant and later a captain in Rogers' Rangers. The elder Noah never served in the military after 1725. Before his death in 1798, he was the oldest living survivor of the fight.
17. Timothy Richardson, the son of John and Susannah (Davis) Richardson, was born in Woburn July 24, 1687. He was married in 1717 to Abigail, daughter of Deacon Edward and Sarah (Walker) Johnson. He was partially incapacitated by his wounds for the rest of his life. He died in 1735. His widow married Daniel Gould in 1747.
18. Josiah Johnson, the son of Benjamin and Sarah (Walker) Johnson, was born in Woburn July 28, 1702. He and his wife Elizabeth had ten children. He was severely wounded in the fight and submitted several petitions to the General Court and was pensioned. He subsequently lived in Woburn and Billerica where he died in 1783.
19. Samuel Whiting, the son of Samuel and Elizabeth (Read) Whiting, was born at Dunstable October 22, 1697. In 1704 his father was captured and held by the Indians for eight years. He was wounded in the fight.

There is no public record of his marriage or surviving children.

20. John Chamberlain, the son of Thomas and Elizabeth (Hall) Chamberlain, was born in Chelmsford March 29, 1692. He enlisted from the town of Groton. He was married to Abigail, daughter of Thomas and Hannah (Whitney) Woods by whom he had six children. The legend of his duel with Chief Paugus is fully covered in the main text of the book. In the years following the fight he was known universally as "Paugus John"
21. Isaac Lakin, the son of William and Elizabeth Lakin, was born in Groton December 11, 1702. He married Elizabeth, daughter of John and Mary (Blood) Shattuck on January 21, 1725. He was wounded in the engagement but survived.
22. Eleazer Davis, the son of Ebenezer and Dinah Davis, was born in Concord March 4, 1702. He married Sarah, daughter of Joseph and Elizabeth (Tarbell) Davis in 1732. He was severely wounded in the fight and lost a thumb. The story of his lone survival in the woods is fully covered in the book. He received aid from the government "*on account of the wounds and smarts received at Lovewell's fight.*" He had six children by his wife Sarah and he died in 1747.
23. Josiah Jones, the son of Nathaniel and Mary (Reddit) Jones, was born in Concord January 19, 1702. During the retreat from the battle, he strayed from his companions and managed to make his way to Saco despite his serious wounds. Near death on his arrival, Doctor Allen nursed him back to health. He managed to reach his home in Concord in late June of 1725. He was disabled for the rest of his life, and received several pensions for his support, the last in 1739 two years before his death in 1741. He left a wife, Elizabeth, and three children.
24. Solomon Keyes, the son of Solomon and Mary, and grandson of Solomon and Frances (Grant) Keyes, was born in Chelmsford May 11, 1701. He married Sarah,

daughter of Ensign Jonathan and Rebecca (Parker) Danforth. The story of his miraculous escape from death in a canoe is fully covered in the main text of the story. In spite of being wounded three times in *The Fight*, he later served in the French and Indian War. He was killed at Lake George, September 8, 1758. A son was also killed in that war. Another son later fought in the Revolutionary War.

25. Seth Wyman, the son of Lieutenant Seth and Esther (Johnson) Wyman, was born in Woburn September 13, 1686. He married Sarah, daughter of Thomas Ross in 1715. He took over command of the company when all seemed lost, and he was given a captain's commission upon his return. After organizing a new expedition, he died from the effects of dysentery contracted during his expedition. He died September 5, 1725. He and his wife had five children.
26. Edward Linkfield married Hannah, daughter of John and Hannah (Parish) Goffe of Londonderry in 1723. He was not wounded in the battle. He and his wife Hannah had a son Benjamin who was indentured to Hon. Mathew Patten of Bedford. The indenture was surrendered in 1755. Subsequently the son lived in Chelmsford, Lancaster and Hinsdale, NH.
27. Thomas Richardson, the son of Samuel and Sarah (Howard) Richardson, was born in Woburn September 25, 1684. He married Rebecca, the daughter of Samuel and Rebecca (Johnson) Wyman. He fathered thirteen children. He was listed as a sergeant in the company, and he was not wounded. He died in Woburn in 1774.
28. David Melvin, the son of John and Hannah (Lewis) Melvin, was born in Charlestown October 29, 1690. His family moved to Concord in 1700. He was not wounded in the fight. Subsequently he was a captain with Col. Willard's regiment at Louisbourg. He was wounded at Louisbourg, and he succumbed to his wounds in Concord in 1743. He was married to Mary,

daughter of Jacob and Susannah (Reddit) Farrar and sister of Jacob Ferrar.

29. Eleazer Melvin, the son of John and Margaret (Shanesberg) Melvin and half brother of David Melvin, was born June 23, 1703, He served as a lieutenant with his brother Captain David Melvin at Louisbourg. He served as an officer in campaigns of the French and Indian War at Lunenburg, Northfield, Crown Point and Norridgewalk. He married Mary Stow, and he died in Concord in 1754.
30. Ebenezer Ayer, the son of Captain Samuel and Elizabeth (Tuttle) Ayer, was born in Haverhill February 18, 1705. In 1726 he married Susannah, daughter of Robert and Susanna (Atwood) Kimball. He was one of the nine men who were not wounded in the fight. He lived in that part of Haverhill that is now Salem, N. H. He died in Concord October 18, 1754.
31. Abiel Austin, the son of Thomas and Hannah (Foster) Austin, was born in Haverhill in 1703. In 1727 he married Sarah Moulton by whom he had ten children. He escaped wounds in the fight; Belknap's History of New Hampshire stated that he was still alive in 1790 and residing in Salem, N.H
32. Joseph Farrar, the son of George and Mary (Howe) Farrar, was born in Concord February 18, 1693. He was one of the nine fortunate men who were not wounded. He lived in Chelmsford where he died in 1733 leaving a widow Mary and five children.
33. Joseph Gilson, the son of Joseph and Hepsibah Gilson, was born in Groton in 1694. He fathered nine children by his wife Sarah. There is no record of his marriage. He was not wounded in the engagement.
34. Benjamin Hassell, the son of Joseph Hassell, was born in Dunstable August 9, 1701. He was the fourth generation of a family who had suffered greatly in the defense of Dunstable. His grandfather, Joseph Hassell, his grandmother Anna (Perry) Hassell, his uncle Benjamin

Hassell, and relatives Christopher Temple and Obadiah Perry were slain by the Indians in 1691. Although there is no record of his marriage, he had a daughter, Adah born in 1734. After leaving the field of battle without orders, he returned to Dunstable with the men from the fort. His neighbors eventually forgave his role in the battle. There is no record of his death.

35. Benjamin Kidder, the son of John and Lydia (Parker) Kidder, was born in Chelmsford, August 11, 1697. He married Sarah, daughter of John and Hannah (Parrish) Goffe. He was left in the care of Doctor Ayer at the Ossipee fort after becoming ill. He died in Bedford in 1746. His son Benjamin served as a drummer with Colonel Blanchard at Crown Point. In 1757, the son was captured at Fort William Henry and died a prisoner at Rochelle in France.
36. Doctor William Ayer, the son of Captain Samuel and Elizabeth (Tuttle) Ayer, was born in Haverhill February 6, 1702. He was the surgeon of the company who was one of the ten men left at the fort. He subsequently was a physician in Haverhill. He was married to Abigail Emerson and died before 1770.
37. Nathaniel Woods, the son of Nathaniel and Eleanor Woods, was born in Groton October 19, 1694. He was the sergeant in charge of the men left at the fort in Ossipee. He returned with the other men after they refused his command to stay at the fort. He married three times, and he died in 1766. His wife Alice survived him.
38. Zebadiah Austin, the son of Thomas and Hanna (Foster) Austin, was born in Haverhill about 1700. He married Sarah Gutterson in 1729. They had eight children. He was one of the ten men in the fort. He later settled in Methuen. There is no record of his death.
39. John Gilson, the son of John and Sarah Gilson, was born in Groton March 2, 1698. He married Mary, daughter of John and Mary (Blood) Shattuck in 1722.

He and his wife had nine children. He was one of the ten men in the fort. He died November 17, 1753.

40. John Goffe, the son of John and Hannah (Parish) Goffe, was born in Boston March 25, 1701. He married Hannah Griggs in 1702. He was one of the ten men in the fort. He later became a colonel, and had a distinguished record in the French and Indian War. He lived in Londonderry and Bedford and died October 20, 1788.
41. Isaac Whitney, the son of Jonathan and Sarah (Hapgood) Whitney, was born in Watertown in 1703. He enlisted from Concord and was one of the ten men in the fort. There is no record of a wife or children. He died in Concord in 1754.
42. Zachariah Parker, the son of Eleazer and Mary (Woods) Parker, was born in Groton January 29, 1699. When the names of Hassell and the ten men at the fort were first released in Chandler's Manchester in 1856, the name Zachariah Whitney and not Zachariah Parker was included. Since Parker was one of the grantees of the Suncook Grant, it can be assumed that he is correctly listed as one of Lovewell's company. There are no further details available about his marriage or when he died.
43. Ebenezer Halbert was a grantee of Suncook. He was one of the ten men in the fort. There are no further details available.
44. Edward Spooney was also a Suncook grantee that was among the ten men left at the fort. He and Halbert sold their grants in the township soon after it was awarded; there are no other details about his subsequent life.
45. William Cummings, the son of John and Elizabeth (Kinsley) Cummings, was born in Dunstable April 24, 1702. Early in the march near Contoocook an old wound became aggravated, and Lovewell sent him home in the company of his kinsman Jonathan Cummings. He was married to Sarah Harwood, sister to the

John Harwood who was killed in the fight. He was a deacon and town officer in Hudson and died in 1757.

46. Jonathan Cummings, the son of Deacon Thomas and Pricilla (Warner) Cummings was born in Dunstable July 3, 1703. He married Elizabeth, daughter of Captain Joseph Blanchard. Lovewell assigned him to accompany his cousin William Cummings to his home after a previous wound-disabled William Cummings. Both men were grantees of the Suncook Township.
47. Toby the Indian. In Symmes *Memoirs* he stated that Toby, after falling lame, was "*obliged to return with great reluctance.*" He was on the roll of the company, and he was given to a share in the Suncook grant. He sold his interest to Benjamin Gale of Haverhill. He was one of several "friendly Indians" who were often used as guides.

BALLADS AND POEMS

"Let me make the ballads of the people,
and I care not who makes the laws."
--Chatham

Although the ballads and poems inspired by Lovewell's Fight never gained much critical acclaim for technical merit, they successfully captured the heroic themes that stirred the imagination of folks in the 1800s. Poems, ballads and song lyrics are not always the best source for historic fact, and unfortunately much of the controversy over particulars of the epic fight originated with careless application of the facts in the stanzas and lyrics of poems and songs inspired by the event. Those who are easily stirred to tears by poignant melodies and insistent rhythms can fully appreciate their power to move mountains when mere words fail. The poems, songs and ballads inspired by Lovewell's Fight are presented here without comment:

According to Fanny Hardy Eckstorm, the Reverend Thomas Cogswell wrote this ballad in 1824. It is written in the style of the ancient Chevy Chase ballad. It was the most popular of the ballads and poems about Lovewell's fight, but the stanzas of the ballad contain a number of factual inaccuracies.

LOVEWELL'S FIGHT, a ballad

--Reverend Thomas Cogswell, 1824

What time the noble Lovewell came,
With fifty men from Dunstable,
The cruel Pequ't tribe to tame,
With arms and bloodshed terrible,

Then did the crimson streams that flowed
Seem like the water of the brook,
That brightly shine, that loudly dash,
Far down the cliffs of Agiochook.

With Lovewell brave, John Harwood came:
From wife and twin babes hard to part;
Young Harwood took her by the hand,
And bound the weeper to his heart.

"Repress that tear, my Mary dear,"
Said Harwood to his loving wife;
"It tries me hard to leave thee here,
and see in distant wood the strife."

"When gone, my Mary, think of me,
And pray to God that I may be
Such as one ought that lives for thee,
And come at last in victory."

Thus left young Harwood wife and babes;
With accent wild she bade adieu;

It grieved those lovers much to part,
 So fond and fair, so kind and true.

Seth Wyman who in Woburn lived,
 (A marksman he of courage true,)
Shot the first Indian who they saw;
 Sheer through his heart the bullet flew.

The savage had been seeking game,
 Two guns and eke a knife he bore,
And two black ducks were in his hand,
 He shrieked and fell to rise no more.

Anon there eighty Indians rose,
 Who'd hid themselves in ambush dread;
Their knives they shook, their guns they aimed,
 The famous Paugus at their head.

Good Heavens! They dance the Powow dance!
 What horrid yells the forests fill!
The grim bear crouches to his den,
 The eagle seeks the distant hill.

"What means this dance, this powow dance!"
 Stern Wyman said, with woundrous art;
He crept full near, his rifle aimed,
 And shot the leader through the heart.

John Lovewell, Captain of the band,
 His sword he waved that glittered bright;
For the last time he cheered his men,
 And led them onward to the fight.

"Fight on! Fight on!" Brave Lovewell said:
 "Fight on while Heaven shall give you breath!"
An Indian ball then pierced him through,
 And Lovewell closed his eyes in death.

John Farwell died, all bathed in blood,
When he had fought till set of day;
And many more, we may not name,
Fell in that bloody battle fray.

When news did come to Harwood's wife
That he with Lovewell fought and died,
Far in the wilds had given his life
Nor more would in their home abide,

Such grief did seize upon her mind,
Such sorrow filled her faithful breast,
On earth she ne'er found peace again,
But followed Harwood to his rest.

T'was Paugus led the Pequa't tribe;
As runs the fox would Paugus run;
As howls the wild wolf would he howl,
A huge bear skin had Paugus on.

But Chamberlain of Dunstable,
(One whom a savage ne'er shall slay,)
Met Paugus by the water side,
And shot him dead upon that day.

Good Heavens! Is this a time for prayer?
Is this a time to worship God?
When Lovewell's men are dying fast,
And Paugus' tribe hath felt the rod.

The Chaplain's name was Jonathan Frye;
In Andover his father dwelt;
And oft with Lovewell's men he prayed
Before the mortal wound he felt.

A man he was of comely form,

Polished and brave, well learned and kind;
Old Harvard's learned walls he left
Far in the wilds a grave to find.

Ah! now his blood red arm he lifts
His closing lids he tries to raise;
And speak once more before he dies,
In supplication and in praise.

He prays kind heaven to grant success,
Brave Lovewell's men to guide and bless,
And when they've shed their heart blood true
To raise them all to happiness.

"Come hither, Farwell" said young Frye;
"You see that I'm about to die;
Now for the love I bear to you,
When cold in death my bones shall lie;"

"Go thou and see my parents dear,
And tell them you stood by me here;
Console them when they cry, alas!
And wipe away the falling tear."

Lieutenant Farwell took his hand,
His arm around his neck he threw,
And said, "brave Chaplain I could wish
That heaven had made me die for you."

The Chaplain on kind Farwell's breast,
Bloody and languishing he fell;
Nor after this said more, but *this*,
"I love thee soldier; fare thee well!"

Ah! Many a wife shall rend her hair,
And many a child cry "woe is me!"
When messengers the news shall bear

Of Lovewell's dear bought victory.

With footsteps slow shall travelers go
Where Lovewell's pond shines clear and bright,
And mark the place where those are laid
Who fell in Lovewell's bloody fight.

Old men shall shake their head and say,
"Sad was the hour and terrible,
When Lovewell brave 'gainst Paugus went,
With fifty men from Dunstable."

The following lyrics were offered for sale within a few weeks of the actual fight at Saco Pond. Fanny Hardy Eckstorm wrote that the elder Benjamin Franklin, uncle to the famous philosopher and statesman, was probably the composer of the lyrics.

SONG OF LOVEWELL'S FIGHT

Of worthy Captain Lovewell I purpose now to sing,
How valiantly he served his country and his king;
He and his valiant soldiers did range the woods full wide,
And hardships they endured to quell the Indian's pride.

T'was nigh unto Pigwacket, on the eighth of May,
They spied a rebel Indian soon after break of day;
He on a bank was walking upon a neck of land,
Which leads into a pond, as we're made to understand.

Our men resolved to have him and traveled two miles round,
Until they met the Indian, who boldly stood his ground.
Then speaks up Captain Lovewell; "Take you good heed," say he:
This rogue is to decoy us, I very plainly see.

The Indians lie in ambush, in some place nigh at hand,
In order to surround us upon this neck of land;
Therefore we'll march in order, and each man leave his pack,
That we may briskly fight them when they shall us attack.

They come unto the Indian who did them thus defy:
As soon as they come nigh him, two guns he did let fly,
Which wounded Captain Lovewell, and likewise one man more;
But when this rogue was running, the laid him in his gore.

Then, having scalped the Indian, they went back to the spot
Where they had laid their packs down, but there they found them not;
For the Indians, having spied them when they them down did lay,
Did seize them for their plunder, and carry them away.

These rebels lay in ambush, this very place near by;
So that an English soldier did one of them espy,
And cried out, "Here's an Indian!" with that they started out
As fiercely as old lions, and hideously did shout.

With that our valiant English all gave a loud huzzah,
To show the rebel Indians they feared them not a straw:
So now the fight began as fiercely as could be;
The Indians ran up to them, but soon were forced to flee.

Then spake up Captain Lovewell when first the fight began:
"Fight on, my valiant heroes! You see they fall like rain:"
For, as we are informed, the Indians were so thick,
A man could scarcely fire a gun, and not some of them hit.

Then did the rebels try their best our soldiers to surround;
But they could not accomplish it, because there was a pond
To which our men our men retreated, and covered all the rear:
The rogues were forced to flee them, although they skulked for fear.

Two logs that were behind them so close together lay,
Without being discovered they could not get away;
Therefore out valiant English they traveled in a row,
And at a handsome distance, as they were wont to go.

T'was ten o'clock in the morning when first the fight began,
And fiercely did continue till the setting of the sun,
Excepting that the Indians, some hours before "twas night,
Drew off into the bushes, and ceased a while to fight.

But soon again returned in fierce and furious mood,
Shouting as in the morning, but yet not half so loud;
For, as we are informed, so thick and fast they fell,
Scarce twenty of their number at night did get home well.

And that our valiant English till midnight there did stay,
To see whether the rebels would have another fray;
But, they no more returning, they made off toward their home,
And brought away they're wounded as far as they could come.

Of all our valiant English there were but thirty-four,
And of the rebel Indians there were about fourscore:
And sixteen of our English did safely home return;
The rest were killed and wounded, for which we all must mourn.

Our worth Captain Lovewell among them there did die;
They killed Lieutenant Robbins, and wounded good young Frye,
Who was our English chaplain; he many Indians slew,
And some of them he scalped when bullets round him flew.

Young Fullam, too, I'll mention, because he fought so well;
Endeavoring to save a man, a sacrifice he fell:
And yet our valiant Englishmen in sight were ne'er dismayed,
But still they kept their motion, and Wyman captain made,

Who shot the old chief Paugus, which did the foe defeat;
Then set his men in order, and brought off the retreat;
And, braving many dangers and hardships by the way,
They safe arrived at Dunstable the thirteenth day of May.

The following elegy by Jonathan Frye's young sweetheart was panned as overly sentimental and cloying. One hopes that Susannah found a new love, married and had a good life. Any parent would be proud to have a thirteen-year-old daughter who harbored within her breast such tender sentiments:

THE MOURNFUL ELEGY
on MR. JONATHAN FREY

--by; Susanna Roger, age 13

Assist, ye muses; help my quill,
Which floods of tears does down distil;
Not from mine eyes alone, but, all
That hears the sad and doleful fall
Of that young student, Mr. Frye,
Who in his blooming youth did die.
Fighting for his dear country's good,
He lost his life and precious blood.
His father's only son was he;
His mother loved him tenderly:
And all that knew him loved him well;
For in bright parts he did excel
Most of his age; for he was young,—
Just entering on twenty-one.
A comely youth, and pious too:
This I affirm; for him I knew.
He served the Lord when he was young,
And ripe for Heaven was Jonathan.
But God did take him from us all,
And lament his doleful fall.
Where'er I go, I hear this cry,
Alas, alas good Mr. Frye!
Wounded and bleeding he was left,
And of all sustenance bereft,
Within the hunting desert great,
None to lament his dismal fate.
A sad reward, you'll say, for those
For whom he did his life expose.
He lifted out with courage bold,
And fought the Indians uncontrolled,
And many of his rebels slew
While bullets thick about him flew.
At last a fatal bullet came,

And wounded this young man of fame,
And pierced him through, and made him fall;
But he upon the Lord did call.
He prayed aloud; the standers by
Heard him for grace and mercy cry.
The Lord did hear, and raised him so,
That he enabled was to go.
For many days he homewards went,
Till he for food was almost spent;
Then to the standers be declared,
"Death did not find him unprepared."
And there they left him in the wood,
Some scores of miles from any food,
Wounded and famishing all alone,
None to relieve or hear his moan,
And there without all doubt did die.
And now I'll speak to Mr. Frye:
Pray, sir, be patient; kiss the rod;
Remember this the hand of God
Which has bereft you of your son—
Your dear and lovely Jonathan.
Although the Lord has taken now
Unto himself your son most dear,
Resign your will to God, and say,
"Tis God that gives and takes away:"
And blessed be his name; for he—
For he has caused this to be.
And now to you, his mother dear,
Be pleased my childish lines to hear:
Mother, refrain from flowing tears;
Your son is gone beyond your cares,
And safely lodged, in Heaven above,
With Christ, who was his joy and love;
And, in due time, I hope you'll be
With him in all eternity.
Pray madam, pardon this advice:
Your grief is great, mine not much less;

And, if these lines will comfort you,
I have my will. Farewell adieu!

In Frederick Kidder's second edition of the Reverend Symmes' *Memoirs* he states that Thomas C. Upham wrote the following poem after a visit to the site of the battle:

STANZAS BY THOMAS C. UPHAM

--New Hampshire poet, 1823

Ah! Where are the soldiers that fought here of yore?
The sod is upon them; they'll struggle no more.
The hatchet is fallen, the red man is low;
But near him reposed the arm of his foe.

The bugle is silent, the war-whoop is dead;
There's a murmur of waters and woods in their stead;
And the raven and owl chant a symphony drear,
From the dark-waving pines, o'er the combatant's bier.

The light of the sun has just sunk in the wave,
And a long time ago set the sun of the brave.
The waters complain as they roll o'er the stones,
And the rank grass encircles the few scattered bones.

The names of the fallen the traveler leaves
Cut out with his knife in the bark of the trees,
But little avail his affectionate arts;
For the names of the fallen are graved in our hearts.

The voice of the hunter is loud on the breeze;
There's a dashing of water, a rustling of trees:
E're the jangling of armor hath all passed away;
No rushing of life-blood is here seen to day!

The eye that was sparkling, no longer is bright;
The arm of the mighty, death conquered its might;

The bosoms that once for their country beat high,
To those bosoms the sods of the valley are nigh

Sleep soldiers of merit! Sleep, gallant of yore!
The hatchet is fallen, the struggle is o'er.
While the fir-tree is green, and the wind rolls a wave,
The teardrop shall brighten the turf of the brave.

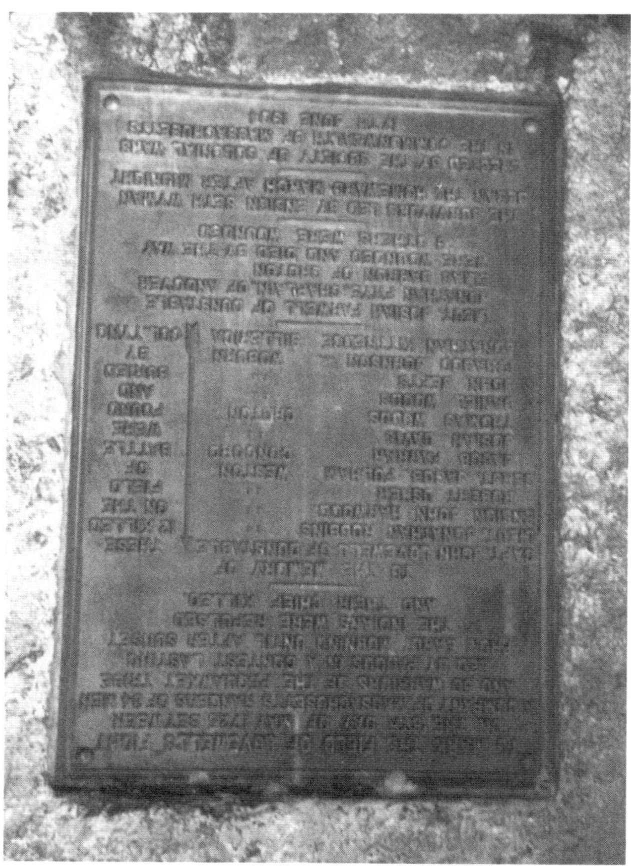

8-3 Battle Monument

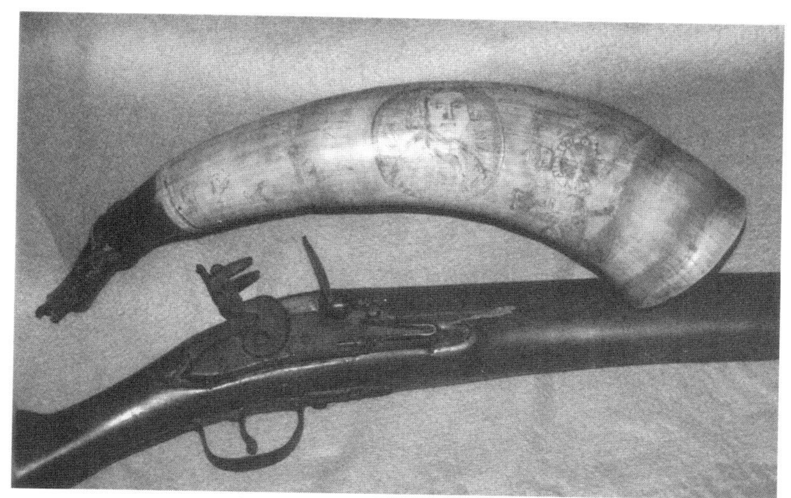

8-1 Nathan Cross musket

8-2 Fort Ticonderoga Rangers

CHAPTER 9

ROGERS' RAID ON ODANAK

We acknowledge no other land but your settlements,
wherever you have built; and we will not be content,
under any pretext, that you pass beyond them—
The lands we own have been given us by the Great Master of Life.
We acknowledge to hold only from him!

--Pigwacket Chief Adeawando
Address to the English at Quebec, 1752

Throughout the course of history, there have been leaders that have irresponsibly plunged their nation into war. They have often done so with little regard to the consequences of their reckless behavior. The refugees of such wars have often been treated as an annoying hindrance to running a war. The attitude always seems to have been—we're fighting a war—we'll worry about the refugees later. The resulting human flow of non-combatants seeking safe haven has always been a problem. The beginning of King Philip's War in 1675 marked the beginning the displacement of New England's indigenous population. During the eight decades of conflict that followed, many of the Native Americans were driven from their native land.

The English, after initially withstanding heavy losses, undertook counter measures that can only be described as ruthless. Their practice of hanging Metacom supporters and condemning others to Caribbean slave markets, as well as their decision to confine "*Praying Indians*" to Deer Island is described in the first chapter of this book. What is less generally known is that many women, children and elders of the Wampanoag, Narragansett, Pequot and other tribes fled their villages to seek refuge with the Penacook, the Cowasuck, the Ossippee and the Pigwacket Indians. At the same time, as the winds of war swept up the New England Coast into Maine, white settlers were forced to flee to Boston in order to escape French and Indian attacks on their villages. By the end of *Queen Anne's War* in 1713, the tide had turned in the English favor, and the pressure of their inexorable advance into native territory continued to create a huge refugee problem for the natives. Their only hope for survival was to seek the protection of sympathetic tribes who were outside the disputed territory.

By the late 1600s, Penacook refugees began to seek refuge with the Schaghticoke (Scaticook) Indians on the Hudson River in New York. The strange story of how Chief Paugus became a Scaticook Indian, and how the English unjustly imprisoned him and his family, has already been related in a chapter on the Pigwacket Indians. According to the historian Gordon Day, the Scaticook Village was a major refugee village in the late 1600s. Among the New England tribes which sought refuge with the Scaticook were the Norwattucks, Agawams, Woronocs, and Potumucks. During their time at the Scaticook refuge, the Mississquoi Chief Greylock recruited warriors from these tribes to help with his raids on the Western Massachusetts settlements of Northfield, Deerfield, Northhampton, Westfield and Rutland, Vermont. By the mid 1700s, however, the Scaticook Indians were forced to seek refuge at the Mississquoi Village in Swanton, Vermont and with the St. Francis Indians in Canada. This steady northward flow of Indian refugees was caused by the burgeoning power of the English, as well as the waning power of the Indians. By 1725, after the Norridgewalk massacre and after the bloodbath at Saco Pond, the French mission village of Saint Francis (Odanak) became an important refuge for New England Indians.

In *Expeditions of John Lovewell,* Frederic Kidder gave a few fascinating clues on the movements of the Pigwacket Indians after the 1725 battle at Saco Pond. Most of the tribe heeded their chief's counsel and followed him to Saint Francis where the other refugees readily accepted them. According to Kidder, the French Governor-General was impressed with Adeawando's diplomatic skills, and he eventually made him one of his favorite advisors. But not all members of the tribe became permanent residents of Odanak. As many as two-dozen dissatisfied Pigwackets returned to their valley after the submission treaty was signed in 1726. Although their whereabouts was not accounted for between 1726 and 1745, there was a reference to a small contingent in a July 9, 1749 entry in the Reverend Smith's journal:

> Several gentlemen (Englishmen) are with the Mohawks, down at St. Georges, treating with the Penobscot Indians about peace. About twenty Saco Indians are in Boston pretending to live with us. In confirmation of this, we find, that, at the treaty of Falmouth in 1749, the Pigwacket Indians are named as being present; but it was decided by the commissioners, that, as they had not been engaged in the war, it was not necessary that they should join in the treaty.

Reverend Smith's letter referred to English and French negotiations at Fort St. George near Bangor, Maine in which a prisoner exchange was being discussed. The letter provided documentary evidence that a few peaceful Pigwackets were living in Massachusetts! A second letter in Kidder's book provided additional proof of the existence of a small band of "peaceful" Pigwackets. It was written by Jacob Wendell, a resident of Boston, but dated New York, 1749. The letter states in part:

> In the beginning of the war with France (1745), some men, women, and children, of a tribe called by us Pigwacket, came to a fort near where they lived, and desired that they might live among the English; for that they desired they might not be concerned in the war; and they lived some time at the fort; but, when war was proclaimed against the Eastern Indians, they were

brought up to Boston, where good care was taken of them by the Government, a suitable place, about fifty miles from Boston, provided for them to live at, where there was good fishing and fowling, and their clothing, and what else they wanted, provided for them by the Government. On the application, this summer, of the Eastern Indians to Governor Shirley for peace, and the messengers promised to call in all the heads of the tribes concerned with them in the war, it was concluded by the Governor, if these Pigwacket Indians desire it, they should go down there; and I am informed by Mr. Boylston, who left Boston some time after me, that he saw those Indians there, and the Commissary General told him he had orders to provide for and send them all down to Casco Bay, where the treaty was appointed; that, I believe, the account thereof may be sent to Canada before now, and the St. Francois satisfied. Thus I have given your Excellency a true account of these Indians; and hope, when the (Canadian) Governor-General has it sent him, he will send home the poor (English) prisoners belonging to this as well as to the neighboring Provinces.

This correspondence referred to negotiations the English were conducting in Quebec with Adeawando and his French sponsors over the release of English prisoners held in Odanak. Adeawando apparently knew about the breakaway band of Pigwackets who were wards of the English. His claim that the English detained this small band of Pigwackets was incorrect. A previous letter from La Jonquiere to Lt. Gov. Phipps stated that the Odanak Pigwackets were infuriated that a band of twenty-six members of their tribe were being held prisoner on an island near Boston. Jacob Wendell's letter was sent to the English negotiators to enable them to counter Adeawando's false accusation that the twenty-eight Pigwackets in Boston were English prisoners.

After peace was declared, this small band returned to Pigwacket Valley. The historian Douglass reported in 1750 seeing small bands of Pigwacket Indians at Ossipee and Fryeburg that included twelve fighting braves. He added that they often traveled to Canada by way of the Connecticut River. The reference to their trips to Canada is a clear indication that this small band of neutral Pigwackets continued to enjoy friendly relations with their more militant relatives.

According to Kidder, this small band went to live at the headwaters of the Connecticut River after the *Treaty of Paris* was signed. At the beginning of the Revolutionary War, certain members of this band petitioned Massachusetts for guns, blankets, and ammunition for thirteen men who volunteered to serve "*on the patriot's side*." The Pigwacket volunteers who fought alongside their former enemies were subsequently rewarded for their service. Early white settlers to Fryeburg recalled Pigwacket elders who lingered in the area; Kidder recalled the names: *Old Philip, Tom Hegon and Swarson*. For these elders, nothing could replace the beauty of their mountain-girded-valley. They clung to their birthright knowing that, when *Brother Owl* came to call their name, the moccasin tracks of their ancestors would mark their trail to the other side.

Over the course of our long narrative about the *Pigwackets,* our focus has been inexorably drawn towards their final destination. In Odanak (*Place of pines*), their identity has merged with the descendants of the many other Indian cultures that call Odanak their home. Odanak is only one of several Abenaki reservations located in Canada and in the United States. A second Abenaki community called Becancour (formerly Wolinak) is located on the south shore of the Saint Lawrence River, about 20 kilometers southeast of Trois Rivieres. The original refugees first lived at a Catholic Mission in Sillery, and they were later given a parcel of land in the "Seigneury de Becancour" that was a gift from the "Seigneur de Portneuf." Becancour has a population of 212 people with approximately 75 actual residents on the reserve. It is administered by the Conseil de bande des Abenakis de Wolinak under the direction of Chief Bernard.

The Abenaki community of Odanak is located on a low bluff beside the Saint Francis River about three miles from its confluence with the Saint Lawrence River. The first Abenaki refugees arrived in Quebec in the mid-1600s. They lived for a time in Sillery, and they later settled near the Chaudiere River. A previous chapter called, *New France,* describes the system by which seigniors (land grants) were awarded to titled people as part of a development program for the New World. A woman named Marguerite Hertel[53] ceded part of her Quebec seigneur to the *Saint Francois Seigneury* where the village of *Saint Francois-du-Lac* is presently located. In 1918 the Abenaki village of *Pierreville*, formerly called the *Indian Reserve*, and later the *Indian Village*, eventually became known as *Odanak* after the local post office was opened.

A sign at the entrance to the reserve advises the visitor that he or she is entering an official Abenaki Indian Reservation, but apart from that, the reservation appears to be a contiguous part of the small community of Pierreville. It is a village of modest homes located in an area that seems chiefly devoted to farming. Inside the reserve, amidst a grove of old trees, a line of carved totem poles along the outer wall of a large building invites closer inspection. For a modest fee, one can spend a fascinating hour or more viewing the exhibits, and marveling at the ability of *The Original People* to live entirely off the natural materials provided by *Mother Earth*. Facing the museum, on the other side of a gravel courtyard under towering trees, is the Mission Church. This too is open to visitors, and the sight of walls covered by woodcarvings that depict the Abenaki cul-

---

[53]Authors' note: The Hertel name was prominent among the names of French officers and soldiers who engaged in the long series of raids against New England settlements. In 1704 Hertel de Roueville together with his four brothers were part of a company of 50 Canadians and 200 Abenaki and Caughnawaga Indians who burned the town of Deerfield, MA. In this midwinter raid they killed 53 and carried 111 men, women and children to captivity in Canada.

ture rewards the curiosity of the venturesome. Earlier church dogma prohibited such ornamentation until Vatican 11 validated the use of local culture and art in Catholic churches. The present Mission Church was built to replace a church burned down by Major Robert Rogers and his raiders in 1759. The town, the museum, the mission church, and the friendly people provide a warm ambience that insures a pleasant visit. For Anglo visitors who might expect to encounter an alien people, it will be a pleasant surprise to discover that Indians are ordinary people—exactly like themselves! The only difference is that they are the descendants of a race of people who came to this continent more than 10,000 years ago!

There are 1,675 people in Odanak with approximately 295 residents on the actual territory of the reserve. Many Abenakis live outside the reserve in neighboring Pierreville. The reserve is administered by the Conseil de bande d'Odanak under the direction of Chief Gilles O'Bomsawin. The tribal council that he heads is part of the Grand Conseil de la Nation Waban-Aki. Twenty-five or more residents of the reserve work in the community under the direction of Chief O'Bomsawin and his council.[54] Forestry plays an important role in the local economy, and the community is well known for it arts and handi-

---

[54]Authors' note: The authors visited Odanak in early October of 2001. We toured the museum and church and conferred with Rejean O'Bomsawin, historian and museum curator. In response to our inquiries about native crafts, he arranged for us to observe a group of Abenaki men making basket "splints" in the ancient way. The raw material was a 12 foot black ash log supported by two short cross logs. Two men wielding the blunt end of axes faced each other and applied alternating blows along the water soaked log in a continuous blur of motion—it was an exquisite demonstration of human skill and dexterity! After scoring a 3-inch wide section, they pried several growth layers off the log, and they meticulously split and separated each year's growth one from the other to obtain the thin splints used in native baskets. The Council distributes these splints to native basket makers in the reserve; they size them and dye them according to their own needs. The workers were amused by our reaction to their "axe ballet"... One young man who spoke English shrugged his shoulders and said, "We've done it that way for thousands of years."

craft production. Individuals in the community do most of the native handicraft work in their homes. In addition to these mainstays, there are residents involved in the manufacture of clothing and furniture. Commercial food distribution and construction is part of the local economy as well.

There are no schools in the quiet community of one hundred eighty four homes, but approximately fifty pre-school, primary and secondary pupils attend schools under the jurisdiction of the Quebec Ministry of Education. There are also sixty residents of the community that attend post-secondary study programs at the university level.

Police service for the village is provided by the Amerindian Police. Drinking water, fire protection and garbage collection are provided by the inter-municipal public service department of Pierreville-Saint-Francois-du-Lac. Odanak has its own sewage system, storm-drain network, and a water treatment basin. Electricity for the village is provided by Hydro Quebec. The Band Council manages a community health care center through an arrangement with Health Canada. Residents also have access to provincial hospitals and other medical services. In addition to the museum and mission church, the community has a community center, a library, and a recreational center. To the casual observer, there is little about the general appearance of the village to distinguish it from other small Canadian towns that dot the landscape of lower Quebec. Its uniqueness lies in the history of its people, and the dark memory of the raid by Rogers' Rangers in 1759.

Major Robert Rogers

The controversial man who is generally credited with forming the first American Ranger units had a unique talent for attracting the limelight. At the same time, his legacy is tainted by the unsavory reputation he earned after his meritorious service in the *French and Indian War*. It is difficult to find an historic figure that has lived a completely exemplary life. Even our greatest heroes are known to have suffered character defects that would doom an ordinary man to the historic dustbin. There are celebrities, however, that because of the limited recall of the public, or through the skillful efforts of image-makers, manage to shake off past scandals and emerge as heroes. Major Robert Rogers is a perfect example of a flawed historic figure whose reputation and image have improved with the passage of time. Despite the sordid record of his civilian life, no one can deny the special skills, energy and courage he demonstrated as a ranger fighting for his country during the Seven Year War—he was a man made for the times.

He was born in Methuen, Massachusetts in 1731, and the dense forests that lay between the frontier settlements and Indian Territory was his early playground. He was a loner who appeared to shun the normal pursuits of his teenage contemporaries. He was an avid hunter who had an intimate knowledge of the trails, waterways, and canoe carryover points between the rivers and streams of New England. He grew up during a period of uneasy peace with the Indians, and he spent a great deal of time in the woods with French and Indian trappers and woodsmen. He not only developed a rudimentary understanding of the Algonquian and French languages, but he readily absorbed the essential fine points of operating in the forest unseen and unheard by the enemy.

As early as 1746, the nineteen-year-old Rogers was undertaking scouting missions in the Merrimack Valley for the local militia, and three years later, he was scouting for Captain Ebenezer Eastman in northern New Hampshire. During this period, he became so enamored with the romantic notion of living in the forest like an Indian that he had no time for the ordinary pursuits of his age group. By 1753 he had built a solid standing as a scout, and he loved the attention his reputation brought him. Whether he knew it or not, the skills he attained as a boy were exactly the singular skills needed for the war that loomed on the horizon. The war that was called the *French and Indian War* on the North American continent was known as the *Seven Year War* in Europe.

The national interests of France and Great Britain placed them on a collision course. They had waged war against one another for fourteen of the preceding forty-five years, and now, after less than six years of peace, incompatible territorial claims put them on an unavoidable path to war once again. England claimed all the land from Newfoundland to Florida, as well as all of the territory between those two points and the Pacific Ocean. France claimed Canada as well as a portion of New England and New York in addition to the entire territory of the Ohio and Mississippi River basins including New Orleans. Like a forest lynx marking its territory with its scent, France built a series of forts from the mouth of the St. Lawrence River to Montreal and Lake Champlain, continuing west to Detroit, and from there down the Ohio and Mississippi Rivers to New Orleans. The two adversaries were like two pits bulls glaring at each other in a fighting arena, each daring the other to attack. Viewed from their relative impact on world history, the previous wars between 1675 and 1726 were mere skirmishes before a major conflict. The winner of this new conflict would control the entire North American continent, and the overseas empire of the loser would be virtually bankrupt. Only an incident was needed to begin the contest, and the French takeover of a new English fort on the Ohio River in 1754 provided that spark.

The twenty-four-year old Robert Rogers was already a veteran when the French and Indian War began in 1755. The traditional training of the British regulars sent to this continent rendered them virtually useless against the French coureurs-de-bois (wood runners) and their Indian allies. The English needed small companies of "*watch and ward*" woodsmen to scout for enemy activity and to warn the frontier settlements of impending raids by the Indians. In this era the raids were coming from Crown Point at Lake Champlain and Odanak in Quebec. If these scouts were able to attack provision supply trains headed to the French forts, or if they could conduct lightening raids on French outposts, that was all the better. By the time the British were ready to begin major assaults on the French Forts, the

State of New Hampshire had a full regiment of "Rangers" that had been handpicked and trained by Rogers.

Rogers' Rangers, as they were called, wore distinctive green uniforms and dashing green berets that set them apart from the English regulars. There was no love lost between the British regulars and the unconventional Ranger units. The official "*Standing Orders for Rogers' Rangers*" were a radical departure from conventional rules of engagement, and the performance of his units in the field was impressive. It is generally conceded that Rogers' original units were the forerunners of today's elite military units that go by such names as Seals, Rangers and Special Services units. The basic tenants of *Rogers' Standing Orders* have survived the years, although they have been edited to reflect an abbreviated, modern version:

1. Don't forget anything.
2. Have your musket clean as a whistle, hatchet scoured, sixty rounds powder and ball, and be ready to march at a minute's notice.
3. When you're on the march, act the way you would if you were sneaking up on a deer. See the enemy first.
4. Tell the truth about what you see and what you do. There is an army depending on us for correct information. You can lie all you please when you tell other folks about the Rangers, but never lie to a Ranger or officer.
5. Never take a chance when you don't have to.
6. When we're on the march we march single file, far enough apart so one shot can't go through two men.
7. If we strike swamps, or soft ground, we spread out abreast, so it's hard to track us.
8. When we march, we keep moving till dark, so as to give the enemy the least possible chance at us.
9. When we camp, half the party stays awake while the other half sleeps.

10. If we take prisoners, we keep 'em separate till we have had time to examine them, so they can't cook up a story between them.
11. Never march home the same way. Take a different route so you won't be ambushed.
12. No matter whether we travel in big parties or little ones, each party has to keep a scout twenty yards ahead, twenty yards on each flank, and twenty yards in the rear, so the main body can't be surprised and wiped out.
13. Every night you'll be told where to meet if surrounded by a superior force.
14. Don't sleep beyond dawn. Dawn is when the French and Indians attack.
15. Don't sit down to eat without posting sentries.
16. Don't cross a river by a regular ford.
17. If somebody's trailing you, make a circle, come back onto your own tracks, and ambush the folks that aim to ambush you.
18. Don't stand up when the enemy is coming against you. Kneel down. Hide behind a tree.
19. Let the enemy come till he's almost close enough to touch. Then let him have it and jump out and finish up with your hatchet.

There were hints of character deficiencies early in Rogers' career. A vague reference was made to his brush with the law on counterfeiting charges. Although the charges appear to have been glossed over in the excitement over his daring achievements in the field, the incident was a portent of things to come. In 1756 Major General Shirley awarded him an unusual honor in Boston when he made Rogers the captain of an independent company of *King's Rangers* that would be on the payroll of the British monarch. Rogers' *Provincial Ranger Company* was one of the King's personal units. This unit was the beginning of the famous corps that later became the famed "Rogers' Rangers." Within a year, nine more companies were added, and Rogers was made "*Major of Rangers*." He and his Rangers were posted to Fort Edwards that was located on the Hudson River below Lake George. He operated out of that base for the remainder of the *Seven Year War.* . Before examining Rogers' famous raid on the mission village at Odanak, it will be useful to describe one of his earlier raids into enemy territory in order to illustrate why he was so admired by the Provincial as well as the British public.

In January 1757, Rogers and seventy-five rangers went north on Lake George traveling on ice skates; at certain intervals they went overland by snowshoe. They were assigned a mission to reconnoiter the French forts at Ticonderoga and Crown Point. Six days out of Fort Edwards, at a point midway between Ticonderoga and Crown Point, they ran upon a train of sledges that were heading south out of Canada. The sledges were loaded with provisions destined for the French forts. In the short engagement that followed, the rangers managed to capture three of the sledges as well as seven men and six horses. Several Frenchmen, however, managed to elude the rangers and make their way to Fort Ticonderoga. Realizing that the garrison would soon learn of their presence, Rogers wisely decided to head for his home base. About two o'clock in the afternoon, a force of two hundred and fifty French soldiers and Indians attempted to surround Rogers and his rangers. During the fight, Rogers was wounded twice, and by nightfall, he had lost twenty of his Rangers to enemy fire. A later report on the action confirmed that the French had lost one hundred and sixteen men in the encounter. With French reinforcements close at hand at the fort, Rogers knew the odds were against him, and he executed a hasty retreat back to Ft. Edward during the night.

His numerous escapes from perilous situations earned him a legendary image that he later exploited to the hilt. On one occasion he was pursued by a large body of Indians up a mountain near the southern tip of Lake George. The summit of the mountain that presently bears his name has a crag on the east side that drops precipitously five hundred feet to the lake. The legend claimed that Rogers walked and slide backwards down the sheer face of the precipice to the lake. Upon tracking him to the spot, the Indians saw two sets of tracks that appeared to lead to the summit from two different directions. Spying the figure of Rogers far below on the surface of the lake, the Indians were said to have attributed his miraculous escape to the will of the Great Spirit, and they abandoned the chase—Such was the Rogers legend! He and his Rangers were in the thick of things for the duration of the war. They were with General James Wolfe in his expedition to Quebec, and they were in the Montreal campaign of 1760. After Vaudreuil surrendered Montreal, General Jeffrey Amherst ordered Rogers and his men west to take possession of the northwestern outposts. Rogers' Rangers also placed a role in *Pontiac's War* (1763-1764), and they were in the *Battle of Bloody Bridge.*

By the summer of 1759, the French were on the ropes. They had abandoned Ticonderoga and Crown Point in July, Fort Niagara surrendered later that month, and Quebec capitulated in September of that same year. After the surrender of Crown Point, the new British commander sent a messenger under a truce flag to make a proposal of peace to the Saint Francis Indians. On the 13th of September, it was learned that the messenger had been taken prisoner and subjected to a great deal of abuse. This insulting act was the final straw for General Jeffrey Amherst. The presence of Rogers and his Rangers at the fort gave Amherst the idea to vent his anger through them. He immediately sent an orderly to Rogers carrying a message for a special mission:

> You are this night to take a detachment of two hundred picked Rangers and proceed to attack the enemy at the settlements of the St. Francis Indians, on the south side of the St. Lawrence River, in such manner as shall most effectively disgrace and injure the enemy and redound to the honor and success of His Majesty's arms. Remember the barbarities committed by the enemy's Indian scoundrels on every occasion where they have had an opportunity of showing their infamous cruelties toward his Majesty's subjects. Take your revenge, but

> remember that although the villains have promiscuously murdered women and children of all ages, it is my order that no women of children should be killed or hurt. When you have performed this service you will again join the army, wherever it may be.
>
> Yours, etc
> Jeffrey Amherst

Rogers followed the general's order at once drawing provisions, powder and ball from the Crown Point commissary, and embarking two hundred of his Rangers in bateaus who began to paddle north on Lake Champlain that very night. They were headed for Mississquoi Bay a distance of almost 100 miles. A more superstitious man might have delayed his departure until after midnight, but not Rogers—the date was September 13, 1759. For the glory seeking Rogers, this was a dream mission. His Rangers faced a long march through enemy territory with virtually no prospect of reinforcements should they encounter trouble. While they were encamped for the night on the 5th day, a keg of gunpowder exploded wounding Captain Williams and several other men who required an escort to make it back to Crown Point. Worse still, the boom of the explosion carried all over the north end of the lake. Undeterred by the mishap, Rogers ordered the reduced force of one hundred forty two men to continue towards Mississquoi Bay. Although the accident had occurred on the fifth day, they managed to reach the head of the lake on the 10th day without being spotted. After hiding the boats up a creek beneath overhanging branches that lined the bank, he left two trusted Indians instructing them to follow his trail and warn him in the event the enemy discovered the concealed bateaus. In accordance with his own standing order to never follow known trails, Rogers avoided the more obvious trail along the Yamaska River.

In the evening of the second day, the two Indians arrived in camp bearing the alarming news that the French had discovered their boats! The enemy force had confiscated the bateaus and provisions, and they had spirited them away under a separate guard; the main enemy force of three hundred fifty French and Indians was in full pursuit of Rogers and his company! A less daring commander would have ordered a retreat, but not Rogers; he was a man who loved challenging situations, and he needed a new triumph like a junkie craves a fix. He convinced his men that they could outdistance the enemy, and that they could still complete their mission and get back without being attacked by the pursuing force. He dispatched ten men to Crown Point with Lieutenant McMillan to apprise General Amherst of the circumstances, and to request that a relief party with extra provisions be sent from Fort 4 at Charlestown, NH up the Connecticut River to the mouth of the Ammonoosuc River near the Coos Meadows. His written request to General Amherst closed with the laconic comment, "*We will be returning that way, if we ever return at all.*"

The raiding party spent nine days marching through the knee-deep water of a vast spruce swamp. At night they contrived to sleep by fashioning crude hammocks out of piles of spruce bows they cut in the forest. Miraculously, they managed to reach their target undetected. Twenty-two day after departing Crown Point they reached the Saint Francis River. According to oral Indian tradition, Rogers and his men forded the river from the left bank to the right bank at a basin nine miles above Odanak, and they camped in a ravine less than 1 ½ miles above the unsuspecting village. To ford the swift moving river, they had to form a human chain with the tallest man upstream and let the tail end of the chain gain the opposite bank downstream. Historical records do not reveal how they managed to execute this maneuver without getting their gunpowder soaked. They had to dive and retrieve a few muskets that were lost in the crossing.

Late on the 22nd day, a scout climbed a tree and reported seeing the village in the distance. Soon after dark, Rogers went forward with Lieutenant Turner and Ensign Avery to reconnoiter the village. A celebration was in full progress at the Indian village, and the rhythmic beat of drums and the chanting of singers were clearly audible in the crisp fall air. The celebration of a wedding, or possibly a harvest dance, lasted well into the night, and many villagers had gone down to the river to sleep. A goodly number of the braves were away on a hunting trip, so many of the revelers were elders, women and children. Rogers and his two companions rejoined the main force about 2 a.m., and after briefing his troop of Rangers, he had the entire force move forward to within three hundred yards of the village. The men shed their packs and squatted or sat resting, the murmur of their low voices muffled by the sounds of the festival. By 4 a.m. the villagers had all returned to their cabins, and a brooding silence settled over the village. The rangers, having been split into three companies, were now positioned to attack the village from three different directions simultaneously. Meanwhile, the slumbering natives reposed in the cross hairs of Rogers' design, oblivious to the impending terror.

With the first hint of light on the eastern horizon, Rogers ordered the assault, and the three companies fell on the hapless village from diverse directions. In the partial darkness, it was scarcely possible to select victims by age or gender, and the Rangers bent to their task with a will to exact the revenge that General Amherst had ordered. In their beds, in their cabins, running for their lives, men, women, and children were slaughtered indiscriminately in a scene that rivaled *Dante's Inferno*. The few who managed to flee to the river were either shot by pursuing Rangers, or their canoes were sunk and they drowned in the river. Rogers later reported that their qualms about performing the massacre were eased when they sighted the scalps of six hundred English victims displayed on poles about the village.[55] After the massacre, Roger's issued the order to burn

---

[55]Authors' note: The claim of 600 scalps on display at the village probably came from Rogers' report of the raid to his superiors, and it leads to a logical question. Since both the English and the French required the actual scalps as physical proof to pay bounty money, would not the Indians have turned the scalps over to the French in exchange for the bounty money? Otherwise how could the French keep their accounts straight? There were reports that certain Indians became experts at "splitting scalps" in order to collect two bounty payments.

the buildings, and by 7 am, the entire village was ablaze except for some storage cabins. A later report by Rogers stated:

> By that time we had killed two hundred Indians and taken twenty women and children prisoners. Fifteen of the latter I suffered to go on their own way, and brought home with me two Indian boys and three girls.

An exhaustive examination of the known facts shows that Rogers grossly overstated the results of his raid. Gordon Day, the respected American historian who specialized in Abenaki history, researched official Canadian archives to check the official records. He put the actual death toll at thirty Abenaki, of which twenty were women and children. In his account he falls short of branding Rogers a liar, writing:

> The facts of Rogers' Raid in October 1759 did not exactly coincide with the version that has been popularized in history. In contrast to Rogers' claims that he killed over 200 and left 20 women and children as prisoners, French observers wrote in internal memos to their chain of command (a source they are unlikely to fabricate the truth), that only 30 Abenakis were killed, and that 20 of them were women and children. Oral history tells us that a Stockbridge Mahican used as one of Rogers' scouts slipped into the village beforehand and warned them of the impending raid.

In the aftermath of Rogers' raid on Odanak, there were a great number of conflicting stories about the event. However, the continuity of the story is best served at this juncture by addressing the Rangers' precarious situation immediately following the raid. Rogers' post raid report reveals a great deal about his immediate concerns:

> When the detachment paraded, Captain Ogden was found to be badly wounded, being shot through the

> body, but still able to perform duty. Six privates were wounded and one Stockbridge Indian killed. I ordered the party to take corn out of the reserved houses for their subsistence home, which was the only provision to be found. While they were loading themselves I examined the captives who reported that a party of three hundred French and Indians were down the river, four miles below us. They also stated that two hundred French had, three days before, gone up the river to Wigwam Martinique, supposing that I intended to attack that place. A council of war now concluded that no other course remained for us, than to return by Connecticut River to No. 4.[56]

There was very little time to rest after the early morning attack, and the men used the time allotted to loot the mission church. They took everything of value including gold and silver relics and belts of wampum before they burned the church. Had they foreseen the starvation they would face during the long march home, they would have brought along more corn from the Indian stores in place of the loot. They crossed the Saint Francis River, and they followed a route that would ultimately bring them to Memphremagog, and finally to the rendezvous at the Coos Meadows. Rogers pressed the detachment hard for eight days until their rations ran out. At that point he divided the party into small units; he reasoned that they might have a better chance to shoot game and provision themselves. He had units march down the east and west shores of Memphremagog in order to divide and confuse possible pursuers. The rangers were instructed to regroup at the junction of the Ammonoosuc and Connecticut rivers, where they expected to find provisions and reinforcements sent up from Fort No. 4 at Charlestown, NH.

A party of Indian caught up to the small band under Ensign Avery two days later, and they succeeding in capturing seven

---

[56] Rogers' Memoir, in *Life of Stark*

of the nine men. Most of a second party of twenty men were also killed or captured included Lieutenants Dunbar and Turner. The captured men were returned to Odanak where they are alleged to have been tortured. After a long arduous trek, the starving men in Rogers' own party staggered into the Coos Meadows expecting to find food. Lieutenant Stevens' relief party with the requested provisions had previously arrived at the rendezvous, but when they heard gunfire from what they supposed to be the enemy, Stevens decided to retreat to his base. They headed back to the fort two hours before Rogers arrived carrying the vital food with them! Gazing incredulously at the still-smoldering fire of their would be rescuers, Rogers' men fired their guns in a vain attempt to signal the relief party back. The starving men were so downcast by the disappointment that several died within a day of their arrival. In the modern army vernacular, these men were the victims of a typical *fubar* (fouled up beyond all recognition). Rogers' journal describing his personal actions illustrates why he was so highly regarded by succeeding generations of Rangers:

> Our distress in the occasion was truly inexpressible. Our spirits, greatly depressed by the hunger and fatigue we had already suffered, now almost entirely sank with us; seeing no resource left, nor any reasonable hope that we should escape a most miserably death by famine. At length I came to a resolution, to push as fast as possible towards Number Four leaving the remains of my party, now unable to march further, to get such wretched subsistence as the barren wilderness could afford, till I could get relief to them, which I engaged to do within ten days. I taught Lieutenant Gant, the commander of the party, the use and method of preparing groundnuts and lily roots, which being cleansed and boiled will serve to preserve live.

Rogers promised his men he would be back within ten days; he took the wounded Captain Ogden and one of the two captive Indian boys with him. He lashed together a crude raft of dead logs, and he endeavored to fashion crude paddles from split slabs of wood. They managed to propel this makeshift contraption down river to Fort No. 4. Two hours after his arrival, boats were dispatched with food for his men at Coos Meadows. Incredibly, after being driven to the limits of human endurance, Rogers went back up the river two days later in the company of men in canoes carrying food to other possible survivors. Of all his daring exploits, his expedition to Odanak was his most celebrated. When his men were all assembled at Charlestown, he marched them back to Crown Point where they arrived December 1, 1759. In view of his heavy losses, it is not surprising that he chose to grossly inflate the enemy body count at Saint Francis. After leaving the place, he had lost three officers and forty-six of his noncoms and men. That is forty-nine out of one hundred and thirty two men—almost forty percent of his force!

As usual, the *only* native record of the event is preserved through their oral tradition. There is a great deal of folklore regarding the "Abenaki Treasures" looted by the Rangers from the Mission Church. In his journal dated December 24, 1759, General Amherst wrote, "A small group returned loaded with "wampum" and lovely things brought back from St. Francis of the Lake." The French Jesuit, Father Maurault, who served as a missionary at Odanak, wrote in 1866, "*The portion of Rogers' booty is estimated at $933.00 and consists mainly of wampum and provisions.*"

Father Charland, in his book, *History of St. Francois du Lac* dated 1942, declared, "*The objects seized by the Rangers were silver plated copper chandeliers, a small statue of Our Lady of Chartres and valuable objects*." Father Gravel in his book *Suagothel* wrote, "*The Church was ransacked and burned, the Rangers took valuable objects, namely a relic containing a gold case, a solid sterling statuette of Our Lady of Chartres and sterling plated chandeliers*."

The noted Abenaki historian Gordon Day personally interviewed Odanak resident Elvine Obomsawine in order to make a permanent record of what amounts to a virtual eyewitness account of Rogers's raid by Indians who were there. The account, that has a ring of authenticity to it, reveals that an Indian from Rogers' party did indeed warn the Indians about the raid. Perhaps, because of the prevailing confusion, or possibly because a young girl's word was discounted by some, the warning was only partially effective:

> And the Indians at that time in the fall were dancing. Already the harvest was all gathered.... And they danced and sometimes celebrated late, dancing and sometimes going out because it was a nice cool night. They rested, some went to smoke and rest. And one, a young girl, a young woman, she did not immediately go in when the others went in. When they went into the council house to dance again that one, the young girl, the young woman, did not go in because it was cool and she stayed outside. She remained longer outside, and it was dark, and when she was ready to go in at the start of the dancing inside the house, when she was ready to go in, then someone stopped her. He said, "Don't be afraid." In Indian, you understand, he said, "Friend, I am your friend, and those enemies, those strange Iroquois, they are there in the little woods (planning) that when all leave for home they would kill them all, their husbands, and burn your village, and I come to warn you." And surely the young woman went into the council house, the dancing place, and she warned the other Indians what he told. She warned what she had been warned. And some did not believe her, because she was so young, because she was a child. Some of them stopped and went home to see about their children and get ready to run away as soon as possible, so they could hide....Father gathered everyone—it was dark, of course in the dark no one kindled a light. They gathered their children in the dark, you can be sure. And they left to hide somewhere where they could not find them. Of

> course it was night at that time and they hid in a big ravine where they could not find them. And that man, the old man, they counted their children to see if they were all there where it was deep. And one had been left! My aunt's grandmother was the one who was missing! And she did not know that she was alone in the house, but already she was awake, and she was sitting at the foot of the bed and she was looking out of the window leaning on the windowsill. She was singing, she was calmly singing (to herself). She did not even know that the others were gone. Suddenly then her father quickly entered in the dark, entering quickly, and he took her-he found her singing, this one. Right away he took her and left as quickly as he possibly could to the ravine-the big ravine that is where Eli Nolet's house (now) is, that's where the ravine is, *At the Pines*, that's what they call it at Odanak, *At the Pines*. And there they hid, the Indians, the Abenakis. And my grandfather, the Great Obomsawin, The Great Simon, he crossed the river, just as the sun was rising. Just as the sun is seen first. He didn't arrive soon enough, and just at that time he is almost across the river when the sun showed. And his hat-something shone on his hat, something (bright) that he wore. And there he was shot down on the other side-he was the only one (to get across). All that were with the houses-well, that was when they burned the village-the others, surely many were killed of the others, all that were with the houses.[57]

General Amherst had sent Rogers on the revenge raid to Odanak at a time when France was in the throes of giving up her New World possession under the intense pressure of British arms. Some historians wrote that Rogers' raid marked the

---

[57]Authors' note: Stories about the *Abenaki Treasures* and recorded oral tradition about Rogers' raid on Odanak are taken from: www. *Ne-Do-Ba (Friends).* The non-profit site run by Nancy LeCompte offers a great deal of useful information about the Abenaki Indians.

destruction of Odanak, but the Mission Village was eventually rebuilt, and it survives to this day. With the surrender of Quebec and Montreal, French influence in the New World was in chaotic decline. In an era when news traveled with the speed of a sailing ship, or through the wilderness on the lips of voyagers, the news of the Vaudreuil's surrender of Montreal had not reached the western forts. The story of how Lord Amherst sent Rogers to occupy the French forts, and Rogers' futile attempts to achieve respectability in civilian life, provide an engrossing climax to this complex man's life.

France made a final attempt to reclaim New France in 1760 with its expedition to retake Quebec. Six hundred Rangers and seventy Indians with Rogers at their head were on hand when Montreal capitulated to Major General Amherst. The Rangers entered the city in the evening of the 8th of September. Four days later Amherst sent Rogers and two companies of Rangers into the Pays d'en Haut to take possession of the western forts. Traveling west in fifteen whaleboats, they arrived at the mouth of the Cayuga River near the present city of Cleveland on November 7th. After intensive negotiations with Chief Pontiac, Rogers negotiated an alliance that allowed him to proceed further west through Ottawa territory. Having shared the sacramental pipe with Pontiac to seal the alliance, Rogers and his two Ranger companies proceeded towards Detroit with fresh provisions and an escort of Ottawa braves. It was an astonishing feat of diplomacy and skill for Rogers to talk his way through territory that that had previously lived under no other banner than the fleur-de-lis. Rogers sent an Ottawa scout ahead to apprise the French commander of the nature of his visit. Belletre, the French Commandant received him skeptically, but with complete aplomb, Rogers was able to convince him to surrender the fort. For the first time ever, on the 29th of November, the British flag flew over the former French fort. Rogers had advanced British interests from Montreal to Detroit without firing a shot—a remarkable achievement! With his characteristic flair for the spectacular, Rogers then attempted to reach Michilimackinac, but the oncoming winter forced him to return to New York where he arrived in February 1761

Two years later he appeared with a small detachment of Rangers at the siege of Detroit. Rogers and his twenty-man relief force were sent from Fort Niagara to relieve the beleaguered Detroit garrison. On the July 31, 1763, he and his men fought in the *Battle of Bloody Bridge,* where the daring of Rogers and his men is credited with preventing the British retreat from being a complete disaster. In a typical heroic episode, Rogers and a few of his men fought off a large force of Indians from inside a civilian house. At the precise moment that the enemy burst through the front door of the house, Rogers and his men ran through a back door and escaped—a typical Rogers' exit! This was Rogers' final campaign of the French and Indian War.

Rogers turned up the next year in Portsmouth, NH where he tried to adjust his renegade ways to civilian life. Settling in Portsmouth was a logical move for a man of Rogers' ambitious nature. It was the seat of government for the New Hampshire Province where a new elite oligarchy had been created around Benning Wentworth and his Anglican Church supporters. Rogers had married the daughter of Reverend Arthur Brown who was rector of St. John's Church in Portsmouth, and a close associate of Governor Wentworth. The governor and his Anglican cronies had bought up the Mason land grants, and the kickbacks they were getting from Wentworth's township grants was making them rich. It is not surprising to learn that Rogers had acquired five hundred acres of land in Concord, NH in addition to three thousand acres of land near Bennington, VT. The land was sold to him for a pittance as a reward for his valuable military service. To all appearances Rogers had become a real estate wheeler-dealer. There are records of numerous purchase and sale agreements during the 1763 to 1765 period that indicate he was heavily involved in land deals, but his subsequent behavior suggests that he was bored with the routine of civilian life.

Apparently bored with his life as a land speculator, in 1765 Rogers went to England where his military fame made him a celebrity He published two well-written books about his military experiences, and he worked his celebrity for all it was worth, rubbing elbows with the English nobility and military elite. He was smitten by celebrity narcissism; he loved attention! In June 1766, General Gage announced the appointment of Major Rogers as Commandant of the garrison of Michilimackinac. When the Superintendent of Indian affairs heard of Rogers' appointment he was beside himself. He characterized Rogers as "*an overly ambitious, vain liar who had been spoiled by excessive flattery, and who was incapable of performing the duties of Commandant of the fort.*"

Rogers arrived at Michilimackinac in August 1766, and he immediately began to demonstrate that his superior, Sir William Johnson, knew whereof he spoke. After General Gage learned about Rogers' reputation, he appointed a Commissary to ostensibly regulate the Indian trade, and to coincidently curtail Rogers' power. Rogers quarreled with the Commissary, and he began to trade illegally with the Indians borrowing heavily to finance his speculation. His official expenditures reached such an unreasonable level that the Superintendent of Indian Affairs was obliged to dishonor them. Rogers' indignation over his imagined grievances prompted him to begin a treasonable correspondence with a French officer. The two renegades cooked up a plan to declare an independent governorship of Michilimackinac and for them to preside over a home government, presumably with Rogers as governor. It was a blueprint for treason! If that scheme failed, the conspirators had an even crazier plan. Rogers planned to steal the post funds as well as rob the white traders, and last but not least—he planned transfer his allegiance to the French in New Orleans! Fed up with his mismanagement and treasonable plotting, Rogers was arrested and taken in chains to Montreal where he was tried and released on a technicality. Undaunted by his disgrace, he decided to sail for England where he thought he might be better appreciated.

In Great Britain, incredibly, Rogers's rap sheet was wiped clean and he flourished in his new role as a martyr as well as a living legend. The public idolized him, and the British press lionized him. He was a darling of the British nobility, and on the occasion of his reception by the English Monarch; he gallantly knelt and kissed the King's hand. His creditors kept their silence in the hopes that he would be able to parlay his popularity to riches and pay back his considerable debts. Emboldened by the naiveté of the public and the British authorities, he boldly finagled his celebrity to secure the title of *Baron*, a title that would insure him an income of 600 pounds a year. As if that were not enough, he also asked to be made a pensioned major in the British Army.

We hear very little of Rogers' activities from 1772 until 1775, but in that year, he turned up in America as a British Major, retired on half pay. His long sojourn in Great Britain, his British military rank, and his aimless wandering from Pennsylvania to New Hampshire caused him to be viewed with suspicion on the eve of the Revolutionary War. His association with Loyalists, his improbable statements to the denizens of seamy taverns, all contributed to his bad reputation. The Pennsylvania Committee for Safety arrested him in September 1775, but he was paroled after pledging never to bear arms against the American Colonies. Yet, despite having given his solemn word not to do so, he tendered his services to the British General Gage in a letter dated November 26, 1775.

On December 2, 1775, he appeared at Dartmouth College in Hanover, NH. He approached President Wheelock with an offer to help secure a land grant for the college, anticipating no doubt to use his political connections in Portsmouth, NH. During his interview, he boasted of fighting two battles under Dey in Algiers—a country he had never visited. Put off by his shabby appearance, President Wheelock nevertheless handled his visit tactfully without making any commitment. After the interview, Rogers went back to his tavern accommodation, and he neglected to pay for his room at the tavern when he left Hanover the following day.

Later that month, he made a written request for an interview with General Washington; he presumably intended to offer his services, but the general declined to see him. Then, after being arrested in South Amboy New Jersey in February 1776, and after being turned over to New York authorities, he asked to be allowed to proceed to Philadelphia where he proposed to offer his services to the Congress. When news of his latest gambit was made known to the New Hampshire House of Representatives, they voted a formal resolution recommending that he be arrested. Addicted to the wine of celebrity and with his life in disarray, Rogers appeared to have run his last bluff.

But he was not quite finished. In August 1776 General Howe of the British army commissioned him Lieutenant Colonel, and he was ordered to raise a regiment of Loyalist Rangers to fight for the British Army—against the Americans! Rogers pursued that task with his customary enthusiasm, and he succeeded in enlisting a full regiment of Loyalist sympathizers. Two months later, he led this inadequately trained regiment in an engagement against his own countrymen at Mamaroneck, New York. The magic was gone, however, and he displayed none of the heroic qualities that had brought him fame. He left the field before the Americans routed his regiment. The British later stripped him of his rank.

The sad details of how the disgraced Rogers managed to escape imprisonment in America and return to England in 1777 are unknown. His wife left him in 1778 citing non-support and infidelity as reasons for the divorce. Little is known of his final years in England where he reportedly died in 1795.

Robert Rogers burning ambition drove him to heights that his character was unable to sustain. The pattern of his life was like that of a 4th of July rocket—soaring to dizzying heights and bursting—in self-destructive chaos that ended in oblivion. Today Rogers is chiefly remembered for forming the first U.S. Ranger unit, and there are several Internet websites that feature *Rogers Standing Orders.* In 1885 Joseph B. Walker peered into the future and accurately predicted how Rogers would be remembered:

When another century shall have buried in oblivion his frailties, the valor of the partisan commander will shine in undimmed luster. When the historian gives place to the novelist and the poet, his desperate achievements portrayed by their pens will render as romantic the border of Lake George, as have the daring deeds of Rob Roy McGregor, rehearsed by Walter Scott, made enchanting the Shores of Loch Lomond.[58]

Wamasit Indian
Tewksbury, Massachusetts

[58]Authors' note: Web site: usgennet.org/usa/topic/colonial/rogers/bio.html. This is one of the ten or more web sources used as research for the chapter on Odanak and Rogers's raid. Joseph B. Walker's article was written for *The Bay State Monthly* published by John N. McClintock & Co. January 1885, Boston, pp. 211-225. Walker's story was retyped and reformatted by Kathy Leigh in August, 2001.

9-1 Entrance to Abenaki Reserve

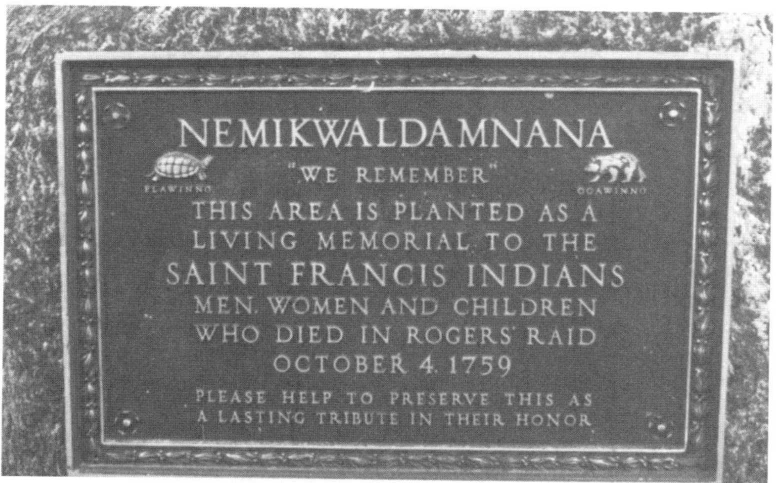

9-2 Memorial to raid victims

EPILOGUE

ABENAKI RESURGENCE IN THE NEW MILLENNIUM

With the English capture of Crown Point and Rogers' lightening raid against Odanak in 1759, the French capacity to mount Indian raids against English settlements was broken. But although the North American conflict ended in 1760, the *Seven Years War* that pitted Great Britain against France and Spain continued for two more years. Under the terms of the *Treaty of Paris* in 1763, France relinquished all claims to her North American colonies and the Abenaki Indians in both Canada and New England became British subjects.

Through almost nine decades the Colonists and the Indians had committed the worse imaginable atrocities in a concerted effort to annihilate one another. Now, with the sound of the war whoop and the cannon silenced, it was time to forgive and forget the past and make a new beginning. But the hearts of the victors held little charity for the vanquished. And the people who had fought so valiantly to defend their ancestral lands now had their own "*trail of tears*" to endure. They had been virtually annihilated as a people! Before contact with the Europeans, the Abenaki population was estimated at approximately 45,000. European transmitted plagues had reduced that number to approximately 12,000 by the time of the Pilgrim landing in Plymouth. At the beginning of the Revolutionary war in 1775, some historians estimated their population as low as 1,000. That figure did not include the Abenaki who had gone to Canada to escape Anglo retribution.

As we have seen, as early as 1720, the authorities had discovered the effective use of bounty payments to reduce the native population. A proclamation by Massachusetts Lieutenant

Governor Phips in 1755 trumpeted a payment schedule that ranged from 50 pounds for live Indian male captives to twenty pounds for the scalps of male or female Indians less than 12 years of age. Females over 12 years brought less money than adult males—they were valued at 25 pounds alive and 20 pounds dead. Governor Phips' bounty notice concluded with the following high-sounding language:

> Given at the Council-Chamber in Boston, this Third Day of November 1755, and the Twenty-ninth Year of the Reign of our Sovereign Lord GEORGE the Second, by the Grace of GOD of Great-Britain, France and Ireland, KING, Defender of the Faith GOD Save the KING.

Once they were classified as British subjects, the English settlers sought other ways to get rid of the Indians. One unofficial method was to round up and transport small groups of Indians to the Canadian border and leave them there with a warning to not come back. It was during this period that some Indians began to conceal their identity and adopt English names and lifestyles.[59] There are many modern Indians descendants that attempt to trace their native roots. When asked about the meager details forthcoming from their families, they will often reply that their parents or their grandparents did not want to talk about their Indian ancestry.

As late as 1920 there were still efforts to control the Native American population. The most notable of these was a *Eugenics Project* that was designed to "eliminate degenerate bloodlines and replenish old pioneer stock." It was a special research program that was actively pursued in the State of Vermont in the 1920s and 1930s. The information that came out of a "Vermont Eugenics Survey" led to a sterilization law in 1931.

---

[59] *Legends of the Pond*, by Alfred E.Kayworth; 1998, (p.109-115): The oral history of Christine (Kukukuo) Dube's family describes how her Abenaki ancestors managed to change their Indian name to Drew and assume Anglo identities in the early 1800s.

According to a 1999 *Boston Globe* article, the law resulted in the sterilization of several hundred poor, rural Vermonters, *Abenaki Indians and others deemed unfit to procreate.*[60]

The Abenaki Nations proved themselves to be remarkably resilient in restoring their population to the pre-contact level. In addition to the Abenaki reservations in Odanak and Becancour, there are several Maliseet Indian reservations in Canada. If one adds the Canadian Abenaki and the Penobscot, Passamaquoddy and Maliseet populations to other Abenaki descendants in New England, a total Abenaki head count of 45,000 is a reasonable estimate. The most obvious signs of Abenaki resurgence are the Indian reservations in the State of Maine. While the confines of an epilogue allows only a limited examination of the Maine Indian reservations, a brief look at the history, the geography, and the administration of the Penobscot, Passamaquoddy, and Maliseet tribes is helpful to an appreciation of their importance to the State of Maine.

The word Penobscot is derived from the Abenaki word *Pan-wampskik* that is literally translated as, "*The People where the river tumbles down over white boulders.*" The Penobscot Indian Nation's reservation is on *Indian Island* located about twelve miles north of Bangor on the Penobscot River. The reservation owns 55,279 acres of land that includes *Indian Island* and other islands in the river to the north. After the passage of the Maine *Indian Claims Settlement Act* in 1980, the Federal Government recognized the Penobscot Indian Nation. The reservation is self-administered by a Tribal Governor, a Lieutenant Governor and a Council. The 1996 census lists 2,093 tribal

---

[60]Authors' note: As early as 1998 Joe Phillips of Mechanic Falls, Maine was mailing out flyers that described how his aunts Dorris James and Gladis Malo had been sterilized during the Vermont project. Joe and his aunts did not learn of their Abenaki heritage until the late 1990s. The revelation that he was the son of Mississquoi Indians from Vermont and that his aunts were victims of a state eugenics program transposed Joe Phillips life. He is currently embarked on a personal crusade to promote truth, a love of fellow man that knows no race barriers and a love of God. He actively pursues his goals through his mailings to interested parties.

members, 500 of whom reside on Indian Island, Olaman Indusa part of their ancient ancestral home. Olaman Industries, Penobscot Indian High Stakes Bingo, and a wide variety of local crafts entrepreneurs provide employment for tribal members. The tribe has the right to elect and seat a non-voting member in the Maine House of Representatives.

The Passamaquoddy Indian Nation has two reservations that are located in Northeastern Maine. The literal translation of Passamaquoddy is "*the people who fish for pollock*" or "*plenty-pollock-place.*" *The Treaty of 1794* between the Passamaquoddy Tribe and the Commonwealth of Massachusetts conveyed the Indian Reservations in Washington County to the tribe. Their lands include Indian Township, Pleasant Point, Pine Island, Nemcass Point, Line's Island and fifteen islands in the Schoodic River, also known as the St. Croix River. Currently, the Passamaquoddy Indian Nation owns more than 200,000 acres of land in the State of Maine. *Pleasant Point Township* is located on a peninsula known to its residents as *Sipayik* (zih-bahy-ihg). The reservation includes most of the land from the junction of Routes 190 and U.S. 1 in Perry to the tip of the peninsula. *Indian Township* is located just north of Princeton, Maine. The 1980 *Indian Claims Settlement Act* contributed significantly to the economic viability of the two Passamaquoddy townships. The administration of the two townships follows the Penobscot pattern. There are more than 2,500 Passamaquoddy residents of whom approximately 600 live on each of the two Passamaquoddy Townships.[61]

The *1980 Maine Indian Land Claims Settlement Act* also recognized the Houlton Band of Maliseet Indians. The 504-member band received a start-up grant that is currently being used to establish essential programs and to purchase up to 5,000 acres of land for a reservation. The tribe has already ac-

---

[61]Authors' note: Both the Penobscot Indian Nation and Passamaquoddy Indian Nation have official web sites that provide in depth insight into their history and their current legal status. A simple web search using the two names will bring up a multitude of web sites that provide a great deal of information on the two Nations.

quired several parcels of land located about three miles north of Houlton in Aroostook County within a mile of the New Brunswick, Canada border. A Chairman and a six-member tribal council are currently administering the band.

The passage of two hundred and fifty years has done a great deal to soften the harsh images of the past. In recent years the American public has been exposed to sympathetic portrayals of the American Indian, and the popularity of such films as *Dances With Wolves* reveals a widespread need to learn and understand more about the *Indian Way of Life* and the spirituality of the *First People*. The large number of web sites featuring various aspects of native spirituality highlights the surging interest in American Indian culture and spirituality. Many devotees to the so-called Indian Way insist that their beliefs are compatible with traditional Christian beliefs.[62] As one might anticipate, there are some natives who complain about the rising number of *Indian Wannabees,* that is to say, those non-natives who want to act like Indians. They complain that, after having given up their lands and culture, the Anglos aim to take away their last unique asset—their spirituality! These negative views can be judged in the same context as the strident opinions of the minority that claim to be still at war with the white man. These fringe elements have the good fortunate to live in a society that allows free reign to their contrary opinions.

For what we sometimes were, we are no more;
Fortune hath changed our shape, and Destiny
Defaced the very form we had before.
--Sir Walter Raleigh

[62]Authors' note: During a visit to an inmate *Sacred Circle of Fire* session at the Concord State Prison in New Hampshire, Al Kayworth asked the Chaplain about a possible conflict between Indian spirituality and Christian teachings. He responded that Indian spirituality is not a religion—it is a *Way of Life.*

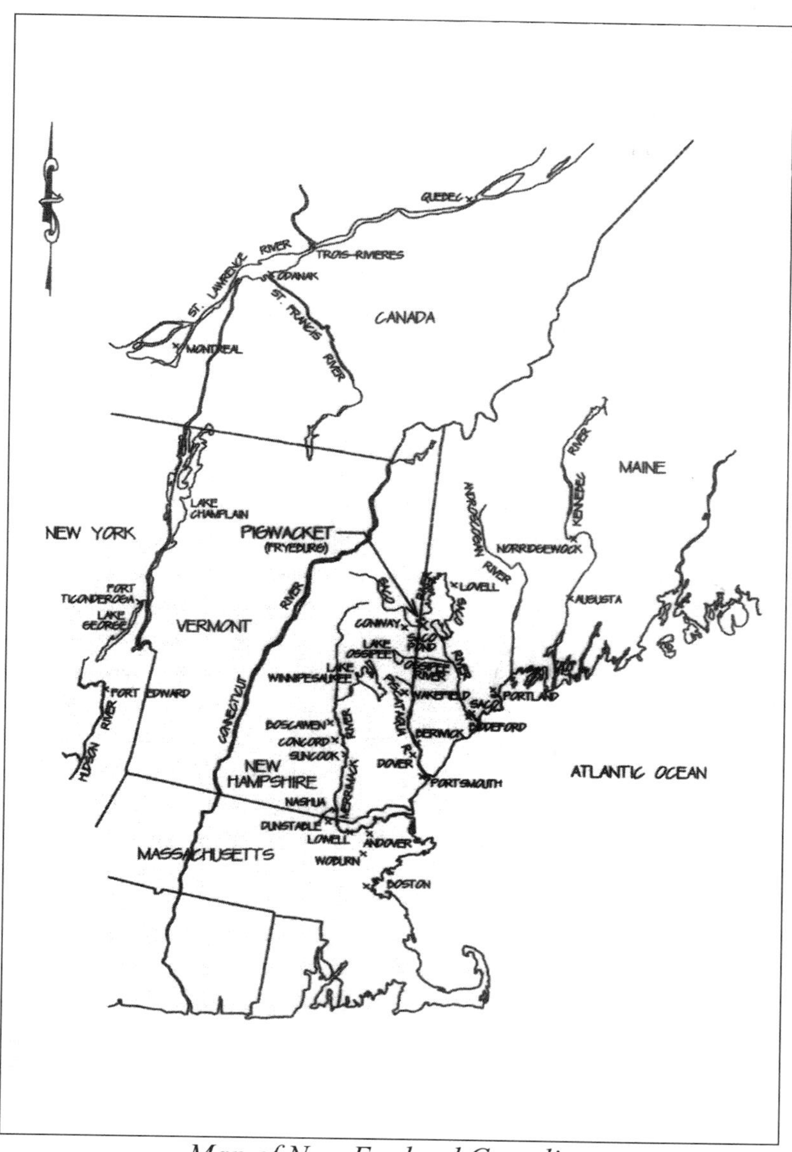

Map of New England Coastline

BIBLIOGRAPHY

Carter, Rev. S. F. assisted by Hon. T.L. Fowler. *History of Pembroke, N.H.* The Republican Press Association, 1895.

Chamberlain, John. *The Indian Fighter at Pigwacket;* Weymouth and Braintree Publishing Company, 1898.

Charlevoix, Rev P.F.X.de Charlevoix, S.J. *History and General Description of New France*; translation by John Gilmary Shea; Loyola University Press, Chicago, IL.

Eckstorm, Fanny Hardy. *Pigwacket and Parson Symmes;* New England Quarterly article, September 1936.

Eckstorm, Fanny Hardy. *Who Was Paugus*; New England Quarterly article, June 1939.

Eckstorm, Fanny Hardy. *The Old Fight at Pigwacket 1725*, City of Bangor Public Library microfilm records F973.25.

Evans, George Hill. *Pigwacket*, Conway, N. H. Historical Society publication No. 1 1939.

Farwell, Frederick Henry and Fanny (Barber) Farwell. *The Farwell Family*, 1929.

Fox, Charles J. *History of the Old Township of Dunstable*; 1846.

Kayworth, Alfred E. *Abenaki Warrior*, Branden Books, Inc. 1998.

Kayworth, Alfred E. *Legends of the Pond*, Branden Books, Inc. 2000.

Kidder, Frederick. *Expeditions of Captain John Lovewell*, Bartlett and Halliday; Boston, 1865

Green, Samuel A. M.D. *Groton during The Indian Wars*, Groton, MA 1883.

Munro, William Bennett. *Crusaders Of New France;* Yale University Press, New Haven, Connecticut, 1921.

Parkman, Francis. *France and England in North America, Volume 11;* The Library Of American.

Nason, Rev. Elias M.A. *A History of the Town of Dunstable, Massachusetts*, Alfred Mudge and Son; Boston, 1877.

New England Genealogical Register. *The Forty Seven Men of Lovewell's Company*, 1909 Vol LX11.

Penhallow, Samuel Esquire. *The History of the Wars of New England with the Eastern Indians,* T. Fleet for S.Gerrish; Boston, 1726.

Symmes, Rev Thomas. Narrative Of The Great Fight, S.Gerrish ; 1725.

Stearns, Ezra S. A.M. *Early Generations of the Founders of Old Dunstable*, George Littlefield publishing, 1911.

Webster, Kimball, *History of Hudson, N.H*; edited by George Waldo Browne; Granite State Publishing Co, 1913.

INDEX